*"The landscape is dead.*
*Gobbled up by the trenches.*
*What is not trench is moon.*
*We dug trenches when it was necessary.*
*Now the trenches are overwhelming and engulfing the men.*
*Trenches appear like inflamed proliferations around battles that got stuck.*
*Foreign bodies can no longer be expelled.*
*And last of all there is gangrene which is eating up the rest of the men.*
*Let pedants and military bureaucrats have orgies in the trenches."*

— Ulrich Sander, *Pioniere – Ein Frontbericht 1914-1918*, Jena 1942, p.207.

# GERMAN AMATEUR PHOTOGRAPHERS IN THE FIRST WORLD WAR

## A VIEW FROM THE TRENCHES ON THE WESTERN FRONT

**Sebastian Remus**

**Schiffer Military History**
Atglen, PA

*Dedication*
*This book is dedicated to my mother Gretel Friedhoff. Thanks for all.*

Book design by Robert Biondi.


Library of Congress Catalog Number: 2008928529.



Printed in China.
ISBN: 978-0-7643-3093-3

We are always looking for people to write books on new and related subjects. If you have an idea for a book, please contact us at the address below.

Published by Schiffer Publishing Ltd.
4880 Lower Valley Road
Atglen, PA 19310
Phone: (610) 593-1777
FAX: (610) 593-2002
E-mail: Info@schifferbooks.com.
Visit our web site at: www.schifferbooks.com
Please write for a free catalog.
This book may be purchased from the publisher.
Please include $5.00 postage.
Try your bookstore first.

In Europe, Schiffer books are distributed by:
Bushwood Books
6 Marksbury Ave.
Kew Gardens, Surrey TW9 4JF
England
Phone: 44 (0)20 8392-8585
FAX: 44 (0)20 8392-9876
E-mail: info@bushwoodbooks.co.uk
www.bushwoodbooks.co.uk
Free postage in the UK. Europe: air mail at cost.
Try your bookstore first.

# CONTENTS

**Photocall behind the front. German gunners posing for a group photo in front of their billet. Group shots sent in letters or as postcards played an important role in the exchange between front and home.**
**Field-Artillery-Regiment 20, 10. Infantry-Division.**
**Côtes Lorraines.**
**August 1915.**

# INTRODUCTION
## Photographing the War: Amateur Photographers and their Photographs

When the First World War began in August 1914 nobody anticipated what was to come. Most soldiers leaving for the war expected to be back by Christmas. However, the war would go on until November 1918 and was going to radically change the face of the new century. The Great War was the first global war of modern mass societies in the industrial age of the rising 20th century. The involvement of entire populations and the unlimited use of modern industry and global resources were to become significant features in modern warfare. Economic capabilities were combined with permanent technical innovation. This resulted in an unprecedented influx of new technical devices being introduced into the battle, a fact that deeply influenced the course and the style of warfare. "The brutal, mud-filled, murderous insanity known as the Western Front" (cit. Tuchman: *Guns* p.438) became the main and most typical battlefield of the Great War and photography became the technical device to preserve its face. Amateur photography is an important part of the visualized legacy of the Great War. Never before had amateur photographers played such a significant role in preserving the collective war memory. In fact, military amateur photography originated in the Great War.

The photos in this book show the Western Front as it was seen and photographed by German amateur photographers serving as soldiers in the trenches. Tens of thousands of German soldiers and officers had their cameras with them in the field and compiled a forgotten treasure of millions of amateur photos. Daily life in the trenches, the devastated landscape of war, dugouts, death, hospitals in small village churches, life in the camps behind the frontline – this is the authentic face of the Western Front as it was witnessed and preserved by the simple view of the photographing infantryman in the trenches. The amateur photos are of an impressive authenticity but do not show – if photos could do this at all – the reality as a whole. Photos tell an ample but never complete story. What was, or perhaps more importantly, what was not photographed can tell us a lot about the photographer and his relation towards his social environment. Looked at in this way the photos contain a message beyond the photographed scene. The photos of the amateur photographer have their limits forced upon them by a kind of moral self-censorship and the conditions of a soldier's life and mission in the trenches. In comparison with the works of professional army or press photographers the view of the amateur photographer is often surprisingly naive and simple but striking nevertheless in its ability of fixing the reality of trench war on film. As a rule decency prevented the soldier from the voyeurism of the horrors of trench war. One seldom sees amateur photos of killed comrades or their mutilated bodies as most amateur photographers hesitated to take such shots fearing to hurt the dignity of the victims and their relatives at home. When hit wounded soldiers were the object of first aid and not of curious photographing by their comrades. There is of course the question of the dead bodies of enemy soldiers. However, even such photos are rarely found in private collections. Some of the few existing photos of this kind seem to contain a sense of the photographer's sympathy towards the victims and served as representatives for the morally disapproved shots of their own killed comrades. On the whole though, most photos of killed enemy soldiers appear somewhat strange and seem to be an expression of curiosity towards a kind of trophy.

Photographic technology during 1914-1918 also had its limits. Action photos of combat, heavy gunfire or the frontline at night are few and far between. The necessary exposure time for the films of that epoch was simply too long for such shots. On top of this, dangerous trench warfare normally did not allow soldiers to roam about taking photos or preparing for the moment of a spectacular shot. The limited space of the trench restricted the photographer's perspective to a few metres and men. During fighting or whilst under fire, the amateur's camera was kept carefully in his field pack. No one in the trenches would have taken the risk of facing a raiding enemy party with a camera in his hands instead of a rifle and stick grenade. This explains why amateur photos show the quieter moments of the deadly life they led in the trenches and not the instant when the infantry went over the top. Such pictures were reserved for professional photographers who could prepare the scene in advance and find a safe place for taking their shots. The amateur photographer was still an actor in the war and not a member of the audience. But even the silent and "idyllic" shots show the reality of trench war at the Western Front. For not only did combat and death mark life in the trenches, so did boredom and idleness, sentry duty and work. Neither armies nor industries, nor the men in the trenches were able to fight and feed a permanent battle. Even the inhuman trench war had to accept human limits.

In the Great War amateur photos were both sent home and used as an object of exchange. Obviously not everybody had a camera and amateur photographers gave copies of their photos to friends and comrades. Many soldiers used photos as postcards to send their relatives back home a view from the front. The addressees were often asked to keep the received photos carefully as part of the soldier's war souvenirs. In the Great War mail was the only form of communication between soldiers at the front and their relatives at home as the soldiers served for many months or even years without home leave. As a result the army postal service was very important for soldiers' morale. The collapse of the army postal service in the course of major operations was always a depressing experience for the fighting men and a nerve-wracking test for the families at home waiting for news and fearing the worst. Whilst most soldiers sent only one long and time consuming letter per week some sent a photo postcard with a few short greetings to assure their families that everything was well nearly everyday. Next to the written word, photos sent in letters or as postcards played an important role in the exchange between front and home. Amateur photos allowed a visual presence of the men at the front and became an alternative way of visualizing the war for the people at home who depended otherwise on the pictures of controlled newspapers and magazines or propaganda films in the cinema. Officially all mail was subjected to censorship by the company officers or special censor departments in the rear area. However, the tremendous flood of mail sent everyday reduced military censorship to mere random tests in the German Army so that sometimes even the date of impending offensives could carelessly appear in a letter. Effective censorship depended on a soldier's willingness to commit self-censorship. In the German Army this generally worked, assisted by a kind of private censorship which meant avoiding telling loved ones back home the plain cruel truth about life at the frontline. This private censorship included the amateur photographs which were always a compromise between showing the world of the front without shocking relatives at home.

The amateur photo became an important part of the soldier's war souvenirs. Many amateur photographers compiled complete series of photo books with written commentaries as a documentation of their service time in the field. Sometimes amateur photographers became something like semi-official regimental photographers who sold single photos to collect money for charity or produced photo books that were issued to the regiment's members or could be bought by the soldiers to commemorate their service time. The interest in these photo books within the forces was deep, prompting divisions and army corps to publish printed versions. These printed photo books covered periods of frontline service or complete sectors of the front and were printed by army or corps periodicals at military printing offices behind the front or by civil publishers in Germany. In 1916 the VIII. Reserve Corps' periodical "*Champagne-Kriegszeitung*" published a series of issues containing photos from the corps' sector at Champagne and the Aisne River. The numbers were compiled by the editors of the corps' periodical then printed in Cologne in Germany and sold to the troops at the front as part of the army welfare service. Another one of these books was "*Zwei Jahre an der Westfront*" (*Two Years at the Western Front*) published by an independent infantry division; it included 323 photos from Artois, Picardie and Lorraine. A remarkable number of 15,000 copies where printed when the book was published in 1917. Such publications served a charitable purpose and the profits went towards the allowance of dependants of soldiers killed in action.

Reviewing literature about the Great War published after the war, the minor role amateur photography played in comparison with the photos of official and professional photographers is surprising. Up to the present times the official perspective still dominates the published visual souvenir of the Great War. The treasure of German amateur photographs survived the time hidden unnoticed in the private photo books of veterans or in the postcard collections of boys or girls who received a new photo postcard from a father or brother serving at the front every week. At the beginning of the 20th century collecting postcards was a common hobby. Oversized albums were used for this precise purpose. When in the 1920s and 1930s many printed regimental histories were published in Germany the authors, usually former regimental officers, illustrated the books with amateur shots placed at their disposal by comrades who had served in the same regiments. Official photography of the time offered only a general view of the war and ignored troop identity and exact data about place names and was thus useless for the regimental history's purpose. However, this was the last time that amateur photos were published on a large scale. Amateur photography subsequently fell into oblivion. Many Word War I photo books have been published since 1918. Until today however nearly all published photo books have relied on official archives and press photo services. Time and time again they have contained photographs taken either by professional photographers who worked for photo journals or for the German Army department for photo and film, the so-called Bufa (*Bild- und Filmamt*) which produced photos and films for propaganda purposes during the war. On the whole these books show highly professional and spectacular shots of a vast variety of topics that would have been impossible for normal soldiers to have taken. However, these books miss one important viewpoint: the simple view and special perspective that only a soldier in the trenches could have.

Amateur photography in the Great War has its technical history too. Photographic technology and war photography was not an invention of the First World War. Like many other technologies of the Great War photography was an advancement of technological devices that had already existed before 1914. However, it was only a few years before the war that these technological devices reached a standard that allowed mass production and common usage, much in the same way as motorised transport and aircraft for example.

The technology to take photos by using mechanical devices and a chemical process had already been invented back in the 19th century and the first pioneers of photography also took the first war photos. The archives of war hold photos from the Mexican War in 1848, the Crimean War, the Civil War and the Franco-Prussian War from 1870. However, at this time photography was the business of specialists who had to handle plenty of heavy and difficult equipment. Photographers of the 19th century traveled on the battlefield with a carriage loaded

**Opposite: German officer with his camera in a mine crater at the Argonne forest. The long exposure time of the films from that time made the use of tripods advisable. But even these tripods were collapsible and portable.**
**Argonne sector.**
**Undated.**

with their photographic equipment and chemical laboratory. Photos had to be developed on the spot shortly after being shot. Some years before the First World War small cameras and comfortable film material which was easy to use became available. To develop a photo all that was necessary were a few bottles of chemicals, two dishes and some water. The photo film normally had postcard or half postcard size. To expose the photo paper only a lamp was necessary and the film was put directly onto the photo paper. To transport the camera in a knapsack, to use it on the battlefield and to develop photos during an hour of leisure in the dugout was no longer a problem for the soldiering private photographer.

Soldiering German amateur photographers began taking photos in the last few months of 1914. Nearly no amateur photos are available from the first months of war. The reason for this is simple; when they entered the field most men expected that the war would only last a few weeks and they simply forgot, or did not bother, to take their camera with them. In October 1914, when the stalemate began soldiers sent letters from the front asking their families at home to send them their cameras or catalogues of photographic equipment so they could place orders. From this time on amateur photographers shot millions of photos. The engineer officer Ulrich Sander refers in his war memoirs to photography as being a "contagious epidemic" in the spring of 1916. His men, engineers of *Pionier-Kompanie* 237, learned how to develop films and fix prints easily (cit. Sander: *Pioniere*, p.154). Even later on, when food, materials and resources were becoming scarcer, the German chemical industry was still producing enough photographic material to allow amateur photographers to keep taking their photos up until the end of the war.

The Trench War at the Western Front had countless faces. Collective memory focuses only on the major battles – Verdun, the Somme, Champagne, and Passchendale – with its bloody attrition of men and material. Ernst Juenger, the famous German writer and veteran, called the material battles of the Western Front a "storm of steel". In his books he describes – like many other German World War I authors – the soldier's experience at the front as being that of a worker in the industrial battle machinery of technical weapons. The trench fighter became a technical specialist of killing in a world of devastation, the gunner a worker serving huge machines producing destruction and death. However, the amount of time spent in high intensity battles and the amount of soldiers involved was actually quite limited on the Western Front, merely a matter of days or weeks in fact. Big battle was only one face of trench warfare. The soldier in the trenches had to cope primarily with the daily needs of life under the conditions of small-scale combat, never-ending work and the duty and dangers of guard service. The routine of exchange between frontline service and reserve duty fixed the pattern of life at the front. His major problems were how to live and how to survive, daily routine, housing, heating and food. Front line soldiers, even at the quiet sectors, lived in a world of devastation where even before the war there had not been enough infrastructure to support the living conditions of thousands of men. Many soldiers spent whole years of their life in the trenches. Living in a community of comrades under trench war conditions became their life. Trench soldiers also had a lot of time which is why the amateur photos published in this book

**The dugout as an improvised darkroom. Infantrymen developing negative films in their dugout. They are using their mess kit and old tins as developing baths.**
**Infantry-Regiment 52.**
**Aisne.**
**1915.**

show the soldiers' daily life in the trenches at the Western Front. It was generally during the quieter moments that the soldier took up his camera. Photos of action in pitched battle are the exception not the rule. It is especially the seemingly peaceful moments of trench warfare that show us the typical face of the Western Front: Everyday routines under the conditions of war, devastation and death.

The Western Front was a world of its own separated technically from the civil world by what the Great War lieutenant and later writer Ernst Juenger called a "storm of steel". Mentally "the front" was separated from the people at home by a spectrum of unexplainable and ambivalent impressions resulting in a kind of speechlessness and self-censorship. Everybody knew that the front was not a peaceful place. But the shocking and ambivalent reality was not communicable in its full extent. Apparently this is still the case today. It is quite possible that this ambivalence of impressions arouses much more irritation in the mind of the modern spectator studying World War I photos today than in the mind of wartime contemporaries who did this ninety years ago. Peaceful and idyllic scenes, like soldiers playing cards in the trenches on a sunny afternoon or smiling infantrymen at work, seem not to correspond to pictures of total destruction and rotten corpses. The amateur's idyllic shots are not propaganda but an expression of the complexity and absurdity of a world of war marked by the extreme contrasts of survival and death. In a battle zone that was ruled by death and destruction, simple work with a shovel to construct protective works against the deadly impact of shells and everyday activities like eating, sleeping and a few leisure hours were a basic condition for the men in the trenches to survive both physically and mentally. Four years of trench war had converted the civil existence of millions of men into war. However, the lengthy stalemate had, to a certain extent, also introduced the normal and vital culture of civil life into the war, blurring the border between peace and war in the minds of a generation.

## Western Front 1914

The failure of the German "Schlieffen Plan" on the banks of the River Marne during the first few days of September 1914 was the birth hour of what would become the monstrous phenomenon known as the Western Front. There was much post-war arguing about the "Schlieffen Plan" in Germany. Defective and mismanaged, the plan led the German Army into the Battle of the Marne where the German offensive in the west reached its "high-water mark" on September 9, 1914. Many critics argued that both the plan and its mishandling by the German Chief of Staff *General* von Moltke, the unlucky nephew of the famous Moltke of Bismarck's times, bore the seed of failure. Awaiting Russian invasion, the German infantry was pressed by Schlieffen to achieve victory in the west within forty-two days while the army and its service of supply depended completely on foot marches and horse transport as the railroad system had been seriously damaged by the retreating French and Belgians. This was Napoleon style logistics while the German Army fought an industrial age war consuming more ammunition and supply per day than a Napoleonic army during an entire campaign. Losses on both sides were also far beyond Napoleonic age standards. The armies clashed along a front of several hundred miles and infantry confronted with industrial firepower clung to old-fashioned tactics. At the beginning of the war the German infantry would usually advance a few metres in close formation, almost shoulder to shoulder, fall down to take cover and fire lying down, then get up and rush forward a few more metres. The dense attack formations produced deadly fire concentrations against the enemy but offered an excellent target for rifle and shellfire at the same time. This resulted in a slaughter of German infantry at Mons and le Cateau when carried out by trained professionals like the British Expeditionary Forces (BEF). But BEF losses under the hail of German rifle fire at Mons and le Cateau were also considerable (cit. Bull: *Trench Warfare* p.45). The French tactics on the battlefields of the Ardennes and Lorraines were not more sophisticated and produced even more losses.

The advancing German Army, already depleted by the tremendous losses of August and September 1914, was additionally weakened by Moltke. Contrary to Schlieffen's original idea he even withdrew forces from the decisive right wing which was in the end too weak to overwhelm the enemy at the gates of Paris. However it is highly questionable whether the road systems of Belgium and Northern France would really have been adequate enough to march and to supply the additional army corps so urgently needed at the German right wing in the Battle of the Marne. At its climax the German offensive cracked at the Marne under the counterattack of the French Army. In addition, nerves were straining to breaking point at the German High Command (OHL = *Oberste Heersleitung*) where Moltke and his staff officers realized their own troops' weakness and feared defeat. After a flawed analysis of the military situation by the OHL representative *Oberstleutnant* Hentsch the German armies were ordered to retreat in order to evade an expected serious defeat. The "Schlieffen Plan" and its failure revealed the strategic problems that would decide Germany's fate in the Great War. The Central Powers were inferior in both men and material and could only become weaker in the course of fighting. Germany was surrounded by a superior coalition of enemies that imposed the naval blockade upon the German coast and cut the country off from world markets. Thus it was no secret that German economic resources were limited and that Germany could not sustain a lasting siege. Germany's military power was also limited. As a consequence the option of simultaneous military operations at different theaters of war was excluded. Consequently the Imperial German Army fought under time pressure and had to decide whether to fight in the west or east.

The French victory of the Marne in September 1914 changed the direction of the battle in the West. After the retreat of the German forces behind the Aisne and Vesle rivers and the successful stabilization of the German line the race to the sea began. The western battlefields were extended more and more to the north till the raging battle reached the channel coast at Nieuwport, culminating in the battle of First Ypres. While the battle in the west raced to the Belgium channel coast the battlefront left behind became static from September-November 1914. The infantry began to dig in. Trenches appeared all over what was then called "the front". "Not only the dead but the living too, were buried now" (cit. Stratz: *Der Weltkrieg* p.82). On both sides of the front the combat strength of the fighting units was exhausted by two months of permanent fighting and far below standard. The depleted forces felt the heavy weight of modern war technology. Exhaustion and intensive firepower finally stopped the war of movement. Between the English Channel and Switzerland stalemate and trench war had begun. The Western Front was reality.

In order to extend the German line to the north new army corps had to be formed in Germany and assembled in Northern France and Belgium. But this needed time. To assist the open northern flank waiting for the arrival of new army corps *General* Erich von Falkenhayn, the new Chief of General Staff of the German Army, asked for the assistance of the armies holding the front at the Champagne, Verdun and Lorraine sectors. On September 25th, visiting the headquarters of Crown Prince Wilhelm's 5th Army at Stenay on the Meuse River,

Falkenhayn asked for local attacks to hold enemy forces at the southern part of the front. Crown Prince Wilhelm refers to this visit in his war memoirs commenting on the origins of the stalemate: Since the second half of September 1914 the lack in men and material had limited the German initiative to local attacks. But the concentration of forces for local operations had depleted the already weakened frontline garrison of all dispensable human force and had resulted in a freezing of the line. Technical means became the main support of the front. In this way, as Crown Prince Wilhelm writes in his war memoirs, the "hated trench war" began (cit. Wilhelm: *Meine Erinnerungen*, p.101-102). This view of the origins of the new form of warfare at the Western Front is confirmed by a 5th Army order of October 1914 ordering *Armee-Abteilung v. Strantz*, which was holding the St. Mihiel salient, to compensate for the lack of men and ammunition by constructing more field fortifications.

The beginning of the stalemate at the Western Front was not a sudden change but a process that transformed war and battlefield, step by step, into a system of fixed positions. Only strongly fortified lines could reduce losses and be defended by a minimum of forces. This allowed the transfer of available forces to the theatres of local operations in order to regain the initiative. Army orders instructed the ground forces to develop the improvised early positions into a sophisticated system of combat and communication trenches. This change was not only tactical and technical it also signalled a change of mentality that demanded new regulations and training for the troops in the line. Trench war proved to be a long process of learning.

An interesting and typical example for this period between August and December 1914 is Infantry Regiment 40, the so-called *Hohenzollernfusiliers*. This regiment had its peace garrison at the city of Rastatt in Baden. After taking part in the recapture of Muelhausen at Alsace on August 9, 1914 the regiment was transferred to the northern Vosges Mountains and took part in repulsing the French attacks at the Lorraine sector in September 1914. In the beginning of October, the *Hohenzollernfusiliers*, like many other regiments, were sent by rail to northern France where the battle at the Western Front was on its bloody move towards the coast. In the German attacks at Vermelles and Festubert the *Hohenzollernfusiliers* again had to pay their bloody toll in the foggy October days when stalemate finished the war of movement for the depleted companies. In spite of the repeated arrivals of new drafts on the battlefield regimental strength was declining steadily. All battalions were far under strength. On October 23 the 7th Company was made up of merely three NCOs and fourteen men. Three months before this company had left Rastatt with nearly 200 men. One day in October at Vermelles cost the first battalion twenty-three fatalities, seventy-three wounded and nine missing soldiers. This was nearly 10% of its original strength in August but in October the battalion was already more than 25% below strength. From originally four companies per battalion three had to be formed. Some companies were commanded by company-sergeant-majors. In December 1914 the few surviving old soldiers of August 1914 saw a complete change of generations in the fighting regiments. The heavy losses of four months of war had left only a few of the "old men" who had left the garrison together with their regiment in the cheering first days of August. Newly arrived drafts of young soldiers filled up the depleted ranks. The regimental history of the *Hohenzollernfusiliers* comments as follows: "So the old soldier died out. A younger generation without war experience took his place and learned their own lessons" (cit. *Fuehren: Hohenzollernfuesiliere im Weltkrieg 1914-1918*, p.124). This deadly change of generations in the fighting forces would be repeated again and again till November 1918. After the war the regimental history of Infantry Regiment 40 recorded ninety-four officers and 3,766 NCOs and men killed while serving in the ranks of the *Hohenzollernfusiliers* at the Western Front from 1914-1918. This number was nearly the strength of the regiment when it left Rastatt in the first days of August 1914.

In October 1914 general exhaustion on both sides of the frontline resulted in stalemate and the trench war began for the *Hohenzollernfusiliers* too. The beginning was hard for the soldiers in the trenches because there was a new enemy: the approaching winter. Wintertime in Northern France was not so much snow and hard frost as months and months of cold weather, rain and mud. Since October 1914 the trench war had not only consisted of the daily fighting against the enemy and the construction of field fortifications but much more than that, of fighting the destructive impact of rain and mud on the trenches, dugouts and men's health. Trenches and dugouts were flooded by rain and mud. Soaked with water, earth constructions collapsed quickly and left the soldiers in their ruined trenches unprotected against shellfire and weather. Trench war became a job for specialists like engineers, miners and carpenters. War became work. Water was the most serious problem in the trenches. Heavy rainstorms or the melting water of thaw could flood trenches and dugouts within hours thus forcing the garrison to retreat onto open ground. In the Vosges Mountains meltwater often transformed trenches into torrential mountain streams. Irrigation ditches, dams and pumps became the weapons used to fight the water and to enable the trench fighter to exist in his muddy world. All kinds of earthworks had to be strengthened by using timber, wickerwork and planks. Whole kilometres of soft ground were bridged with dug boards. Next to construction work, locating and transporting building materials became a big business. In the course of the war engineers piled up large depots of materials behind the frontline to supply the front with all the building materials it needed.

October-November 1914 was however a time of improvisation. Infantry Regiment 40 can again be cited as a typical example of this period. In the winter of 1914/15 the *Hohenzollernfusiliers* held the line at Loretto Hill some kilometres west of Lens at the Artois sector. In order to make traffic possible in their sector the *Hohenzollernfusiliers* had to construct 3200 metres footbridges. For this construction effort they needed thirty wagonloads of piles and fifty-seven wagonloads of planks. Planks and girders were taken from the ruined, or by these activities ruined, houses of the nearby villages and towns Liévin, Angres and Lens. For the construction of first and second line dugouts 135 wagon loads of timber alone were removed from deserted buildings. The wire obstacle consumed forty wagonloads of sharpened piles. Finally, in January 1915, after months of intensive labour the positions of Infantry Regiment 40 were protected by an uninterrupted obstacle and all trenches were six feet deep. 225 loopholes with metal plates, shell splinter proof sentry posts, bomb proof dugouts for three companies in each battalion sector; hundreds of sandbags, plenty of weather resistant ammunition boxes and five ship bells for alarm purposes completed the position. But this elaborate result of engineer's skill and soldier's labour could be destroyed by heavy shell blasts within a few minutes. The Western Front developed its face and character in the winter of 1914/15. Engineer officer Ulrich Sander justly called this new form of war "an ammunition and constructors war" (cit. Sanders: *Pioniere*, p.229). On both sides of the line the soldiers constructed with shovels and picks what was to become their damp underground world for the next four years. The following years saw a process of perfection of trench war construction that produced nearly impregnable positions and a never-ending trial to break the impregnable wall which was called the Western Front.

But in spite of the difficulties of wintertime, endless labour and permanent small-scale warfare this winter was also a period of reorganization and recovery for the exhausted armies. On November 26th, 1914 the order of battle of the German forces at the Western Front was reorganized. Three army groups (*Heeresgruppen*) were formed. The "*Heeresgruppe Kronprinz von Bayern*" (Army Group Crown Prince of Bavaria) became responsible for the northern part of the front running from the channel coast to the battlefields of the Somme and commanded the 4th Army at Flanders, the 6th Army at Artois and the 2nd Army at the Somme. In the central sector between Oise and Champagne the "*Heeresgruppe von Heeringen*" was in command of the 1st Army on the riverbanks of the Oise, the 7th Army at the Aisne-Vesle riverfront and the 3rd Army on the chalky fields of the Champagne. Compared with the two other army groups the southern section of the German front was much longer and extended from the Argonne forest to the Swiss border. This sector was controlled by the "*Heeresgruppe Deutscher Kronprinz*" (Army Group German Crown Prince). The commander of this army group was the son of the German Emperor Wilhelm II. Crown Prince Wilhelm was responsible for the 5th Army holding the sector north of Verdun, the *Armee-Abteilung von Strantz* at the St. Mihiel salient between the Meuse and Moselle rivers, the fortress of Metz, *Armee-Abteilung von Falkenhausen* holding the frontline at Lorraine and the northern Vosges Mountains and *Armee-Abteilung Gaede* at the southern end of the Western Front from the southern Vosges Mountains to the Swiss border. The army group commanders were still army commanders too, retaining the command of their respective army which they had controlled since the beginning of the war. Crown Prince Rupprecht of Bavaria commanded the 6th Army, *Generaloberst* von Heeringen the 7th Army and Crown Prince Wilhelm commanded the 5th Army. The army groups did not form new staffs, but the 6th, 7th and 5th Army staffs had to fulfil both jobs; controlling an army and an army group at the same time. The main purpose of the army groups was to control the army group sector, to form army group reserves for the respective army group sector in order to deal with critical situations and the relief of exhausted troops. This reorganization was a response to the unsatisfying command system of the first months of the war. During this period the armies at the Western Front had acted quite independently under direct command of the German High Command. The 1st German Army (Kluck) was under the control of the 2nd (Buelow) but such a provisional arrangement could not compensate for the level of command lacking between a passive OHL and uncoordinated army commanders. The Chief of OHL *Generaloberst* von Moltke did not exert close control over his advancing armies. When the German armies approached the Marne the German supreme headquarters were 300 kilometres behind at Koblenz. As the HQ consisted of a staff of 1000 people, including the Emperor and the chancellor, a transport capacity of eleven trains was needed to move the headquarters. But overcoming personal and political restraints in order to move the headquarters further west proved even more difficult. While the political leadership and chancellor Bethmann-Hollweg argued against a move of the HQ to Luxembourg the Emperor pressed Moltke for a shift to the armies' right wing. Against all resistance the HQ was finally moved to Luxembourg. Moltke and the operations department were billeted at a former girls' school that offered even worse working conditions. A staff officer reported that tables in the small rooms were improvised and lighting was not available. Candles and petrol lamps had to be used at night. And most of the staff's work had to be done at night (cit. Stratz: *Der Weltkrieg* p.52). Communications were not better. There was no telephone communication between the majority of army headquarters and wireless was quite unreliable. Reports from the armies arrived late and outgoing orders were rendered obsolete because of the rapidly changing situation. Although the Emperor made a trip to the 4th Army's sector in the Champagne on September 7, Moltke did not visit his "far distant" armies before September 11 – a trip by car of 4-5 hours! At this time the Marne battle was already lost. To exert any influence on his army commanders Moltke relied on sending special representatives to the forward army headquarters. The representatives were to collect updated reports and were authorized to give orders on behalf of the supreme headquarters. One of these representatives was Oberstleutnant Richard Hentsch who played such an unlucky role in the decision making process during the battle of the Marne in September 1914. The distance between the OHL and the army headquarters and the insufficient lines of communication resulted in a serious lack of battle command and coordination. The disaster of the Marne arose from the lack of reserves and this failing structure of command. The implementation of army groups was designed to improve the German command structure. However, by March 1915 the army groups were already being dissolved and armies and army detachments were placed back under direct OHL control.

## Western Front 1915

From 1915 onwards strategists of both opposing camps were divided into two fractions and debated uncompromisingly the problem of where to focus the war effort and which theatre of war would bring victory: Westerners and easterners. The question of whether to first win the war in the west and then finish off the enemy in the east, or vice versa, plagued both groups. The westerners argued that absolute victory could only be achieved by beating the main adversary at the decisive Western Front. The easterners proposed an alternative path to victory by attacking the weakest partner of the hostile coalition with limited forces. For Germany this was Russia, for the Allies Turkey or the Balkans. The easterners' idea was to break up the hostile coalition by knocking out the weakest member and saving valuable blood which had already been so lavishly shed by the Western Front generals. On the German side this never-ending struggle lasted up until 1917 when the revolution in Russia finally solved the problem. The limited forces and permanent Allied pressure allowed the German army offensive operations at one theatre of war only. The Allies, repeatedly frustrated by their efforts at the Western Front, embarked on their eastern projects at Saloniki and Palestine till the end of war.

The Western Front was an absolute priority for France. Holding the Western Front was the basic prerequisite for the national survival of France. After losing major parts of Northern France, including its valuable coalmines and industrial facilities to the German invader, France was forced to take a last stand. As in Germany a never-ending struggle between westerners and easterners also took place on the British side. Westerners, like Sir Douglas Haig who took over the BEF Command in late 1915, argued that only a victory on the main battlefield in Belgium and Northern France would decide who were to be the victors of the war. They argued for a full-scale engagement at the Western Front in order to destroy the main enemy: Germany. Easterners, like Winston Churchill, referred to Britain's natural role as a naval power capable of engaging the enemy anywhere in the world at his weakest strategic points to achieve decisive victory with a minimum of effort and losses. The British and French Supreme Commands never focused their efforts either on the west or on the east but pursued both strategic concepts. Notwithstanding their general superiority in men and material this splitting of resources resulted in heavy setbacks for the Allies. At the same time as attacking several times at the Western Front Allied expeditionary corps tried to break the Central Powers by hitting their weakest allies, Turkey and Bulgaria, only to find the same frustrating stalemate at the Gallipolli peninsula, the Saloniki bridgehead and Palestine which they had hoped to avoid. There was never any concrete decision either way as Britain pursued overseas expeditions right up till the end of war whilst simultaneously fighting the main war in Northern France.

At the beginning of 1915 the issue of where to focus German offensive power – on the Western or the Eastern front – became the crucial question of strategic priority for the German Chief of Staff Falkenhayn. The problem was Germany's limited military power that allowed offensive operations at one theatre of war only. For Falkenhayn, even with a reorganized and increased German Army at hand, the idea of making a second attempt at breaking British and French resistance, with the threat of overwhelming Russian manpower behind, would be a perilous risk. Falkenhayn opted instead for a strategic push at the Eastern Front to quash the Russian armies while still holding ground in the West with a minimum of forces and activities there limited to local operations. Early in January 1915 Falkenhayn made his decision and prepared the defence at the Western Front for 1915 by issuing orders on January, 7th and 25th in which he formulated his doctrine for the defensive battle.

The existing frontline in Belgium and France would become a fortified and well-organized line of defence that enabled the German garrison to resist even lengthy attacks of superior British and French forces. The German High Command took it for granted that an attack in the West was impending. Falkenhayn intended to send as many troops as possible to the East to take part in the offensive. As a result the garrison troops at the Western Front were reduced to an absolute minimum. To give them a strong hold in the defensive battle the frontline divisions had to construct a strongly fortified frontline position. The weakness in manpower was to be counterbalanced by strength in firepower. Machine gun nests were built of concrete; they were to serve as centres of resistance from which the enemy could be stopped by flanking fire. Wire obstacles were constructed fifty metres in front of the trenches but still close enough to be controlled by the trench posts. The Germans quickly realized that the increasing enemy artillery firing at high trajectory was able to pulverize every position if enough guns and shells were available and if observed fire was possible. But the real consequences for the infantry could not be grasped completely. The infantry was assembled in the main line of resistance and it was ordered to hold the trenches at all costs. Every metre of the trench lost to the enemy should be retaken by immediate counterattacks. Behind the frontline trenches the construction of a support line was ordered; it was meant to provide shellproof dugouts and covered communication trenches for the reserve and counterattack forces. The network of the communication trenches allowed the troops to move in the trenches covered against fire or to evacuate heavily shelled trenches. Communication trenches offered room for the construction of dugouts behind the exposed line of main resistance. The question of the construction of rearward lines which were designed to stop breakthroughs when counterattacks failed became a point of debate. Some German Army commanders at the Western Front argued against the construction of rearward lines because they feared that the resistance of the frontline forces would be weakened if the men were continually aware that there was still another line of defence behind them. Experience confirmed that this fear was unjustified and loss lists taught that the inflexible doctrine of holding a trench line crowded with infantry at all costs carried a high price in blood and fatalities. The lack of labour units meant that German combat forces in the West had to undertake the tremendous task of construction work and transporting material themselves. In the first half of 1915 the construction effort focused on the improvement of the frontline trenches that were to become the centres of resistance. The improvement of the frontline positions was a cause of real stress for the troops; they worked for months mainly at night, directly in front of the muzzles of the enemy's guns. In May 1915 *General* Falkenhayn ordered the construction of a rearward line about 2-3 kilometres behind the frontline positions. The underlying idea was that the Allies would be forced to rearrange their artillery concentration before being able to attack the next of the successive lines. The German positions were in a permanent process of construction for over a year. By the summer of 1916 these constructions had developed to the standard of a veritable fortress with concrete shelters, deep dugouts and several lines of wire obstacles. These measures gave the war at the Western Front its typical character of siege warfare.

The battle on the Western Front in 1915 was a time of improvisation. The German system of defence was in a process of progressive development up until 1917 when it reached its peak with the flexible defence in depth. Faced with this development British and French attack tactics underwent a process of improvement, learning from terrible failures. The first test of battle at the Western Front in 1915 took place in the Champagne where the French Army attacked the German 3rd Army's sector between Souain and Perthes with five army corps on February 21st. It was the first time that the German trenches lay under drumfire. When the battle had ceased in March all preliminary French gains had been lost to German counterattacks. Crown Prince Wilhelm mentions in his war memoirs that his staff officers wondered how France could bear such heavy losses in men (cit. Wilhelm: *Meine Erinnerungen*, p.125). The Champagne battle was still going on when the First British Army, under the command of General Sir Douglas Haig, attacked on March 10th-12th at Neuve Chapelle. Using overwhelming manpower – 30,000 Britons against 2000 German defenders – to attack a narrow sector, the breakthrough and taking of Aubers Ridge seemed to be a sure bet. This was not however to be the case. Shattered by unprecedented heavy artillery preparation the German line collapsed. But for the British battle plan, set on a schedule of succeeding rushes, stops and preparatory fires, the failure of the attacking forces on the flanks and the deadly fire of some German rearward machine gun nests broke the momentum of advance. Opportunities were missed because of the inflexible British plan and command system. Battalion commanders who suggested alterations in conformance with the battlefield situation were denied all freedom of action. Corps headquarters several miles behind the battle line insisted on direct battle command but depended completely on unreliable telephone communications. Without real-time information and with a chain of command that needed hours in order to transfer orders to the battalions and companies, direct higher battle handling became impossible. As a result the British troops were forced to rely on precise timetables. Fixed timetables were an inflexible instrument for handling permanently changing situations on the battlefield. Without an operational leadership the collapse of timetables resulted in soldiers being left in the trenches unsupported and unguided from the rear. But the failing leadership, which was criticized in the trenches as "château general ship", turned out to be a general problem of battle control which was never solved in the Great War. Military technology, especially the unprecedented effect of artillery and rifle fire, had mercilessly outrun the communication techniques by cutting the information flow and the chain of command the moment battle began. At Neuve Chapelle the German line was broken and the front line garrison smashed. But the British troops had to wait for hours for new orders from the 4th Corps and they lost their chance while the German resistance recovered from the first surprise. German reinforcements were given enough time to occupy a system of rearward strong posts from where the superior firepower of the German machine guns stopped any further enemy advance. But German reinforcements came too late to counterattack at once. The following day the British resumed the attack, this time without preparation, against an unlocated German line of unknown strength which was in fact much stronger than on the first day of attack. Three rushes resulted in failure and losses. On the third day the German counterattack took place. The attacking German reinforcements faced the same problems as the British on the second day and they also failed. The battle ended as a battle of lost opportunities, setting the pattern for what was to come on the Western Front and revealing the basic tactical problems of trench warfare.

Neuve Chapelle was the first step on a path of trial and error. The Allies had to improve their offensive tactics, to understand the defensive power of the German line and to find the instruments to break it. As a first but still insufficient measure mortars and mountain guns were allotted to the infantry to deal with the deadly machine guns. British General Headquarters saw the key to offensive success in a detailed preparation including careful registration by artillery. On April 4, 1915 the French CinC Joffre issued his directive for general offensives which was quickly captured and carefully studied by the Germans. Placing the stress on attack and intensive artillery preparation, Joffre's order rejected the effectiveness of surprise attacks. To achieve superiority in every phase of attack each division was allotted a narrow sector of between 1200-1500 metres where a steady flow of reinforcements filled the battlefield. Advancing in dense waves and following in close succession this human flow was supposed to keep the attack moving. But in the test of battle the relentless concentration of forces would ultimately turn out to be counterproductive. At each divisional sector 3600 men were crowded on an area of 1200x170 square metres and the units became mixed up completely. When this densely crowded infantry went over the top and became exposed to German gun and machinegun fire the battle developed into a mere slaughter, as would happen in the next Champagne battle in the autumn of 1915 (cit. Schwarte: *Die militaerischen Lehren des Grossen Krieges*, p.33-34).

On the other side of no-man's land Neuve Chapelle lessons were also learnt. In June 1915 the German Inspector General of the Engineers' Corps (*Gen. Insp. des Ing. und Pion. Korps*) issued the manual "war experiences of field fortification" recommending the construction of two positions separated by 1-2 kilometres and consisting each of several trench lines between 50 and 100 metres apart. Important spots were to be converted into strongpoints and it was emphasized how necessary flanking fire from machine gun posts was. Concrete dugouts were to provide the infantry with shellproof cover. Obstacles were to be constructed close to the trenches at a distance of 20-30 metres only and in different strips that were to be 6-10 metres wide. Close cooperation between infantry and artillery was vital (cit. Schwarte: *Die militaerischen Lehren des Grossen Krieges*, p.32). Acting on "war experiences of field fortification" Falkenhayn ordered a deepening of the system of obstacles and trenches and the construction of a second line of trenches. This second line of trenches was planned as a rearward live-in trench offering the German garrison bombproof shelters, living facilities and covered communications. Machine guns were carefully posted in concrete shelters to rule no-man's land by flanking fire. The frontline trench was held only by sentries. The bulk of the forces remained in the second line ready to man the first line immediately in the moment of alarm. The first line was still to be held at all costs – this was an inflexible doctrine that would cost many German soldiers' lives in 1915/16. This double front trench system would finally develop into the classic German deep defence system used at the Western Front in 1917.

German activities on the Western Front in 1915 were restricted to local operations and defensive actions. The 2nd Ypres battle marked a new step in the escalating battle at the Western Front when on April 22 the Germans attacked behind a cloud of poison gas. Unprotected against the asphyxiating gas the allied infantry flooded back and the line collapsed but there were no German reserves available to exploit the opportunity. The use of poison gas could have been the chance for a strategic breakthrough but the attack was planned by the German Command as a kind of experimental local operation. In April 1915 gas was not yet a calculable weapon but it was to become so in the near future.

Even the French and British could only launch major offensive operations for a limited time before manpower and ammunition ran low. In the meantime, between the big pushes, the Allies held the enemy under permanent pressure with a run of never-ending local operations. But even series of local attacks could not prevent the fact that major parts of the front developed into so-called quiet sectors. Moreover in the higher ranks opinions differed about the sense of pressing the enemy by never-ending local combat activities. The German OHL had some doubts concerning the effect of such men and material consuming operations that did not achieve decisive results and argued for a defensive strategy behind improved positions. Falkenhayn had to use his limited military power carefully in face of the pressing demands of the different theatres of war. Local attacks were often inspired by the forces in the line who were trying to improve a tactically difficult or uncomfortable situation. Facing limited forces and ammunition stores the German higher staffs had to consider carefully if the expected gains justified the expenses in life and ammunition. Tacticians at the Western Front argued against passiveness as a tactical pattern making the German soldier a victim of the overwhelming technical means of the French and British armies. Well-planned and prepared local pushes should hurt the enemy, destroy his offensive build-up and keep the spirits of the own forces up. So-called quiet sectors often proved unreliable in the moment of sudden crisis because the garrison would be in a daze caused by the quiet life they led under the protection of their shelters. The French Army Command embarked on more aggressive politics and pressed its forces to a permanently offensive attitude. Trench war was considered to be a passing phase. This view was shared by the French Field Marshal Foch who describes trench war in his war memoirs as "a confession of powerlessness, merely a crisis in the conduct of war" produced by the development of firepower which made defence superior to attack (cit. Foch: *Kriegserinnerungen* p.195). According to this theory the trench war would last as long as no belligerent side was able to launch an attack strong enough to subdue the increasing power of defence. The French troops were not even allowed to improve their positions because it was feared that this would promote a defensive mood in the men who were destined to liberate French territory from the occupation by the German invader. Lacking in well-designed and elaborate positions the living conditions, comfort and security of the French trench fighter were far inferior to his German counterpart who lived and fought in a sophisticated system of permanent entrenchments.

More trials were to follow: the battles of St. Mihiel salient in April, Loretto Hill, Aubers Ridge and Festubert in May. Some weeks later the French Army attacked in the dense woods of the Argonne forest and at crucial points like Vauquois Hill at the eastern flank of the German Argonne position in June. In July the Muenster valley in the Vosges Mountains saw intensive fighting on some hilltops. Major parts of the Western Front were set aflame again in September when on the 25th the British and French launched a coordinated attack near Loos at Artois and in the Champagne. Twenty-one French divisions attacked the front of the 3rd German Army between Aubérive and Massiges and tried in vain to break through. In spite of superior numbers only the first German line was taken at the tremendous price of 130,000 men lost. Despite the growing power of the artillery preparation the development of British advance tactics proved to be mere mass attacks consisting of wave upon wave of men who were slaughtered by the deadly firepower of the German defenders. The French Army had their own tactics; methodical bombardment of the enemy positions and attacking objectives limited to some hundred yards away. Day and night bombardments that went on for several days would wear down enemy fortifications and morale. The intensive preparation left no room for the momentum of surprise and converted attacks into a programme of slow and systematic progress that aimed at reducing German resistance. Artillery advanced to be the main instrument of the coming attrition warfare leaving the infantry the role of mopping up the broken enemy positions. Tactical and technical progress focussed mainly on artillery during the following years.

In the autumn of 1915 the German infantry at the Western Front had to face the beginning of the Allied strategy of attrition warfare. Attrition warfare developed as a result of battles that had got stuck but could not be stopped for political reasons. In the fighting of 1915 both sides learned that reserves and speed were key problems of the stalemate at the Western Front. On the 19th century battlefield a battle lasted just a few days and only tactical reserves, which were waiting on the battlefield for the proper moment to interfere, were involved. At the Western Front of 1915 the battles lasted for weeks and the strategic reserves of the defender, which came by rail from far away theatres of war, arrived on the battlefield within a matter of days. The tremendous defensive firepower and the slow advance of the attacking forces prevented any strategic breakthrough as long as the defending enemy had reserves at his disposal. Haig would face this problem at the Somme, as would Ludendorff in 1918, when enemy reserves arrived on the battlefield in time and frustrated all attempts to achieve a strategic breakthrough. The reason for this problem was simple. In spite of mass armies and industrial warfare the maximum speed of offensive operations was still only walking speed on the shell-torn battlefields of the Western Front while logistics profited from railway speed. This meant that the defender assembled his reserves faster on the battlefield and reorganized his defence quicker than the attacker could destroy it. Moreover, the attacker's advance was delayed by the destroyed battle zone which he had to pass on his way to the intended breakthrough point. As a result a strategic breakthrough and victory were possible only after a complete exhaustion of the enemy reserves. To cope with this problem successfully Foch developed a refined strategy of attrition that he explained to Field Marshal Raymond Recouly after the war. As long as the enemy had enough reserves at its disposal it would be useless to push back parts of the enemy front or to achieve a tactical breakthrough. The attacking forces would come to a dead end where the supply situation would deteriorate in accordance with the increasing deepness of the penetration. In this critical moment the attackers would be confronted with fresh enemy reserves that had arrived on the battlefield in time to prevent the breakthrough. Foch's solution was a series of offensives which would exhaust the strategic enemy reserves. The effect of the offensives would increase proportionally to the attrition of the hostile reserves. In the late summer of 1918 Foch used this strategy successfully (cit. Recoully: *Foch Erinnerungen*, p.59-61, 81-83). Similar ideas can be found in Falkenhayn's concept for the Verdun battle and in Ludendorff's succession of attacks in 1918. Both failed and were later seriously criticized. Only Foch succeeded in 1918 when he profited from the general exhaustion of German manpower.

## Western Front 1916

For the German Supreme Command the Western Front was the decisive theatre of war and time was considered to be the crucial factor. Germany's conduct of war was however contradictory to this conviction. Instead of seeking a decisive victory in France, as it did only in 1914, 1916 and 1918, it focused on the Balkans in 1915 and 1916, on Russia in 1915-1918 and even on Italy in 1917. This apparent inconsistency was however illusory. As a result of a lack of men and material the German leaders were in fact forced to pursue this conduct of war. Although the army had been successfully increased from 3,900,000 men on August 1, 1914 to 8,200,000 men on September 6, 1916 (Volkmann: *Der Grosse Krieg*, p.241) and a war industry that was capable of supplying this expanding army had been organized, there was no doubt within the German General Staff that in the long-term Germany's resources were inferior to the Allies' potential. In the course of 1916 the Allies finally overtook the Germans in mass production and use of artillery shells. The Prussian ministry of war was blamed for this state of affairs. The German infantry suffered under restless enemy shelling whilst the scarcity of artillery ammunition reduced the effectiveness of German heavy guns. Previously the superiority of the German Army's heavy guns had been one of the reasons for success in battle. For the conduct of war this meant that in 1914 and 1918 the German Army had only a slight superiority of forces at the Western Front. However, superiority at the Western Front was the basic prerequisite for successful battle and the relentless endeavour of Falkenhayn and his successors, Field Marshal Hindenburg and Quartermaster *General* Ludendorff, was to regain this superiority. As a result Germany fought the First World War under serious time pressure. Schlieffen had already realized this and had proposed his ill-fated "Schlieffen Plan" as a solution to the predicament. The aggravation of this time pressure could not be ignored by his successors in 1915-1916 when the Allies launched repeated attacks with ever increasing forces at the Western Front. German resources in men, money, raw materials and industrial capacities were limited and dwindled away under the conditions of blockade and attrition warfare. The German people lived with the feeling of being under constant siege. Surrounded by hostile countries the German nation felt the consequences of the British blockade that was increasingly cutting off Germany and its allies from the world markets and its resources. Food shortages began in 1915. The Central Powers were forced to depend on their own industrial capacities and natural resources. The consequences for the territories occupied by the Germans were very harsh. Germany intensified the exploitation of the occupied territories and their populations. Prisoner of war (POW) labour was mustered up for agriculture and construction work. Behind the Western Front thousands of Russian POWs had to dig rearward positions suffering from malnutrition and lousy living conditions. Collecting raw materials and agricultural produce and organizing labour became the main business of the German military administration in the occupied countries in order to feed the demands of Germany and its allies.

Compared with the German side the Allied resources in men and material were nearly unlimited but not yet organized into armies and converted into war material. Hundreds of thousands of men could be recruited from the British and French colonies. The complete production of the world markets was at their disposal if they could pay. This would result in a tremendous public debt for France and Britain seriously destabilizing post-war national economy. However, the Allies needed time to build up the full weight of their military power. This applied especially to England which had had to increase her tiny professional army up to a million men. Britain's engagement at the Western Front developed from holding a minor force with which to assist their French ally, politically and morally, into a full-scale engagement of seventy divisions. Never before in history had Britain had such a large army in the field, draining the country's manpower and industrial resources in a futile attrition war. In 1915 considerable numbers of volunteers enlisted to form what was later called Kitchener's New Army. But in 1916 conscription had to be introduced in Britain too. There was no other way for the British Army to cope with the drain of men at the Western Front. In the summer of 1916 the new British Army was ready for its push at the Somme.

The First World War was the first war of the modern industrialized world. Modern societies were able to send millions of soldiers into the field equipped with all the technical equipment and supplies that modern industry can produce. Railway transport made it possible to move men and supplies to every battlefield within days allowing an uninterrupted line of supply. The nearly unlimited production capacities of modern industry led to an escalation of warfare and resulted in a battle of attrition at the Western Front where the industries of two coalitions struggled for supremacy. The basic feature of industrial warfare was the mass use of men and resources and a permanent process of innovation of technical equipment. The basic tactical problems consisted of the superiority of firepower and the lack of transport. Keegan summarizes the problem with "the simple truth of 1914-18 trench warfare is that the massing of large numbers of soldiers, unprotected by anything but cloth uniforms against large masses of other soldiers, protected by earthworks and barbed wire and provided with rapid-fire weapons, was bound to result in very heavy causalities among the attackers" (cit. Keegan: *The First World War*, p.293). It could be added that the defender suffered similar loss rates. Modern artillery and the machine gun won the superiority of firepower on the battlefield and made moving troops a costly operation. At the Western Front defence turned out to be superior to attack but no less costly. After winning some hundred metres of shell-torn ground attacks were sooner or later stalled by stiff resistance but at the cost of tremendous losses for both sides. While the defender killed thousands of attackers with his machine guns when they went over the top he himself was exposed to the annihilating effect of the attacker's well observed artillery shelling. Without overwhelming artillery support and technical equipment the modern mass army was unable to attack successfully. But neither the German nor the Allied armies possessed the necessary motorized and armoured transport capacities to move mass armies and their vast amount of equipment in the field which was what was needed if a breakthrough was to be achieved. Therefore it was far more the problem of attacking and movement than the success of defence that produced the stalemate at the Western Front. The result was the war in the trenches. Later on the truck and the tank would solve this problem and end the stalemate. But from 1914-1918 the invention and development of heavy motorized transport and armoured vehicles were still in their early phases.

In 1916 the question for the German Supreme Command was yet again where to focus their strategic priorities. For Germany this was really a question of victory or defeat. Most German military leaders agreed that the Western Front was the decisive theatre of war. But in comparison with the Eastern Front the west offered no promising options for offensive operations. For Falkenhayn the bloody failure of the Allies' attacks in 1915 was a warning. The repeated use of overwhelming forces by the Allies at the Artois and in the Champagne produced nothing more than tremendous losses. In addition the Allies had concentrated the bulk of their arms and armies at the Western Front. After nearly one and a half years of war the Western Front had grown into a veritable fortress. Despite these unfavourable conditions *General* Falkenhayn opted for an offensive in the west; the attack against Verdun. Expecting no serious crisis at the Eastern Front, in Italy or on the Balkans and recognizing the Allied disaster at Gallipoli, Falkenhayn decided that the time was ripe for an attack in the west; all the more so because there was the real prospect of a major Allied offensive in the summer. To forestall the expected Allied offensive Falkenhayn chose to begin the Verdun attack early, in February 1916, in spite of the difficult conditions on the battlefield caused by the cold and wet winter weather. The fortress of Verdun was the strongest part of the Western Front and formed the northeastern pillar of the French line. Stiff resistance from the French Army was thus expected and in fact when it commenced on February 21, 1916 the battle of Verdun became the first real and long lasting battle of attrition. There are contradictory sources about whether Falkenhayn had actually planned to conduct the battle of Verdun from the beginning as a battle of attrition to "bleed the French Army to death" with limited effort on the German side, as Falkenhayn later claimed in his memoirs. The "Christmas Memorandum" in which Falkenhayn, after summarizing the strategic situation at the end of 1915, discusses the options for 1916 and develops the concept of a battle of attrition at Verdun, is only available in the printed edition of Falkenhayn's war memoirs. The original draft is lost, as most other documents of the German Army Command were destroyed in the air raids against Potsdam in 1945. Except for a few pages all of Falkenhayn's private papers were lost in 1945. The German *Reichsarchiv* expresses some doubts about the originality of the "Christmas Memorandum" in the German official history "*Der Weltkrieg*". Even the staff of the *Reichsarchiv* was unable to locate the original "Christmas Memorandum" when compiling the Verdun volume in the 1920s (cit. *Reichsarchiv*: *Der Weltkrieg*, vol.10, p.2). Obviously, whatever strategic idea Falkenhayn had was never clearly communicated to the German military leaders at the Western Front. When the 5th German Army attacked on February 21st the army leader Crown Prince Wilhelm did not believe that attrition would be the final goal of the offensive. His Chief of Staff von Knobelsdorf only became a strong supporter of the idea of attrition in the course of the battle. (cit. Wilhelm: *Meine Erinnerungen*, p.158, 169, 186-189, 228-229). Other army commanders, like the Bavarian Crown Prince Rupprecht, derived the impression from the meetings with the OHL that Falkenhayn himself did not know what he really wanted (cit. Rupprecht: *Kriegstagebuch*, p.427). Moreover the tactical details of attrition – how to inflict serious losses on the enemy with a limited loss of one's own men and material – were never openly discussed between the military leaders and Falkenhayn either. The use of overwhelming artillery on a limited battlefield to destroy the French Army was no new idea and the French responded in the same way, making the battle as costly for the German as it was for the French infantry.

On February 21, 1916 the German infantry went over the top and within days pushed their way into the belt of forts that surrounded Verdun. After several days of remarkable progress and the spectacular taking of Fort Douaumont by a couple of men on February 26 the French resistance collapsed and the way into the fortress' centre was open. But losses were high in the German ranks too and reserves were not available to relieve the exhausted infantry. French reserves arrived in time and in the ruins of the village of Douaumont the Germans met the stiff resistance that would become typical for the battle at Verdun. The chance for a quick victory at Verdun was definitely lost. In spite of new German successes in the following weeks the battle got stuck in the triangle of Fort Douaumont-Fort Vaux-Fleury. Within the limited space of this triangle the battle saw more impressive acts, the taking of Fort Vaux for example and the desperate fight for the ruins of Fleury. In the summer of 1916 the infamous triangle became the grave for tens of thousands of men. The trench war transformed into a crater war. The infantry, dispersed in the shell holes, nearly died of thirst in the summer heat. The shelling cut them off from supply and relief and even the task of bringing bottles of Selters water from the caves of Fort Douaumont was a death mission. Rain turned the shelled earth into groundless mud drowning anyone loaded heavily with arms and ammunition that fell into a flooded crater. At this cratered triangle a new kind of fighter appeared. Dispersed in shell craters the men fought a desperate fight for survival alone or in small groups under never-ending gunfire. The newly introduced steel helmet became the symbol for these lonely fighters against the overwhelming horrors of a technical world. Gunfire at Verdun reached an unprecedented peak of destructive power. The construction of a trench system or communication trenches in the stony soil became nearly impossible. What was dug with exhausting labour in the night was extinguished by bursting shells during the day. Relief or the transport of supplies in the heavily shelled ravines at Verdun was even more dangerous than the existence in the craters.

In the final days of February the French resistance nearly collapsed but the lack of fresh German reserve forces prevented a decisive blow. Although promised to the 5th Army by Falkenhayn these reserves were not available. This resulted in the later thesis that the Chief of the General Staff of the German Army was in fact not interested in the quick capture of the fortress of Verdun. Flanking fire from the western banks of the Meuse River forced the German 5th Army to attack there too. For months "Hill 304" and "Dead Man's Hill" became the scene of more desperate fighting. The battle of Verdun began to consume both the French and the German Army. And the real crisis at the Western Front was still to come.

On July 1, 1916 after seven days of drumfire the Allied attack at the Somme began. The Somme was Douglas Haig's first battle as commander of the BEF at the Western Front. Haig, who would later become a disciple of attrition war, expected a breakthrough as far as Bapaume. Cavalry was at hand to take over. But it was the Somme that was to turn quickly into the second big battle of attrition at the Western Front. While the attack in the French sector was quite successful, for the British 4th Army the ill-fated "first day of the Somme" was a debacle. Months of preparation, seven days of shelling and one million shells had apparently pulverized the German positions. However, although the trenches had been flattened and the dugouts had been reduced to mere holes in the earth when the shelling ceased the attacking infantry found the barbed wire at many places untouched and German infantry emerged from their half buried underground shelters to receive the British with a deadly hail of machine gun fire. Instead of passing a decimated and stunned enemy the British infantry, burdened with sixty pounds of equipment and advancing upright in successive lines over the shell torn ground, met full-scale battle and often massacre. Within one day 20,000 men were killed and 40,000 were wounded which meant a death rate of 20% of the attacking forces. The resulting confusion meant that it took the British generals some time to fully understand what had happened and why. Haig and the 4th Army's staff were still unaware of what had happened one day later and discussed the continuation of the attack while the decimated battalions reorganized and counted their losses. The artillery preparation was impressive but nevertheless insufficient. The amount of heavy guns and high explosive shells used was inadequate and the shrapnel which was destined to cut the wire failed, leaving the job to the infantry.

The offensive continued. Falkenhayn realized that despite the defensive success of July 1st the crisis at the Somme was still to come. Colonel von Lossberg, who had come from the Champagne where he had distinguished himself in organizing a flexible defence in the battle of autumn 1915, was ordered to take over as the 2nd Army's Chief of Staff. The British Command replaced the failing strategy of general attack by operations with local objectives, limited in both time and effort. However, overwhelming gunfire battered the German resistance. Months of rising and decreasing battle activity followed. The war of attrition and German inferiority in men and material took their toll on the men fighting in the shell holes. In September and October the German infantry's power of resistance showed the first signs of weariness. Considerably more ground was lost to the enemy than in July. In the end the Army Group Crown Prince Rupprecht of Bavaria counted a battle-period of forty-seven days when the Somme battle ceased in the mud of November 1916. For the Allies the result was disillusioning: On a length of twenty-six miles a pocket had been pushed five to eight miles deep into the German frontline and forty square miles of shell torn desert were occupied. Bapaume and Peronne were still behind the German line. This was far beyond the breakthrough so eagerly expected in July 1916. But the real victory was the attrition imposed on the German Army. The famous German military writer *General* Schwarte described the balance of the fighting of 1916 as follows: "Verdun as offensive battle, but much more the Somme as defensive battle had shattered the German armies' fighting power" (cit. Schwarte: *Geschichte des Weltkrieges*, p.254).

In the summer of 1916 the initiative was taken over by the Allies. The never-ending pressure at the Somme, the collapse of the Austrian forces in the face of the Brussilow offensive in Galicia and the situation in Italy led Romania to pick this favourable moment to enter the war on the Allies' side. In the autumn Germany was facing a serious crisis and Falkenhayn's method of leading the German war effort was in disrepute. On August 28th, 1916 Field Marshal Paul von Hindenburg and *General* Erich Ludendorff succeeded Falkenhayn in the command of the German Army. The "heroes of Tannenberg" initiated serious changes at the Western Front. To deal with the crisis German warfare in the west was reduced to defensive operations. The attack at Verdun was cancelled. Major forces were sent from the West to Galicia and Romania. The armies at the Western Front had to focus their efforts on more effective defensive organization and the development and training of defensive tactics. The Western Front received command structures which would remain typical in the years that followed. The General Headquarters had its command post at Charleville and later, in 1918, at Avesnes. Emperor Wilhelm II. had his own headquarters at Kreuznach. These were later moved to the famous resort Spa in February 1918. The front line sectors of France and Belgium were under the command of different *Heeresgruppen* (army groups) that formed an operative command structure under the control of the OHL. The Crown Prince of Bavaria Rupprecht and his army group called "*Heeresgruppe Rupprecht von Bayern*" commanded the forces of the northern part of the Western Front. The 6th, 1st, 2nd and 7th Army were under his command. The middle section of the front in the west was under the command of the Prussian Crown Prince Wilhelm and his "*Heeresgruppe Deutscher Kronprinz*". This army group controlled the 3rd and 5th Army and the frontline forces in Lorraine and Alsace which were grouped in army detachments, the so-called *Armeeabteilungen*. At Lorraine the "*Armee-Abt. C*" held the front. Further south in the Vosges Mountains and in upper Alsace the "*Armee-Abt. A*" and the "*Armee-Abt. B*" were in position. The Army Group "*Deutscher Kronprinz*" held the line between Reims and the Swiss border totalling 400 kilometres. Expecting the French offensive at the Aisne and in the Champagne in spring 1917 the army group lost control of the "*Armee-Abt. C*", "*A*" and "*B*" and became responsible for the 7th Army which gave this army group a more westerly orientation. The Army Group Command and the Command of the 5th Army were identical up until November 25, 1916 when the OHL ordered their separation. Deprived of tactical questions the army group staffs were smaller than the army staffs and consisted of a Chief of Staff, four staff officers, two adjutants, two administrative officers and officers for special arms. The 4th Army, which formed the northern flank of the German Western Front at Flanders under the command of Herzog Albrecht von Wuerttemberg, was independent. In spring 1917 Herzog Albrecht took over "*Armee-Abt. C*", "*A*" and "*B*" from the Army Group "*Deutscher Kronprinz*" and formed the "*Heeresgruppe Herzog Albrecht*" at the southern part of the Western Front.

Each army or army detachment consisted of three to six corps. This depended on the different sectors and the respective conditions there. Additionally, the armies were responsible for supplying the war zone and for its administration. The supreme army quartermaster and the Etappen-Inspektion carried out the administrative work. The average number of divisions under army command at the Western Front was fifteen, under corps command 2-4 divisions. Originally the army corps was the basic strategic and administrative unit in the German Army consisting of two divisions each which were permanently under corps' control. But the warfare at the Western Front showed that this method of organization was unsuitable. Armies and corps held a special sector of the frontline for long-term periods and in this way they became stationary. According to the army corps sector's size and the intensity of the fighting exhausted infantry divisions holding the line had to be relieved after several days or weeks by divisions available and suitable for the mission. In its respective sector the corps command became the supreme organization acquainted with the local conditions. As well as the layout and construction of the positions and the coordination of the fighting divisions the corps' responsibilities included the administration of the sector. The corps staff had to organize the service of supply and the construction and maintenance of roads, railroads and depots, the billeting of the troops behind the front and the hospitals. From 1916 the corps were no longer designated by their original Roman numbers but were instead called *Gruppe* (group) in combination with the sector's name. For example, the XIII. *Wuerttembergisches* Army Corps holding the sector of the "Hindenburg line" north of St. Quentin was called "*Gruppe Caudry*" for a year and a half. The forces on both sides of the Meuse river in the Verdun sector were designated as "*Maas-Gruppe West*" and "*Maas-Gruppe Ost*". The permanent exchange of divisions in the line required strict control of the group's sector. This was especially important when confronted with a problem that had not occurred during the first half of the war. During 1915-1916 divisions held their sectors at the Western Front for long periods of time. Now the infantry lost interest in carefully constructing the positions. Even mere rumours about relief reduced labour activities considerably. Many regimental histories record the insufficient construction of positions that were taken over from lazy predecessors. Understandably it was quite depressing for a trench garrison to have to leave their newly well-constructed trenches and dugouts to the benefit of others while they themselves had to take over a worse sector. Many regiments experienced this several times and this had a detrimental effect on morale and motivation.

Under the conditions of Western Front trench war the divisions were in a permanent process of being relieved and exchanged, and they were given big responsibilities regarding relief, military justice, decorations, holiday and training. From the beginning of 1915 the divisions became the smallest self-contained formations of all arms. Even active divisions completely lost the traditional connection with their original peacetime army corps and exchanged permanently together with the sector the commanding corps staff. The infantry division developed into an all arms force of infantry, artillery, machine guns, mortars, train, signal service including divisional sausage balloon, medical and veterinary services and field recruit depot. The battalion size field recruit depot of each division trained permanently approximately 900 recruits and convalescent soldiers ready to be sent to the front when required. The idea of the field recruit depots was to provide replacements quickly and to improve military training by close contact with the fighting forces and their experience. Training camps in Germany could not provide that. When the division moved the field recruit depot followed providing the division with a constant source of trained replacements to maintain the divisional strength at an average of 300-500 officers and 12,000 men. The divisional command structure was quite simple. The divisional commander was head of the division, assisted by his staff of approximately twenty-five officers. He was responsible for all aspects of command and administration and issued his orders to the infantry brigade commander and the divisional artillery commander. The former was responsible for all divisional infantry forces; the latter commanded all artillery units including the heavy artillery in the divisional sector. Special arms such as heavy artillery and mortars, mining companies or labour units were under order of the army or group and stationary in their respective sectors. These units were only temporarily placed under the command of the division in accordance with orders and the military situation.

The German infantry fighting in the trenches was organized in regiments. Approximately 3000 officers and men fought under their respective regimental flag. However, the average regimental strength decreased as the war went on because of the high losses and the lack of recruits. Originally each division had four infantry regiments. In the autumn of 1916 the size of the divisions was reduced to three regiments to increase the number of divisions and make them more practical. Each regiment had three battalions numbered I., II. and III. Like the army corps battalions were designated by Latin numbers in the German Army. Four companies and one machine gun company formed a battalion. The twelve companies of the regiment were numbered from 1-12. Officially they were 250 men strong but under combat conditions their average strength was 160 and this decreased in the autumn of 1918 down to forty rifle bearers. In August 1918 infantry battalions were reduced to three companies but they received an increased number of machine guns. The all-arms pattern of infantry organization converted the battalion commander into a kind of "little division commander", as Walter Bloem recalled in his war memoirs when he took over a battalion in spring 1918. Bloem wrote that the strength of his companies had declined from 250 in 1914 to only 120 riflemen in February 1918. But firepower became even stronger when six light machine guns were used per infantry company and when an artillery battery, mortar and machine gun company, engineers and signal service were attached to each battalion. The machine gun companies were already added to the infantry battalions by order of the war ministry from August 25, 1916, founded on the experiences of Verdun and the Somme. In 1916/17 each machine gun company had six guns. These weapons were designated as close combat assistance for the infantry. For commanding his complex all-arms battalion Bloem had a battalion staff consisting of six officers and two medical officers including an engineer and a signal officer. In 1915 a battalion staff consisted only of the battalion commander, his adjutant and a battalion medical officer (cit. Bloem: *Das Ganze halt*, p.515-516).

In regimental organization the machine gun companies of the infantry regiments were numbered 1-3. Each infantry company was divided into three platoons, each platoon into four sections and a section consisted of two groups forming the smallest tactical subdivision of eight men and one lance corporal. Four stretcher-bearers were attached to the company. Originally a regiment was commanded by a colonel, a battalion by a major, a company by a captain and a platoon by a lieutenant. However, serious losses in the officers' corps lead to a situation where on the whole a major was responsible for the regiment, a captain for the battalion, a lieutenant for the company, and the platoons were lead by sergeant-major-lieutenants, acting officers or vice-sergeant-majors. The regiment was the military home and identity of the German World War I soldier. Old regiments had traditional names like "*Leibgrenadier-Regiment*" or "*Hohenzollernfuesiliere*" and two individual regimental numbers. The first number was the number of their home state, for example Baden, Bavaria or Prussia. The second was the German Army number. Regiments raised later in the war received only the German Army numbers but even these newly raised regiments developed their own identities and traditions and called themselves the regiments with the "high street numbers". This referred to the high regimental number they had been designated compared with the low numbers of the older regiments. The Treaty of Versailles forced Germany to disband most of its regiments after the war. However, this did not end regimental traditions. Conscious of its tradition nearly every German regiment published a printed regimental history and held periodical regimental meetings to remember their deeds and their victims. The regimental tradition was assisted by social organisations, so-called Hinterbliebenenfonds (pension funds for widows and orphans) which supported disabled comrades and widows and children of killed members of the regiments.

## Western Front 1917

1916 ended with the stabilization of the situation for Germany. But Hindenburg and Ludendorff were forced to realize that the exhausted German army would have to embark on a defensive strategy in 1917. The new OHL had shown its ability to cope with the crisis. The Verdun project had been cancelled and after months of combat the stiff German resistance had prevented an Allied breakthrough at the Somme. The front in the east and in Italy was stabilized. Romania was beaten and occupied. Nevertheless 1916 had put enormous pressure on both the manpower of the German Army and its material resources. The 5th Army lost much of the ground that had been occupied by months of bitter fighting within a few hours during two surprising defeats at Verdun on October 24 and December 15. However, the real warning was the loss of 11,000 POWs. Most of those captured on this occasion were taken prisoner unwounded, a fact which confirmed the huge loss of morale within the ranks of the exhausted German army and revealed serious deficits in the tactical organization of the defence. The will of the men in the trenches to fight to the bitter end was obviously shaken. The Army Group *Deutscher Kronprinz* reported on the low morale of the forces to OHL and called for a realistic analysis of the problem (cit. Wilhelm: *Meine Erinnerungen*, p.251-252). According to this report the inflexible defence battle (fought in a system of connected resistance lines throughout the main position with immediate counterattacks by reserve forces) was insufficient. After the loss of the main position confusion usually set in. The Army Group Command stressed that it was not the quality of positions which led to success in battle but skilful defensive combat and the general morale of the forces. Summarizing its report the army group states: "Good troops will hold on even in bad positions but inferior troops will loose even good positions." This summary anticipates a dramatic change in the tactical thinking at the Western Front. New ideas for defensive battle had to be developed and troops trained in order to cope with the expected Allied offensive operations in 1917.

Two years of stalemate and the experiences of Verdun and the Somme formed a new style of trench war. The fighting in a dense system of trenches, craters, dugouts and obstacles demanded well trained and motivated specialists who could handle, both tactically and technically, the different arms of trench war; hand grenades, machine guns, light mortars, signals and gas protection. The role of the rifle was disputed. While the men in the trenches preferred the hand grenade for close combat the higher commands still believed in the use of the rifle. Storm troopers became the new tactical organization for attack and counterattack to deal with the demands of a new more flexible style of trench war. 1915 and 1916 were characterized by the static defence of positions. Orders emphasised that the loss of trenches or parts of the line was to be avoided at all costs. The bulk of infantry forces, concentrated in the forward trenches, were exposed to the destructive power of the overwhelming Allied guns. But these tactics were to blame for high losses. At the end of 1916 new tactical ideas found their way to the trenches. An intensive exchange about actual combat experience between the fighting troops and the higher commands produced more flexible tactics that defined the battlefield not as a line but as a deep zone of resistance. The ideas were laid down in the newly published manual "*Grundsaetze fuer die Fuehrung der Abwehrschlacht im Stellungskriege*" (*Principles for Defensive Battle in Trench War*) issued to the troops for training purposes. This zone of resistance formed a deep network of guns, machine guns and counterattack forces increasing in strength in its rearward zone. Only sentries would occupy the forward line. Untenable positions were prepared for evacuation. Dispersed groups of trench fighters, the so-called storm troopers, were to avoid the main impact of hostile gunfire and attack forces and use every moment of confusion of the enemy to regain lost ground. 1917 saw the coordination of the infantry battle with artillery, aviation, armour and chemical warfare. A combined all-arms battle was proposed. The deep defence concept was not only tactical but operational also. On top of the preparation of a deep defensive zone armies and groups were to post only a minimum of divisions in the line to make as many divisions available as possible behind the front for counterattack operations. These so-called "*Eingreifdivisionen*" (division in reserve) were to fight a flexible and aggressive defensive battle. Their basic operation was the counterattack in order to repel any enemy penetration or breakthrough.

The machine gun became the dominant weapon on the battlefield. Handled by a trained crew a single machine gun was able to block the advance of a whole battalion. Each defensive sector was patterned by a dense and deep network of machine gun posts that could pour their deadly stream of metal into every part of the sector. Flanking fire and mutual cover of machine guns became a basic principle. A sophisticated layout of obstacles was designed to draw the enemy infantry into ambushes and traps where the machine guns waited. Attacking infantrymen had only two weapons to subdue machine guns; the hand grenade and their own bodies. Waves of attacking infantry often simply flooded the machine guns by eating up the hail of machine gunfire with their never-ending flood of attacking bodies. It was not without reason that the infantrymen called themselves "gun food". The success of an attack often depended on a simple technical failure or on overheating having jammed the gun and stopped the fire. To finish off a machine gun post with hand grenades was only possible in close combat. By the end of 1916 the superiority of the machine gun in trench warfare was undisputed. Storm troops were trained not to attack machine gun posts directly but to pass by and attack them from the rear side. This did not reduce the power of the machine gun but it did give the infantry attack a new chance for success.

The winter of 1916/17 saw the formation of special training centres behind the front to teach the lessons learned in 1916 for an effective defence in 1917. Back from the Somme in October 1916 the Fuesilier-Regiment 40 organized a storm trooper school behind its sector at the Champagne front. The training area consisted of a typical system of trenches for training. There, officers and men of resting battalions were taught and trained in storm trooper tactics. Training centres like this were formed everywhere behind the Western Front. Additionally officers, non-commissioned officers (NCOs) and men of the *Hohenzollernfusiliers* were sent to the army mortar school at Vouziers to train using the light mortar, another weapon which was destined to improve the fighting power of the infantry. Other members of the regiment attended special courses on signal service or gas protection. In this way the defensive battle of 1917 was prepared for by the German Army all along the Western Front.

On March 16th, 1917 the German Army took the initiative and made their first strategic move at the Western Front: The "Alberich Operation". Here they retreated, within a few days, to the "Siegfried line". The Allies called this rearward defensive line the "Hindenburg line". It ran from Arras, passing Cambrai and St. Quentin, to the Aisne River between Soissons and Vailly. Fatigue parties, Russian POWs and civil construction companies had been constructing this line since the second half of 1916 but in March 1917 it had not yet been completed. Nevertheless the "Hindenburg line" formed a veritable fortress and successfully repelled all attacks until the British 4th Army broke the line in September 1918. The retreat shortened the German line by twenty kilometres and made several divisions available for the flexible strategy of counterattack operations. The German retreat was an unpleasant surprise for the Allies because they entered a completely destroyed area robbed of all infrastructure. Before the German Army left the area between Arras, Peronne, Roye, Noyon, Soissons, St. Quentin and Cambrai, all buildings, roads, railroads, bridges and even wells and orchards were systematically destroyed. Everything that could have had any use for the Allied forces was blown up or transferred to the east. Directly in front of the "Hindenburg line" a belt fifteen kilometres deep was razed completely. What the Allies found when they slowly pursued the retreating German forces was the so-called "Somme desert". Life or military operations in the "Somme desert" were impossible for many months to follow.

The German retreat to the "Hindenburg line" caused the Allied attack plans and preparations for 1917 to collapse. At a meeting at the French headquarters in November 1916 the Allies' representatives agreed to start the offensive for 1917 in February. The British Army was to attack at the northern banks of the Somme again while the majority of the French Army was to attack between the Somme and the Oise River. West of Reims a second push was planned to support the main offensive. On December 12, 1916 General Nivelle succeeded Joffre as Supreme Commander of the French armies. Nivelle was the hero of Verdun where his forces had delivered a decisive blow against the enemy on October 24, 1916 and recaptured the famous Fort Douaumont. Nivelle, with his newly developed tactics, appeared to be the military leader who could break the deadlock at the Western Front. His tactics managed to coordinate infantry and artillery with the aid of fixed timetables and a rolling barrage. What had been successful at Verdun on a minor scale was to be repeated by a combined Franco-British attack between Arras and Reims on a large scale offensive operation designed to pierce and smash the German front within 24-48 hours, achieving the decisive victory in the west.

However, as in 1916 at Verdun, the German Supreme Command again forestalled the Allied operations when the German Army retreated to the "Hindenburg line". This time the British and French armies lost major parts of what they had planned to be their battlefield between Arras and Noyon. For some time they even lost contact with the retreating enemy between the Somme and Oise rivers. The Allies had to alter their plans and were forced to reorganize their build-up for the offensive operations in 1917. This gave the Germans two more quiet months for their defensive preparations. The new Allied plans set down attacks at the Western Front where it was still possible after the German retreat; on both flanks of the "Hindenburg line" at Arras and the Aisne-Champagne sector. The breakthrough at the flanks of the "Hindenburg line" was to bypass this formidable fortress and result in the collapse of the central part of the German line. Under the command of the new French Commander in Chief General Nivelle, the British Commander in Chief, Sir Douglas Haig, and the British forces attacked the 6th German Army near Arras on April 9, 1917 a few days in advance of the French main push at the Aisne and Champagne. The British attacked at a front of thirty kilometres and achieved considerable success in the first few days. Some of the German divisions collapsed and plenty of booty and POWs were captured. The planned breakthrough however failed. The fighting lasted until May resulting again in attrition and the capture of a salient, eight kilometres deep. Nivelle planned the main push at the Aisne River and in the Champagne. The new French leader relied on a new tactical concept that had already been successfully used on a limited scale at Verdun during the last few months of 1916. Trusting in the overwhelming artillery power of the French Army he intended to pulverize the German front with an unprecedented amount of shellfire. Accompanied by tanks and marching at close distance behind a moving barrage the infantry were to subdue any hostile resistance. Careful organization and fixed timetables were planned to transform the French Army into a machine of destruction. Parts of the enemy line were to be bypassed and taken from the rear. The large-scale performance of this tactical pattern would thus bring the awaited strategic breakthrough and final victory for the Allies. Hopes ran high in the spring of 1917.

On April 16, 1917, after ten days of intensive artillery preparation, the French Army attacked and within a few hours the attack proved to be a complete failure. The Germans had been warned and were prepared. The German OHL had received the first hints of an impending Aisne-Champagne offensive in mid-February when German storm troopers had raided French positions at the Champagne and captured an order of the 2nd French Infantry-Division. Ludendorff refers to this valuable booty in his war memoirs (cit. Ludendorff: *Meine Kriegserinnerungen*, p.324). This information was confirmed when on April 5th the 10th Reserve-Division successfully raided the French positions at Sapigneul and captured the attack orders of the French 5th Army containing the French order of battle and details about the 5th Army's targets and tactics (cit. Wilhelm: *Meine Erinnerungen*, p.272). When the guns of the

French artillery opened fire on a length of 100 kilometres between Soissons and the centre of the 3rd German Army east of Reims on April 6th the Germans were prepared. The attack hit the Germans on both sides of the historical city of Reims between Condé and Brimont at a length of forty kilometres and one day later between Berru and the Suippe valley near Aubérive at a length of twenty kilometres. Local gains were paid with hecatombs of killed and wounded men. The medical service failed to cope with the flood of wounded soldiers and German counterattacks disputed any trench captured by the French infantry. The results were so depressing that at the end of the first day of battle there was talk in the French staffs of stopping the operation. However, the British leaders Haig and Lloyd George insisted on the continuation of the general offensive. In the following weeks the breakthrough operation degenerated into a battle of attrition which was characterized by limited attacks. The fruitless fighting lasted until the end of May. At the end of the battle the first German line had only been partly taken by the French forces, the second line remained untouched.

In May 1917 General Nivelle resigned from his post and the morale of the French forces cracked after the disastrous results of the Nivelle-Offensive. Hopes for an end to the war were shattered and replaced with a deep depression. For some weeks, major parts of the French Army were mutinous and represented no reliable force of resistance against a German attack. However, the German Army remained passive. German military intelligence failed and nobody on the German side realized the opportunity at hand. It was some months later before the German Supreme Command learned of what had happened on the other side of the Western Front. German ignorance and the general strategy to stay on the defensive at the Western Front in 1917 saved the French Army when whole units disobeyed orders to go into the trenches. Red flags appeared and soldiers assembled to form councils like in revolutionary Russia. Sixteen army corps were involved in mutinous activities. Military courts and the wise handling of the army by Generals Petain and Foch restored the situation. In June the crisis was under control but the French Army had to abandon all plans for offensive operations in the following months.

The British Army had to take over the active role for the Allies at the Western Front alone. It was not until June 7th that Haig found out about the crisis of the French Army in a meeting with Petain and how important it was for the British to divert the Germans from the demoralized French Army. As the French Army was inactive Haig was free to decide where to strike and came back to his old Flanders project. At Flanders attrition warfare would approach its climax. Before taking the offensive from the Ypres salient the dominating Messines Ridge at the southern flank of the salient had to be cleared from the Germans. General Plumer's 2nd Army prepared this operation for a long time by tunnelling and mining the ridge. On June 7th at 3:10am, after ten days of intensive shelling, nineteen gigantic mines went up and devastated major parts of the ten miles long German position on the Messines Ridge. The blast killed the German trench garrison and the tremendous noise it made could be heard in southern England. The ridge was captured within one day but German counter-attack divisions prevented Plumer's troops from linking up with the Ypres-Lys Canal and the Lys River line. On June 14 the battle was finished when Plumer realized that a general regrouping of his artillery would be necessary for any further advance. But for his guns the cratered Messines Ridge was impassable.

Six weeks after the capture of Messines Ridge and after intensive preparations the British Army was ready again. Flanders was destined to be a British show and it was the declared mission to clear the Flanders coast from German submarine bases. General Gough's 5th Army, assisted by the 2nd British Army on its right flank and by the 1st French Army on its left flank, was to attack from the Ypres salient. The aim was to push the German 4th Army, under the command of *General* Sixt v. Arnim, from Passchendale Ridge. Passchendale Ridge formed a semicircle east of Ypres and closed the Belgian plain for the British advance. Expecting a decisive defensive battle the defence specialist Lossberg was designated as Arnim's Chief of Staff. After tremendous shelling, which converted the Ypres salient into a fire spewing semicircle, and several delays caused by bad weather, the British infantry went over the top in the early morning of July 31st. Within two days the 5th Army's troops had advanced 1000-2000 metres. The infantry was assisted by tanks which got hopelessly stuck in the shell torn Flanders mud while the infantry found itself in front of the German main line of resistance where a network of enemy machine gun posts blocked any further advance. German counter-attack divisions appeared on the battlefield and reversed the Britons' gains. Rain made the situation even worse, anticipating the troops' suffering in mud and water that was still to come. Four days of futile fighting followed until a break of several days occurred. The British needed time to relieve their exhausted troops and to re-supply them. This would become the pattern of battle for the following months. Periods of intensive shelling and fighting alternated with days of relative calm. The Germans designated these combat periods as six different battles, while the crucial days were called great battle days. When the fighting died down at the end of November the German 6th Army counted sixteen great battle days. Already in the first days of August the Flanders offensive, later called Passchendale with reference to the ruins where the battle met its climax, turned into an attrition battle, probably the biggest ever fought at the Western Front. The battle that had been meant to take the enemy position degenerated into "a brutal, troublesome and frontal moving of the front", as military author Stegemann wrote (cit: Stegemann: *Geschichte des Krieges*, vol.3, p.476). In September Haig changed tactics and embarked on local attacks with limited aims reducing a general offensive to an advance in single steps of 1000 yards each. The positive effect was that the British infantry did not outrun their own artillery and were not exposed to German counterattacks thus making the German defence tactics ineffectual. Moreover the German counter-attack divisions had to now launch their counterattacks under unfavourable conditions against British troops awaiting them in the newly captured positions which were already prepared for defence and which were under the cover of British artillery. Stegemann characterizes this stadium of battle as follows: "Therefore the battle in the area of the immediate front became a merciless manslaughter" (cit: Stegemann: *Geschichte des Krieges*, vol.3, p.481). But at the same time the pace of battle was reduced to a microscopic level. Places that were finally taken in the course of the fighting – Langemark on August 17, Passchendale on November 6 – were only an expression of a microscopic perspective seeking presentable returns for the unimaginable bloodshed. But a hundred square miles of flooded and shell torn ground could never repay the tremendous losses. The real mission of Passchendale, to wear down the German Army, was unjustifiable because, for political reasons, Haig, the responsible British military leader, could not confess that the path to victory was through simple manslaughter.

Passchendale was the tragic and shocking climax of attrition warfare at the Western Front. Politicians and people in Britain were shocked when they realized what had happened there. At the same time however Passchendale was the logical result of three years development of strategic thinking which tried to achieve victory merely through the use of ever increasing artillery fire. Until Passchendale all tactical thinking was only a supplement for the artillery that ruled the battlefields of the Western Front mercilessly. Battle preparation and battle at the Western Front degenerated into a slow and mechanical process without any tactical secrecy or surprise that reduced strategy to a simple trial of strength. Because of their undecided character battles lasted weeks, sometime even months. But even after three years of battle the material strength of both camps was still balanced, though victory was denied to any camp. Time was ripe for a revival of tactical and strategic thinking to overcome the technical factors, which had produced the stalemate in autumn 1914, and shift the balance of power once and for all. New ideas for the offensive battle were developed in both camps and sophisticated tactical principles gained a foothold with the higher staffs. The new thinking focused on surprise and a short artillery preparation that would only last for a few hours but hit the enemy like a hurricane. This new type of battle led to a new level of intensification of the fighting at the Western Front *designed to* speed up the battle and result in a decisive victory.

The German Army tested its new principles for the offensive battle not at the Western front but in the east and in Italy. Only a few hours of a hurricane like bombardment – orchestrated by the famous artillery leader colonel Bruchmueller – preceded the moment in the early morning of September 1st, 1917 when the German 8th Army, under the command of *General* Hutier, crossed the Duena River and within three days took Riga, the capital of Kurland, clearing the northern part of the Eastern Front of the Russians. At the same time the 11th Isonzo Battle left the exhausted Austrian Army in a rather unfavourable situation at the Italian front. Crisis would be imminent if the Italians attacked again. The German OHL decided in favour of an offensive solution and sent troops to the south. *General* v. Below's German 14th Army formed the spearhead at Caporetto when German and Austrian divisions attacked at the Isonzo River on October 24. The Austro-German forces pushed back the Italian Army sixty-five miles down to the Piave River and captured 275,000 POWs and 2500 guns. Caporetto was an unprecedented catastrophe for the western Allies. Both Hutier and Below proved to be experienced specialists of offensive battle. The former would command the 18th Army at St. Quentin and the latter the 17th Army, opposite Bapaume, in the German Army's spring offensive which smashed the British 5th Army at the Somme in March 1918.

At the Western Front it was the British Army that introduced the new style of battle when it attacked the "Hindenburg line" near Cambrai on November 20. While the Germans relied on short hurricane bombardments and sophisticated infantry tactics, the British embarked on their tank force to secure surprise and speed. In both camps artillery specialists had developed pre-registered gunfire to reliable standards so the batteries no longer had to depend on the treacherous method of establishing their fire accuracy by observed shelling before the actual battle, which normally announced each offensive to the enemy at the Western Front. Surprise was now able to play a role in the battle. The Cambrai operation had its origin in an initiative of brigadier General H. Elles, the Tank Corps' commander, who had been looking for an opportunity for his tanks to be used. At Cambrai the Tank Corps were to attack under conditions that would be suitable for the tanks: Surprise, unbroken terrain and a larger number of tanks. General Byng, commanding the British 3rd Army, agreed to Elles' proposal, as did Haig, when the Flanders offensive turned into inglorious attrition. Haig urgently needed a "compensatory success of any sort" to end the campaign of 1917 (cit. Keegan: *The First World War*, p.369). 300 tanks were to attack on a seven-mile front, being closely followed by the infantry that was to break the "Hindenburg line" in one rush. Near Cambrai the "Hindenburg line" consisted of three sucessive lines. The infantry's job was to mop up all remaining enemy resistance after the advancing tanks had passed by. Unobserved by the Germans, the tanks assembled secretly behind the British line and attacked in the early morning of November 20, 1917. Surprise and success were spectacular. Stunned by a hurricane bombardment that hailed down on them, the Germans were pushed back by the British to the outskirts of Cambrai within four hours. The German infantry had only stick grenades to fight the tanks with. Only in the centre near Flesquières, where the 51st Highland Division attacked, were a dozen tanks destroyed by German artillery when passing the ridge. The "Hindenburg line" was on the edge of breaking when the British cavalry charged to complete the breakthrough. But unbroken wire and pockets of resistance forced the British horses to turn round. Even without achieving the intended breakthrough there was much rejoicing in Britain. The battle however was not over. Up until the end of November Byng's Army launched repeated costly attacks to achieve the desired breakthrough. Losses in men and tanks rose. The battlefield was littered with burning wrecks. Bourlon Wood and Fontaine-Notre Dame became the focus of battle. Newly arriving German reserve divisions blocked the British advance. On November 30 the German 2nd Army had assembled twenty divisions opposite the Cambrai salient and struck back. The increased German infantry and artillery was now up to ten times bigger than the forces which had opposed the British on November 20. The commanding German *General* v.d. Marwitz, a famous cavalry man and now commanding the 2nd Army, turned local counterattacks into an operational pincer operation to cut off the British salient. Fifty minutes of hurricane bombardment preceded the attack which hit the surprised British 3rd Army and forced it to cede most of the captured ground and even some of the own old positions by December 4th. When the fighting ceased in mid December, the frontline took the shape of a double salient – the British salient opposite Marcoing and the German salient opposite Gouzeaucourt – which Keegan said appeared as a "symbol of the precarious balance of power at the Western Front at the end of 1917" (cit. Keegan: *The First World War*, p.371).

In the second half of 1917 the French Army had overcome its crisis of morale enough to be ready for local operations. On August 20 the Germans were pushed back at Verdun to their line of departure of February 1916. The German Verdun operation was thereby finally liquidated. Further west at the Chemin des Dames Ridge the French Army pierced the German line at the exposed Laffaux corner on October 23, and in the following weeks it forced the German 7th Army to evacuate the ridge and to take up a new position on the northern Ailette bank. Both operations had only local character but they showed that General Petain, commanding the French Army, had coped successfully with his troops' crisis of morale and that the French Army was back as a fighting force.

1917 turned out to be a success for the German defensive strategy at the Western Front. Several offensive operations of the Allies, who had been fighting to achieve the final breakthrough, had resulted in exhausting attrition battles and nearly caused a collapse in morale in the French Army. The Russian revolution and the subsequent collapse of the Russian Army raised hopes in the Central Powers' camp for the future. Nevertheless time was working against Germany. The entry of the United States of America in March 1917 improved the financial and industrial strength of the Allies and opened the prospect of U.S. troops' intervention in the European theatre of war. For Germany 1917 was a year of growing food and equipment shortages ("*Mangel*") and the bitter feeling of having to hold out ("*Durchhalten*") against a world of enemies. "*Mangel*" and "*Durchhalten*" became the catchwords of 1917 and the prospects for the future were even worse. Life at the frontline became even harder. Food rations were low and of bad quality. Clothing, equipment and weapons were in a permanent process of deterioration without adequate replacements and supplies being available. Substitutes, so-called "*Ersatz*", had to be used for lacking raw materials to produce food and equipment. Presents with food and clothes sent by mail from the families at home became rare. In 1917, after the food shortages of the terrible "*Steckruebenwinter*" (winter of turnips) of 1916/17, people at home had nothing else left to send to their boys at the front. Weapons and personal clothes and shoes were in no better condition. The rifles were so used up that the barrels were completely worn out. Jackets, trousers, coats and shoes were repaired countless times.

On top of the lack of raw materials and the limited industrial capacities Germany had a growing problem with manpower. According to the Peace Strength Law of 1912, an annual contingent of 305,000 recruits for colour service was necessary to maintain army and navy before the outbreak of war. Hostilities in the Great War exerted a heavy drain on Germany's manpower which forced the army to intensify recruiting and call up more men much earlier than was usual. Each annual recruit contingent provided the German armed forces with approximately 500,000 men. During the war the "*Ersatzkommissionen*" (recruiting offices) responsible for recruiting and the medical examination of recruits were able to send between 400,000 and 500,000 young men from the annual recruit contingent to the armed forces to fill the ranks. Medical standards were reduced and age limits softened to muster up enough of the badly needed recruits.

Mobilization in August 1914 brought up fifty-one active divisions and thirty-two reserve divisions to war strength by calling up reserve soldiers and using the surplus of reservists in the depots. The class of 1914 (born in 1894) together with the "*Ersatz Reserve*" (Supplementary Reserve), the so-called "*Restanten*" (men not called up with their respective class) and plenty of volunteers produced more than a million men to fill up the ranks and to raise two series of newly formed reserve divisions and corps by the end of 1914. After a rather short training period of three or four months the new drafts of the first series of reserve forces were sent to the front in Northern France and Belgium to take part in the race to the sea and in the first battle of Ypres in the autumn of 1914. There, the heavy fighting at the tiny village of Langemark produced the Langemark myth, the heroic sacrifice of the German youth called up for service in the field. The second series of newly formed reserve divisions were sent out in February 1915. The Naval Corps was formed at the same time and was to hold the coastal sector at the northern end of the Western Front in Flanders under the designation "*Flanderncorps*". But the losses of the winter campaign and the ensuing battles at the Western Front in the following spring exerted new pressure on German manpower. The need for artillery and more flexibility in moving and relieving infantry divisions resulted in the creation of nineteen new divisions by using the fourth regiments of the already existing divisions in March and April 1915. This method would provide regiments for the newly formed divisions till 1917, when all divisions were reduced to the three-regiments' standard. "*Landwehr*" and "*Landsturm*" – all men between twenty-nine and forty-five liable for military service – were enlisted. The younger men replaced losses in the active and reserve divisions, the older were incorporated into Landwehrdivisions for service at non-active sectors or in the "*Landsturm*" for guard duties behind the front. The class of 1915 (born in 1895) was called up between April and June, the class of 1916 (born in 1896) already between August and November 1915. For the class of 1915 this was half a year early, for the Class of 1916 nearly one year early. In the German Army each class was usually called up in October when the new recruits were twenty years old. But in 1915 each class was already reduced by the percentage of young men who had volunteered in 1914/15 – a circumstance that sometimes produced strange problems later on. One of the youngest recruits was Gerhard Scholtz, who volunteered at the age of fifteen and served from October 1914 onwards at the Western Front. While he was fighting as an acting officer with his battery at the Somme in July 1916 police visited his mother in Germany because her son did not report when called up for the medical inspection of his class in 1916 (cit. Scholtz: *Die Schlacht im Westen*, p.98). The serious losses of the only half trained drafts of 1914 caused the German Army to prolong training from four to five months. But the heavy losses of 1915 and the lack of new drafts induced the military administration to carry out stricter medical examinations to reduce the number of recruits declared unfit for military service. To find new replacements first time men were combed out from the large group of retained men. These men, so-called "*Reklamierte*", were allowed to stay at home because their skilled occupations were needed for industry and agriculture. Thus in August 1915, in spite of serious losses, the German Army had increased the forces in the field by up to 170 divisions.

The class of 1917 (born in 1897) was called up eighteen months before it was due from January till May 1916, only to be consumed by the slaughter at the Western Front in the summer of that terrible year. Some of the recruits who had enlisted in 1916 received training for three months only, so that they could quickly fill the depleted ranks of the divisions that were fighting at Verdun and at the Somme. Originally planned to bring about victory at Verdun, the year of 1916 became a year of military strain and manpower crisis for Germany. Verdun and the Somme, the crisis at the Eastern Front and the impending entry of Romania into the war increased the need for new mobile field divisions again. The OHL decided to form thirty-four new divisions in the second half of 1916. Independent battalions, regiments newly raised from *Ersatz* units, and again fourth regiments were amalgamated to form new divisions. To strengthen the new divisions experienced regiments were transferred from their old divisions that received newly raised regiments in exchange. The field artillery for the new divisions was obtained by a general reduction of the field batteries from six to four guns. But the manpower crisis worsened at the end of 1916 and made the draft of the class of 1918 (born in 1898) necessary. This class had been already called up two years before their time between September 1916 and January 1917. This meant that most of the recruits of the 1918 class were between eighteen and nineteen years old when they entered the trenches after four months' training. After replacing losses thirteen new divisions were again formed at the beginning of 1917. To provide a skeleton of experienced soldiers for these newly raised units, consisting mainly of immature young men of the 1918 class, each experienced company of the Western Front had to send ten men. But their young rank and file marked the new formations of 1917. One of these divisions fought under the nickname "*Konfirmandendivision*" (Confirmee Division).

But the following drafts were even younger. The class of 1919 (born in 1899) was called up between January and June 1917, two and a half year in advance of its normal time. At the end of 1917, in spite of the serious losses of more than three years of combat, the premature call up of conscripts had pushed the total fighting strength of the German Army up to 6,000,000 men of all ranks, excluding the new drafts still under training in Germany. This was a total of 241 divisions. The peace strength in 1914 had been 840,000. But this impressive increase and the divisions set free by the collapse of Russia at the end of 1917 were still not enough to cope with the demand for more manpower at the front. The class of 1920 (born in 1900) had to be called up in the spring of 1918 and was enlisted in the following months. In 1917-1918 more and more very young faces appear on the Western Front photos. Losses in frontline officers were also extremely high. Walter Bloem refers to this problem in the third volume of his war memoirs "*Das Ganze – halt!*" When he took over command of the second battalion Infantry Regiment 12 in February 1918, on the eve of the great offensive in the West, most of his platoon and company officers were between seventeen and eighteen. The lieutenant commanding the mortars was twenty-three and thus already one of the "older" officers. Bloem, who was himself forty-nine years old, wrote that with his grey hair he felt himself to be a strange apparition in amongst these young men to whom he referred to as "minors" (cit. Bloem: *Das Ganze halt*, p.515-516). After the high losses of the failed German offensives in the spring and early summer of 1918, the manpower crisis reached its peak on the German side. The German High Command, under Hindenburg and Ludendorff, was forced to break up more and more under-strength divisions. The men of these divisions were used to replace the losses of other depleted divisions fighting often with only forty rifles per company.

The practice of the German Army Command, forced upon the army by the heavy losses, to call in the annual classes initially a few months in advance and finally two and a half years in advance of their normal time resulted in an increasing number of very young soldiers, often of a lower physical standard, in the ranks of the German combat forces. In normal circumstances each German male was liable for military service from between the age of seventeen and forty-five. Liability for service in the active forces began however only with ones twentieth birthday. Already in 1916 most of the new drafts entering active service were only nineteen years old. The average age of drafts between 1917-1918 was seventeen years old. This generation had already experienced two and a half years of malnutrition and shortage and was physically very different from the peacetime youth of 1914-1915. Forced to increase their numbers the German Army deteriorated in quality. It had a growing percentage of very young and old soldiers while the soldiers of average age, from 20 to 28, were consumed by combat losses. It was not only losses however that exerted pressure on German manpower. To raise the peacetime army from 840,000 up to six million involved creating new formations, especially of light and heavy artillery. Infantry battalions increased by 3 1/4 times their original number but field artillery batteries by 4 3/4 times and foot artillery batteries by 5 1/2 times. The increase in divisions was higher but this was only due to the reduction of regiments from four to three per division since 1915. Thus increasing quantity was paid with a reduction in quality which would be deeply felt in 1918.

## Western Front 1918

After the successful German counterattack at Cambrai several quiet months followed at the front between the English Channel and the Swiss border. No major operations took place until March. The collapse of Russia in the autumn of 1917 opened the prospect of a complete change at the Western Front for the German military leaders. By transferring divisions from the Eastern Front the German Army was able to take the field in the west with as many divisions as the Allies for the first time since 1914. Growing shortages in men and material and the successive arrival of U.S. troops at the European theatre of war were an obvious warning for the German OHL that there was no time to waste. The German Supreme Command decided to attack. Months of intensive planning and preparation began. The OHL ordered army groups and armies to devise plans for possible attack operations. Since the first meeting at Mons in November 1917, Hindenburg and Ludendorff had discussed options for different attack projects with the army group staffs. At the end of January Ludendorff decided to attack the British Army in Northern France. The operation plan promoted an attack against the southern British flank near St. Quentin and a following push in a northwesterly direction to split the Allies and cause the collapse of the British Army. The attack was planned for the middle of March and was to take place as early as possible to head off any preventive Allied attack.

As in the winter of 1916/17 the German Army again went through a phase of intensive training and reorganization. But the training in the winter 1917/18 focused mainly on attack tactics. In order to achieve a rapid and decisive offensive success in battle a quick breakthrough of the enemy positions had to be achieved. Surprise and speed would forestall any expected counterattacks by enemy divisions in reserve. However, after a careful review of the experiences of attack operations at the Western and Eastern Fronts in the preceding campaigns the OHL and army groups designed a training program for the German attack forces. Individual training of the infantryman was combined with exercises on company, battalion, regimental and divisionary level. Special emphasis was placed upon close cooperation between infantry, machine guns, mortars, artillery, aircraft and tanks. Storm troops were trained to attack in dispersed groups and were equipped with infantry guns and portable mortars to destroy hostile machine gun posts by direct shooting. Effective use of the signal service and chemical weapons were also taught. The divisions arriving from the Eastern Front underwent intensive training to become accustomed to the conditions of the Western Front at special army training centres. The artillery officers learned new tactics for artillery preparation at artillery ranges and in schools. Inspired by the ideas of *Oberst* Bruchmueller, the OHL planned only short hurricane bombardments of enemy positions in order to secure the effect of surprise. Only three hours of well-directed artillery and mortar fire of an unprecedented intensity would break the enemy lines and open the way for the attacking infantry. Organized in groups the artillery would be able to concentrate firepower at the decisive points. The firing of high explosives and gas shells would be combined. Gas was especially intended to paralyse the hostile artillery. The artillery's mobility and their ability to pass trenches and craters in the zone of destruction without delay was very important. Special batteries had to accompany the storming infantry to assist directly in the breaking of resistance centres and enemy strongholds or to deal with tanks. The officer's training schools had to change their program completely. Every army formed a special reserve of officers up to regimental level to cope with the expected officers' losses. Special attack divisions were selected. These divisions received additional equipment and manpower at the expense of the second-rate divisions destined to hold the quiet sectors. The German Army had already lost the ability to keep the entire army running on a high level of efficiency and was forced to differentiate between elite and second-rate divisions.

On March 21st, 1918 the German Army delivered the first blow to win the war at the Western Front: "Operation Michael". At 6:30 am thousands of German guns and mortars opened up fire along a front of eighty kilometres between Arras and La Fère. At 9:40 am, after three hours of intensive shelling, the infantry of the 17th, 2nd and 18th Armies went over the top on this misty morning. Fog, smoke and gas covered the battlefield. Within hours the first British position was captured, the second was penetrated at several spots. But the resistance of the shattered British troops was not yet broken and caused increasing losses in the German ranks. In the evening of the first day the German storm divisions had penetrated approximately six kilometres deep and had left behind the zone of destruction. Fatigue parties and railroad construction companies followed up to bridge trenches and shell craters for the artillery and the columns of the service of supply. The supply for the advancing armies depended on the quick reconstruction of the destroyed roads and railroads. The following week saw an advance of the German forces that had not been experienced at the Western Front since 1914. In the pursuit of the British forces the River Somme was crossed and Peronne, Ham, Roye, Noyon and Montdidier occupied. But the final target, which comprised the occupation of Amiens and the separation of the British and French armies, could not be achieved. As the Allied resistance increased the German impetus weakened. At the end of March an increasing number of Allied reserves arrived at the battlefield forming a new, well-organized front that stopped the German advance. The possibility of a victory and the phase of a collapsed Allied defence faded away. After an advance of sixty kilometres the German troops were exhausted. The losses in killed and wounded men were high. Only inadequate supply and ammunition reached the infantry and artillery. Working parties and railroad construction companies failed to bridge the "Somme desert" in time. The reconstruction of the destroyed road and railroad networks was beyond their capacity. The lack of trucks and fresh horses meant the service of supply was unable to cope with the traffic conditions and the growing demands of the troops. Instead of the hoped for breakthrough "Operation Michael" produced only an oversized salient.

However, *General* Ludendorff was determined not to lift the pressure from the shaken enemy. After transferring the attack artillery to the north, the German 6th and 4th Armies delivered the next of a whole series of pushes against the Allied front in Belgium and France in the sector of the River Lys on both sides of the city of Armentières on April 9th. The strategy was the same as that used in March and the result was also disappointing. Passschendale and Messines ridge, the severely disputed battlefields of 1917, were taken and Bailleul and Estaires were occupied. The attack culminated in the capture of the dominating Kemmel Hill southwest of the city of Ypres by the *Alpenkorps*. However, a strategic success was again denied to the German Army.

The German Supreme Command felt that time was pressing. German resources of men and material were limited, and the attacks at the Somme and at the Lys rivers had already consumed much of the valuable resources available for the attacks. The threat of U.S. forces arriving in increasing numbers at the European theatre of war became more real with every week. However, the German Supreme Command still underestimated the monthly rate at which U.S. forces were disembarking in France. Crown Prince Wilhelm wrote in his war memoirs that the OHL clearly recognized that losing the initiative at the Western Front would mean losing the war (cit. Wilhelm: *Meine Erinnerungen*, p.315). Ludendorff however still believed the best way to achieve victory was to destroy the British forces in Northern France. But after the attacks in the Somme and Lys sectors the military situation prevented a new opportunity for a third attack against the British. At the deserted Somme salient the build-up of a logistical base and the necessary infrastructure for attack operations would need weeks. A pursuit of the attack in Flanders would meet the concentration of enemy reserves, including French divisions, and would result in a costly battle of attrition. To draw the Allies' attention and their reserves to the south the OHL promoted a diversionary attack at the Chemin des Dames. The Chemin des Dames sector was by its topography and its well-constructed system of trenches a strong position. At the time however it was only held by second-rate or exhausted troops, including some shattered British divisions who had come from the Somme and the Flanders battles. A surprise attack from the sectors of the 7th and 1st German Armies at the Chemin des Dames to reach the Aisne near Soissons and the Vesle River would open the way for a later attack of the 18th Army in the direction of Compiègne to improve the southern flank of the Somme salient. The final result would be a consolidated line that could be held with limited forces, thus giving full freedom of action to the OHL for the final attack in Flanders. One month of preparation preceded the offensive. Passing the cratered Chemin des Dames Ridge with its destroyed mountain roads proved to be a serious challenge for the artillery and the service of supply and demanded special preparations and equipment.

At two o'clock on the morning of May 27th, 1158 batteries opened up their preparatory fire between Vauxaillon and Brimont. Three and a half hours later ten German divisions crossed the Ailette swamps and climbed up the slopes of the Chemin des Dames Ridge where the enemy was taken completely by surprise. Within a few hours the 7th Army took the ridge while the 1st Army crossed the Aisne-Marne channel. In the evening, after an advance of twenty kilometres, the German divisions reached the banks of the Vesle River. The Allied defence had collapsed completely. Misled by the unexpected extraordinary success, the German Supreme Command decided to seize the opportunity and stipulated new far-reaching aims, including a Marne River crossing, for the originally limited attack. After breaking the shattered enemy resistance, the Ourcq River was crossed and the cities of Soissons and Fère en Tardenois captured on May 29th. One day later, the IV. Army Corps reached the Marne River between Château-Thierry and Dormans and a few river crossings were taken. But as in March and April the Allied resistance recovered. An excellent railroad system helped the Allies to bring more and more reserve forces into position including American divisions. These forces finally stopped the German advance at the banks of the River Marne in the first days of June. Within four days the German 7th Army had advanced sixty kilometres and captured 50,000 POWs, 600 guns and 2000 machine guns. But again it was not a strategic victory, and moreover the supply situation of the salient was critical. The supply of the Marne salient depended completely on the limited capacity of horse-drawn transport and trucks. The railway line Laon-Soissons was the only railway leading directly into the bulge. But the destruction of the railroad tunnel north of Margival made this railway unusable. The German railroad engineers would have needed six weeks for the reconstruction of the tunnel. Therefore the control of the railroad centre at Reims on the left flank of the attack forces was thought to be crucial for supplying the advancing German divisions. But this important railroad junction was still in the hands of the enemy. Between the railway station St. Erme and Chaudardes a new railroad was under construction to connect the railhead Laon with the railroads in the Marne salient. For the critical supply situation of the Marne salient this solution was more than insufficient.

To connect the Somme and the Marne salient and in the hope of breaking enemy resistance in front of the 7th Army by a flanking manoeuvre, the 18th Army was ordered to attack between Montdidier and Noyon. The 18th Army's attack met an already prepared enemy on June 9th. Instead of achieving another breakthrough to open the way for a deep advance, the German thrust hit the Allied line frontally and pushed it back twelve kilometres to the banks of the River Matz. Shells of the German field artillery burst in the streets of Compiègne. But the result of the operation was only of local importance. Sixty kilometres northeast of Paris the German offensive between Montdidier and Reims came to a halt. The first days of June 1918 saw the culmination of the crisis at the Western Front. In consolidating the line, the Allied leaders coped successfully with the crisis and laid the foundations for regaining the initiative in the near future. But the German Army was still able to deliver a final blow.

The situation of the 7th and 1st German Armies in the Marne salient was critical. Due to the lack of efficient railroad connections the supply situation was insufficient. Both armies held an extended line with long dangerous flanks. The German infantry was too exhausted to dig a deep network of trenches. Large-scale enemy counterattacks were expected and the Allied forces increased. U.S. divisions arrived in quick succession at the Western Front. To reduce the pressure on the Marne salient and to do as much damage as possible to the Allied fighting power, the German OHL decided to attack at Reims. By attacking on both flanks of the city, a strong enemy force would be trapped and annihilated. The capture of the railway junction at Reims would open new lines of supply for the Marne salient. The offensive was planned as a large scale encircling operation involving three German armies at a front of 120 kilometres. Starting from the line Château Thierry-Cambrecy, the 7th Army was to attack on the right flank in a south easterly direction along the Marne, take the Marne River crossings at Epernay and meet the 1st Army near Châlons. The 1st Army passed Reims and the mountains south of the city to attack along the Vesle River in the direction of Châlons. To cover this arm of the encircling movement the 3rd Army had to attack in the Champagne between Prunay and Aubérive and to advance with its right flank to the area south of Châlons. But Hindenburg and Ludendorff did not expect to achieve a strategic victory at the Western Front by this offensive. The advance would be stopped at the Marne. The aim of the attack was to destroy the enemy's fighting power and to draw French reserves from Flanders to the central front. There at Flanders the final blow to crush the British Army was planned to take place in August.

The attack at Reims was fixed for June 15th, 1918. The success of the offensive depended on surprise and speed. But the necessary intensive preparations needed six weeks. In the meantime French, British and American forces launched a series of local attacks at the Western Front. The already exhausted German army felt an increasing pressure upon its own decreasing resources. In the preceding offensives many thousands had been killed or wounded, and the Spanish influenza had depleted the German ranks even further. On July 10th the Army Group German Crown Prince received the first warnings of an impending French offensive near Villers Cotterêts. However, the deep forests of this area prohibited efficient reconnaissance. Combat activity and artillery fire increased all over the front. In the evening of July 14 the 1st and 3rd Armies' Chiefs of Staff confirmed to the army group commander Crown Prince Wilhelm that the secret of the attack preparations had been kept successfully.

The Allies were however informed, and they were well prepared when on July 15th at 4:40 am the German storm troops went over the top. Deserters had betrayed the attack. The Germans found the first French position evacuated. Thus most of the German artillery preparation had fallen on empty trenches. In the second position the stiff resistance of French divisions halted the attack. In the evening of the first day of battle the OHL recognized the complete failure of the manoeuvre and the attack of the Army Group German Crown Prince and the 3rd Army was cancelled. On the following day the renewal of the attack by the 1st Army was also stopped. Only the 7th Army made six kilometres progress at the southern slopes of the Marne valley after crossing the river on heavily shelled boat bridges. But for the troops in the Marne bridgehead the situation was hopeless. Again it was on the banks of the River Marne that the German offensive reached a turning point.

In the morning of July 18th, 1918 the Allied Supreme Command under Marshal Foch regained the initiative. Without preceding artillery preparation French and American infantry divisions attacked the western flank of the Marne salient. Assisted by hundreds of tanks and covered by a rolling barrage, French and U.S. forces broke the German resistance and advanced eight kilometres. In the following days the growing pressure against the flanks of the Marne salient forced the 7th Army to evacuate the bridgehead on the southern banks of the Marne River as a first step. But the Marne salient was untenable in the long run. By August 3rd the complete salient was evacuated, and the 7th Army had retreated to a new position along the riverbanks of Aisne and Vesle between Soissons and Reims. The pressing threat of an impending German offensive against Paris was lifted from the Allied High Command.

But further north Foch prepared another blow against the 2nd Army to push back the German salient at the Somme. The successful attack of Canadian forces east of Amiens at Villers-Brettonneux on the foggy morning of August 8th, 1918 and the following collapse of the German line sealed the German defeat and marked the beginning of the general retreat of the German Army at the Western Front. In his war memoirs Ludendorff called August 8th "a black day for the German Army", not only because of their declining fighting capabilities, but much more because the morale of the German Army was in an obvious process of deterioration (cit. Ludendorff: *Kriegserinnerungen*, p.547-552). The last months of 1918 saw a collapse in morale of an increasing number of German units at the Western Front. After the highflying hopes for a victory in the springtime the ensuing disappointment and the permanent stress under which they lived and fought had taken their toll and morale was low. The heavy losses of the spring offensives reduced many German divisions that had been involved in the attacks down to 20% of their original strength. Company strength of many infantry regiments was down to forty rifle bearers to whom no time for rest or recreation could be allotted. There were no sufficient replacements for lost men or material available on the German side. The very small number of replacement troops coming from Germany was reduced by desertion, and many soldiers who were coming back from a few days holiday in Germany hung around at the railheads and in the rear area to delay the return to their regiments. Ludendorff estimated in his book "*Kriegfuehrung und Politik*" that several hundred thousand deserters and draft-dodgers loitered behind the Western Front during this time (cit. Ludendorff: *Kriegfuehrung und Politik*, p.154). Many newcomers were unwilling to risk their life or health in an obviously lost war. The strike of the ammunition workers in Germany inspired single mutinous units to greet still reliable forces entering the line with the battle-cry: "Strike". However, it was not only the morale of many of the individual soldiers that began to crack in the final months of the war. The German military order and control by officers and military police slackened in the rear area too. Collapsing traffic control and rear area services resulted in chaotic traffic conditions and left soldiers on leave unguided and sometimes even unfed for many days on their ride by train to Germany. In his memoirs Crown Prince Wilhelm recounts a trip to visit the troops of his army group near Charleville where he met one of these mutinous trains between Waulscourt and Givet on November 7th. The train stood on the open track and red flags were flown from the wagons. Several hundred soldiers were rioting in the wagons. Crown Prince Wilhelm ordered the soldiers, who were mainly Bavarians on their leave trip from Flanders, to leave the train, and restored order and discipline by appealing to their honour. A seventeen-year-old soldier decorated with the Iron Cross told the Crown Prince what had happened: They had been on the train for three days, unfed and with no officers on board. Crown Prince Wilhelm had "the strong impression that if the situation in Germany and the rear area had not been out of control these men would not have become mutinous" (cit. Wilhelm: *Meine Erinnerungen*, p.265-267). Most war memoirs of German officers refer to such mutinous behaviour and rioting German soldiers. It is remarkable that most of these reported mutinous events or chaotic situations occurred in connection with the absence of officers and NCOs. But most of the officers who witnessed such events and described them in their memoirs forget to tell the reader that they themselves did not interfere to restore order like Crown Prince Wilhelm did at Waulscourt. The collapsing order behind the German line in the final months of war seems to have been accompanied by a surprising passivity of German officers and military police and by a complete lack of will to enforce discipline by martial law or executions, as the French Army had done to suppress the mutiny in 1917. In the frontline the majority of the combat forces remained reliable where they were still under the control and the guidance of their officers. The infantry officers did not depend on martial law. Social control and social cohesion in the companies or platoons still proved to be sufficient to maintain discipline and order as had been the case in the preceding years of the war. Accustomed to the discipline and motivation of its infantrymen the German Army finally became the victim of its functioning social cohesion as it left the army officers mentally unprepared to react vigorously and brutally in the moment of mental crisis and collapse.

The general retreat began in the second half of August. Passing a system of prepared rearward resistance lines the German soldier fought a series of delaying actions. One of the most important rearward positions was the so-called "Siegfried line" or, as the Allies called it, the "Hindenburg line". The dense belt of trenches and wire ran from Arras in a southeasterly direction to the Aisne River between Soissons and Reims. This line was already part of the Western Front between April 1917 and March 1918. After fighting for months at the devastated area of the "Somme desert" without shelter and prepared trenches in the line or inhabitable quarters behind the front, the shattered German forces put their hopes on this line, expecting to find strong positions and powerful artillery to back their resistance and stop the retreat. On September 2nd the Army Group Crown Prince Rupprecht of Bavaria made a new stand at the "Hindenburg line". But holding the position turned out to be only a short-term delaying action. On September 19, 1918 the British Fourth Army together with U.S. forces crushed the German defences at Bellicourt, where even the Somme channel as part of the defence could not help the depleted German regiments to stop the Allied advance. Other more or less prepared rearward resistance lines waited to receive the retreating German troops: Between Ypres and Arras the "Wotan line", forming the northern flank of the "Hindenburg line". Forty kilometres further east was the system of the "Lys-Hermann-Hundig-Brunhild line" which ran parallel to the old Western Front from the Lys Channel in the north to the Meuse River in the middle part of the Western Front. Eighty kilometres behind this system lay the nearly unprepared "Antwerpen-Maas line", which had its northern end at the port city Anvers, passed Belgium and followed the Meuse river to meet the old frontline at Verdun. Further down the Western Front the "Michel line" was prepared for the evacuation of the St. Mihiel Salient. For a last line of resistance the German OHL planned to occupy the "*Grenzstellung*" (border line position) that protected the German border between the German city of Aachen and the fortress of Metz in Lorraine. But this position existed only as a sketch on the general staff's maps and never came into action.

In the summer of 1918 Allied superiority in men and material was confronted with nearly total exhaustion on the German side. The German offensive operations in the spring of 1918 turned out to have been a deadly gamble: In trying to force a decisive victory Hindenburg and Ludendorff had expended the last reserves of men and material available to the German Army. The attempt of the German Supreme Command to gain a final victory at the Western Front with a series of deep offensive operations was ultimately revealed to be nothing more than a large-scale battle of attrition. Which was precisely the battle the German Army could not win. The big push at the Somme on March 21st, 1918 was hard, but not hard enough to break the British Army at the Western Front. The German HQs regarded the collapse of the British Army and the splitting of the Allied front as the prerequisite for victory. What "Operation Michael" failed to achieve could not be won by the following attacks in Flanders, at the Marne and in the Champagne sector. Germany, with its resources pushed to their limit, could not win this final phase of attrition war at the Western Front, as an American Army was entering France to build up its troops to a force of several million men. The strength of the different armies fighting at the Western Front in September 1918 illustrates the desperate situation for Germany. The German Army had 197 divisions at the Western Front, but only fifty were really combat-worthy to fight a total of 220 Allied divisions. In detail:

| | |
|---|---|
| American Army | 42 |
| British Army | 60 |
| French Army | 102 |
| Belgian Army | 12 |
| Italian Army | 2 |
| Portuguese Army | 2 |

This comparison gives an incomplete impression of the precarious situation of the German Army because the U.S. divisions were more than twice the size of a German peace standard division. But the German divisions were far below their peace standard at this time. In October 1918 the combat strength of some divisions of the Army Group German Crown Prince was reduced to 1000 rifles. However, after half a year of intensive fighting the French and British divisions were also depleted. Therefore the combat strength of British and U.S. divisions was themselves unequal. With the fighting power of forty-two divisions the AEF was able to hold a hundred miles of the Western Front while the BEF, commanding sixty divisions, had a sector of only ninety miles under its control. Nevertheless Allied superiority was unquestionable.

Because of the lack of men and material that would have been necessary to occupy the positions even the prepared resistance lines could not help the German forces to stop the Allied advance. All that the men on the battlefield could do was to stiffen the resistance and to fight delaying actions. Especially at the Meuse-Argonne sector the American Expeditionary Forces had to fight their way through a system of lines against obstinate German resistance in September and October 1918. Further north the Allied armies pushed the German forces out of the occupied French and Belgian territories step by step. On October 1st the Allies entered St. Quentin, on the 2nd Lens and Armentières, on the 12th Laon, and on October 18th Zeebrugge, Ostende and Lille were evacuated by the Germans. Still not really believing in the victory in 1918, Foch, who had been Supreme Commander of the Allies since March 26th, pressed his exhausted armies to attack everywhere at the Western Front. Plans for a campaign in 1919 were already prepared but the prospect of another winter in the trenches was not an attractive one. Foch hoped to provoke the expected collapse of the Germans by not allowing them any time for recovery. This was the climax of attrition war at the Western Front. The German line seemed to be close to collapse. Realizing the real situation and losing confidence in their troops' ability to hold firm the German military leaders Ludendorff and Hindenburg urged their government to offer an armistice to the Allies. On October 5th Prince Max of Baden, the new chancellor, approached the U.S. president to mediate a peace settlement to avoid any further bloodshed. But fighting did not cease until November 11th, 1918 at 12:00 pm when the guns fell silent at the Western Front. The last shots were fired at a line already far from the trenches, running from Gent to Mons, Charleville, Sedan, Verdun and Thiaucourt from where the old frontline still ran undisturbed to the Swiss border.

## Topography of the Western Front

German trench soldiers developed a special relationship to infamous battlegrounds of the Western Front where they held their trenches for months or sometimes even years. The major parts of the line in Belgium and France were the scene of fighting for several years. Different sectors became feared and notorious in the troops' minds according to the topographic conditions and the combat intensity. After several turns in the line the trench fighter was well acquainted with the special dangers and horrors of these sectors. The need for orientation in the complex world of trenches and destruction and the soldiers' relation to the respective sectors or places found their expression in new names created by the men who served in the trenches. Many places received nicknames which ridiculed the horrors or characterized the military or topographic importance, or simply converted French names into names more suitable for the German tongue. The men of Infantry-Regiment 27, for example, called the Chemin des Dames "*Schmenkerdamm*". In the autumn of 1914, in the line south of Ypres, the engineers of *Pionier-Kompanie* 237 (119. Infantry-Division), whose recruiting area was the coastal districts of Northern Germany, translated the name of the severely contested village Wytschaete as "*Wueste Scheisse*" (terrible shit). In the slang of this engineer unit's home country this sounded quite similar. At Verdun, Fort Douaumont dominated the central part of the severely contested battlefield. Already a few days after the beginning of the offensive in February 1916 the attacking troops referred to the fort as the "coffin lid". This nickname was tragically confirmed by the desperate fighting that ensued. Quickly captured by the Germans, Fort Douaumont became the objective of repeated heavy French counterattacks. But the nickname became notorious when 650 men of the German garrison were killed in the fort by the accidental explosion of old French ammunition dumps in the casemates. The dead bodies had to be buried by the survivors in the cellars of the fort. Intensive shelling prevented the evacuation of the dead bodies or of burying them outside of the fort. The trench war transformed the Western Front into a zone of devastation. The most devastated area was the Somme sector, which got a really significant nickname. The sector had already been destroyed in the Somme battle in 1916. In their retreat to the "Hindenburg line" in March 1917 the German forces annihilated everything which could have been useful for the British Army: Houses, streets, railways, bridges; even fruit trees and wells were burnt or exploded. Afterwards the ravaged area was called the "Somme desert", uninhabitable for friend and foe.

The Western Front extended over 475 miles from the channel coast at Nieuwport to the Swiss border. Forming a strip of destruction that was 20-30 miles wide, the frontline cut its way through Western Belgium and the northern and eastern parts of France. On its course to the Swiss border the front passed a wide variety of landscapes that gave each sector its characteristic face and imposed very different living conditions on the soldiers. While living and fighting in the trenches, the soldiers had to cope with topographic and climatic conditions ranging from the flat and muddy plains of Flanders, where the high ground-water level often prohibited even the construction of regular trenches, to the Vosges Mountains, where trenches and dugouts had to be cut into the barren rock at an altitude of up to 1200 metres. And the war at each sector was also quite different. Depending on the respective topographic conditions and the strategic importance of the sector some parts of the Western Front became the focus of battle for longer or repeated periods, like Flanders, the Artois, the Somme and the Champagne, while others fell asleep after some initial fighting in 1914/15, as happened at St. Mihiel, Lorraine or the Vosges Mountains and the Alsace. Due to the limited number of available troops, only the creation of passive sectors allowed the French Army to withdraw the troops that were needed for offensive operations at the active sectors. The Germans economized men and guns by converting their trenches into a formidable fortress in the west to send as many men as possible to the Eastern Front. A continuous simultaneous battle along the complete Western Front, as it was fought in August and September 1914 bringing about tremendous losses, was impossible. There were simply not enough men, guns and ammunition. Additionally, "cushy sectors" served for the recuperation of exhausted troops. However, the "cushy war" at these quiet sectors was still very much a real war, killing and wounding tens of thousands of men and devastating the area. On so-called quiet days a regiment at the Western Front counted in its sector the impact of an average of 500 shells fired by enemy guns and mortars against positions and communication trenches. Between the English Channel and the Swiss border, on each quiet day, the German OHL recorded the loss of 1000 men who were killed, wounded, or simply got sick.

## Flanders Sector

Flanders was the northernmost sector of the Western Front where the frontline was anchored at the channel coast in the dunes east of Nieuwport. Running approximately forty miles south from this city to Armentières, the Flanders sector included parts of Western Belgium and Northern France. Flat plains and high ground-water level and its general lack of remarkable topographic features characterized Flanders. Owing to the high water level which was generally between three and four feet below the ground, the trenches and dugouts were mercilessly filled with water. The trench soldiers depended on breastworks and concrete shelters for protection and billeting that were constructed on the muddy ground surface. These pillboxes, varying in size from machine gun posts to platoon shelters, were camouflaged and difficult to spot for the British artillery observers. But the concrete shelters were nevertheless quite vulnerable against repeated direct hits by heavy artillery. Concrete shelters became death traps when shells found their way through the mud to the box's bottom side and exploded there, overturning the pillbox. Its inhabitants were buried alive when the pillbox fell on the entrance side closing the exit with impenetrable mud and water. Only a few flat hills and ridges offered better conditions and valuable observation posts, and in the muddy Flanders plain they were of outstanding strategic value. Notwithstanding all preparations with sandbags and duckboards the intensive shelling turned the Flemish countryside into a pattern of water filled craters and groundless mud, for which Flanders became notorious after Passchendale. After the shells had destroyed the carefully designed artificial irrigation system nobody could stop the water regaining the ground.

Two remarkable rivers crossed the Flemish plain. The Yser River, flowing from south to north parallel to the frontline between Ypres and Nieuwport and the Lys River, which crossed the battlefield between Armentières and Menin. The Yser River between Nieuwport and Dixmuide became a considerable barrier when the Belgian Army flooded the western banks of the river in the final days of October 1914. By opening the sluices at high tide and closing them at low tide the Belgians converted the area west of the river into an impenetrable zone and forced the Germans to abandon their bridgehead on the western Yser bank, while they themselves used the railroad embankment farther west as their forward line.

The city of Ypres was the most important town of the Flanders sector. This historic commercial town with its medieval brick buildings was situated in the centre of a rich and cultivated province dotted with villages, single country-houses and cottages, surrounded by parks and fences. The farms formed square-shaped courts enclosed by walls and water ditches. A system of thick hedges separated fields and enclosures for the cattle. Draining-ditches and canals crossed the country. Centuries of cultivation had left no open ground. Soon the intensive artillery shelling converted the landscape into a desert of shell torn mud.

In October and November 1914 the war entered Flanders. The German Chief of the General Staff Falkenhayn tried to break the Allied left flank one last time and sent his newly recruited reserve corps into battle. In the battle at the Yser and in the first Ypres battle the Germans failed, and as a result the German offensive in the West was stalled. Between Nieuwport and Ypres the frontline became static and ran generally from northwest to southeast, passing Dixmuide at its eastern side and the Houtulst forest at its western side. Near Langemark the frontline changed direction. This place became renowned in November 1914 when young German reserve regiments undertook the last costly assault to break the Allied flank. This bloody onslaught later created the "Langemark myth" in post-war Germany that celebrated a generation of young students sacrificing themselves for their country. At Ypres the front formed the famous Ypres salient, a fourteen-mile semicircle surrounding the city's eastern outskirts. The British Army held the town while the Germans dug in on a belt of hills and

**Below: Typical views of the Western Front – The northern end of the Western Front at the Belgian channel coast with the German trenches in the dunes at Lombardzijde. This position at the beach was called the "Seestellung".**
**Lombardzijde, Flanders.**
**Undated.**

**Opposite: Typical views of the Western Front – The Flanders sector. A fork in the road at a tiny shattered Flanders village. Mist, wet ground and brick houses were typical for this flat country.**
**Flanders.**
**Undated.**

ridges rising up to 30-80 metres above sea-level and overlooking the British position in the salient by 15-65 metres. This semicircle of rising ground consisted of the Pilkem spur running southeast from the village of Pilkem, the Menin Ridge halfway between Ypres and Menin, and the Messines Ridge with its highest points at Wytschaete and Messines. Messines Ridge was a dominant position, rising up to eighty metres at Wytschaete. From this ridge every movement in the British trenches at the Ypres Salient could be observed. No major British offensive could prevail without taking Messines Ridge first. In 1917 when the British Army launched its Flanders offensive Messines Ridge was its first objective. On June 7, 1917 Messines Ridge was the scene of one of the greatest mining operations that took place at the Western Front. In the early morning nineteen mines containing approximately one million pounds of high explosives went up under the German positions. Menin Ridge was the central part of the German position. Rising up only sixty metres above the adjacent country, this ridge sent north an arm of only fifty metres altitude, ending at the village of Passchendale. In autumn 1917 Passchendale Ridge, site of the second German line that had been blocking the British advance for weeks, became the symbol of attrition warfare. Opposite Messines Ridge lay another hill where the battle focused in April 1918 when the German Flanders offensive reached its climax: Kemmel Hill. After breaking the British front and capturing Armentières the possession of Kemmel Hill and the adjacent ridges was to seal the fate of the Ypres Salient. The German "*Alpenkorps*", especially trained mountain troops, attacked and took the hill. But French divisions arrived in time and blocked any further advance of the Germans. Ypres was again saved.

## The Artois Sector

The Artois sector extended over a length of twenty-five miles between Lille and Arras. The frontline passed between Armentières and Lille and ran in a southwestern direction to La Bassée. There the German position formed a salient around this town, leaping some three and a half miles forward into the Allies' front, and crossed the Aire-La Bassée Canal. From the canal the frontline led south, past the western suburbs of Lens and reached the southern end of the sector at Arras. In 1915 and 1917, when the Allies focused their attack operations on the Artois sector, the frontline underwent some alterations. The salient at La Bassée was reduced by British attacks in 1915, and the Carency bulge southwest of Lens disappeared when the French took Notre Dame de Loretto Hill and the adjacent villages in the same year. The British captured Vimy Ridge on April 9, 1917, pushing back the German frontline between Lens and Arras by approximately four miles.

The Artois sector was part of the industrial and mining zone of Northern France. Its part occupation by the German Army was deeply felt by French industry. Already in 1914 the Germans had captured the majority of French coal resources when they occupied the mining areas of Lorraine and Artois. The mining area of Bethune-Bruay was also under permanent threat. It was still in the hands of the French but only five miles behind the British trenches and under the guns of the German long-range artillery. The mines of Bethune-Bruay played a crucial role in French war production. 70% of the French wartime coal consumption was hauled there, and coal was of great importance in the Great War, as it was the basic energy used to run industry and railroads. As a densely populated industrial zone the Artois sector was an exception at the Western Front. In general it passed only rural areas of Belgium and France. The Artois was dotted with coalmines, winding towers, factories, steelworks, smokestacks and extensive areas of working-class estates. The miners' and workers' quarters were located in the direct neighbourhood of their factories and mines and were called colonies while the mines were designated by numbers. A dense net of railroads connected the industrial sites with the major cities Lille, Bethune, Lens, Douai and Arras. Situated only a few miles away from the frontline they all suffered from shelling or accidental explosions. On January 10, 1916 a terrible catastrophe took place at Lille, where a whole neighbourhood was destroyed when a German ammunition dump exploded, killing hundreds of civilians in their crumbling houses. For the troops the Artois sector was an unpleasant place. Many regimental histories refer to the poor and crowded billets found in the small working-class houses and remember a generally depressing environment. But the deserted and destroyed factories and mines provided plenty of construction material making trench and dugout construction easier. The Artois industrial zone was a typical example of a densely populated industrial area in the beginning of the 20th century. It offered only low living conditions to the working class, as was the case in Manchester and the Ruhr too.

In 1915 and 1917 the Artois sector became an active front. The Allied effort was guided by the general idea of a pincer movement to take the German bulge in Northern France by its flanks. 1915 saw the first combined attempts of the British and French armies undertaken with insufficient artillery support and reserves against a German front that was becoming impregnable. In 1917 the pincer movement took on a strategic scale when the French and British offensives were carefully coordinated. The French attacked at the Aisne while the British arm of the pincer started at Arras.

At the Artois sector the battle focused at the La Bassée salient with Neuve Chapelle and Festubert on its flanks and the Lens salient with Loos on its northern flank and Notre Dame de Loretto Hill in the southwest. Together with Vimy Ridge, Notre Dame de Loretto Hill formed a system of ridges rising up to 165 metres at Loretto Chapel and 140 metres west of Vimy. The ridges controlled the frontline between Lens and Arras and overlooked the Douai plain by approximately 100 metres. Both hills were separated by the Carency River and formed a steep slope on their eastern side. The German Army had occupied the ridges since 1914, thus prohibiting any advance and observation from the Allies. For them control of the ridges was the key to dominating the Douai plain. In May 1915 the French Army attacked at Notre Dame de Loretto Hill, where, before the war, a gentle chapel had attracted pilgrims. After months of intensive fighting, Loretto Hill and the adjacent villages Souchez, Ablain, Carency and Neuville were all under French control. The Canadian Corps took Vimy Ridge after intensive preparations two years later. On April 9, 1917 the Canadians' surprise attack trapped parts of the German trench garrison in their deep dugouts and subdued the resistance successfully. The Easter Battle of Arras was a shock for Ludendorff and Hindenburg because the Vimy Ridge position was considered to be impregnable. The new principles for defensive battle had not yet been completely understood by the German troops and their leaders. The British learned their lesson, too: With intensive preparation they believed even "impregnable" positions could

**Opposite: Typical views of the Western Front – The Artois Sector. Main road of the destroyed village Liéwin. This sector was an important industrial and mining area of France. Trench war took place between factories, mines and working-class estates.
Liévin, Artois.
1917.**

Liévin.

be broken. Vimy led the way to spectacular success at Messines Ridge and to tragedy at Passchendale.

## The Somme Sector

The Somme sector constituted the most extended battle zone at the Western Front. It formed a triangle with Arras at its top, Montdidier at its left flank and St. Quentin at its right flank while the base was fixed on the northern banks of the Oise River. The River Somme, that gave the name to this sector, crossed the battlefield diagonally and passed on its way St. Quentin, Ham, Peronne and Amiens. Shell-torn ground, deep obstacles, trenches, dugouts and 205 ruined villages and towns covered the approximately 200 square miles that made up the "Somme desert". In 1914 and 1915 the Somme was deemed a "cushy front". After the retreat of mid September 1914 – even Amiens was under German control for a few days – the frontline stabilized, and for more than twenty months the Germans had time to turn their positions into a chain of nearly impregnable fortresses consisting of several lines of trenches and deep dugouts. An example of such a fortress was the Schwaben Redoubt at Thiepval whose underground cellars could resist even heavy bombardment. As they were fixed on the tops and slopes of the gentle hilly countryside of the Somme the German trenches profited from overlooking the enemy positions.

Beginning at Arras and running generally south, the Somme front vaulted as a vast salient into the Allied positions between the villages of Monchy aux Bois and Fricourt opposite Albert. The salient was crossed by the Ancre valley between Beaumont-Hamel and Thiepval. Both villages constituted veritable fortresses and were situated on exposed hilltops on the opposing riverbanks, thus towering above the valley by approximately seventy metres. Forming the right German flank in the battle of the Somme, both places resisted successfully against repeated British attacks. Thiepval was taken on September 26th, Beaumont-Hamel and the adjacent notorious Y-ravine not before November 13th, 1916. La Boisselle and Fricourt at the southern flank of the salient were also exposed and notorious positions. At the former spot the Amiens-Bapaume road crossed the frontline, and at the latter spot the trenches changed direction for approximately six miles to the east and formed a right angle that left Fricourt under fire from both flanks. Both places overlooked the surrounding countryside and as a result became the scene of intensive mining. To this day extended zones of mine craters exist there, including Lochnagar Crater south of La Boisselle which was fired on July 1st and produced a crater of eighty metres diameter and twenty-two metres depth. At Maricourt the frontline again changed direction back to the south and formed a second right angle, leaving the French trenches there as exposed as the German ones were at Fricourt. Maricourt was the junction between the British and French armies when the Allies went over the top on July 1st, 1916. At Curlu the frontline crossed the Somme River. The swampy river course at the bottom of the deep and winding valley could be overlooked from a height of fifty metres from the neighbouring hills and steep slopes. Passing between Rosières and Chaulnes, the front went straight down south through what was in 1916 the French sector of the Somme battle. West of Roye at the village of Andechy the German position formed another salient protruding a few miles into the Allies' line before changing the direction towards the southwest, and after passing Lassigny on the west side reached the Oise River south of Noyon.

On July 1st, 1916 the peaceful time at the "cushy" Somme came to an end. After months of preparation and seven days of bombardment British and French infantry went over the top and opened the "Battle of the Somme". By mid-November 1916 British and French infantry conquered in repeated charges, each of which took place after tremendous drumfire, eighty-five square miles of shell torn country dotted with heaps of bricks that had formerly been villages like Pozières, Bazentin, Montauban, Longueval or Guillemont in the British sector or Maurepas, Dompierre, Ablaincourt or Maisonette Ferme in the French sector. Little woods like Bernafay, Thrones, Deville and High Wood became the contested focus of battles, but they had long ago been reduced to mere stumps and shell holes. The Somme battle ended in the middle of November 1916. The German Somme salient was reduced to the Gommecourt salient between Arras and Bapaume. South of the Gommecourt salient the Somme offensive produced a new Allied salient between Thiepval and Chaulnes which vaulted deep into the German line. From its northern flank at Thiepval the front ran directly east to Sailly-Saillisel, where it changed direction towards the south, heading to Peronne. This town was still in German hands, but it was under the guns of the French who were holding the dominant position of Maisonette Ferme. At Maisonette Ferme the frontline went southwest to Chaulnes.

After months of intensive fighting both sides were left in unfavourable positions without trenches and dugouts. At the beginning of the winter season the troops had to live in mud filled shell holes exposed to the wet and cold winter weather of Northern France. The length of the winding frontline overexerted limited infantry strength, especially that of the German Army. In autumn 1916 the German OHL decided to construct a new more favourable rearward position, the "Hindenburg line". It ran in a general southeasterly direction from Arras to Laon and passed Cambrai and St. Quentin on its way. This new line reduced the length of front and thus saved valuable troops. Between St. Quentin and Cambrai the "Hindenburg line" was fixed at the St. Quentin Canal. This obstacle strengthened the position considerably. The vulnerable spot of the canal position was Bellicourt where the canal disappeared inside a tunnel for two miles, thus forming a natural bridge over this obstacle. In September 1918 Bellicourt would be the key for Rawlinson's 4th British Army to break the formidable "Hindenburg line". In March 1917 the German Army retreated to the new position and its comfortable shelters. The complete infrastructure of the evacuated area had deliberately been destroyed before and nothing was left for the following British troops. This area was called the "Somme desert".

The "Hindenburg line" held firm until March 1918. Even the surprise attack of 300 tanks at Cambrai on November 20th, 1917 failed to achieve a breakthrough. The German counterattack retook most of the captured ground. On March 21st, 1918 the "Hindenburg line" became the starting line for General Ludendorff's last push to win the war. Three German armies attacked and smashed the British 5th Army under Gough; they advanced nearly as far as they did in 1914. Ten miles east of Amiens, the important railroad junction for the northern part of the Western Front, the German advance was stopped leaving the Germans stranded in their self-produced desert. Now the Germans suffered from the same supply problems and lack of shelter under which the British troops had suffered. In autumn 1918 the Germans retreated to the "Hindenburg line" a second time but this time the supposed impregnable position failed to stop the British Army.

## The Aisne Sector

After the retreat from the Marne in September 1914, the German Supreme Command ordered General Kluck's 1st Army and General Buelow's 2nd Army to occupy a position on the northern banks of the Aisne River between Noyon and Reims. But British and French forces soon succeeded in crossing the river and getting a foothold at the eastern part of the Aisne sector where they climbed up the southern slopes of the Chemin des Dames Ridge. Intensive fighting took place at the Aisne bridgeheads in autumn 1914. When the British corps left for Flanders the French Army occupied the whole sector. In September 1914 the 7th German Army took over and held the sector till 1918. The French focussed particular attention on the Aisne sector because it was the sector of the Western Front closest to Paris. Until the spring of 1917 the Aisne sector was a typical "cushy front". This changed in 1917 and 1918 when first the French Commander in Chief Nivelle, and later the German Supreme Command, brought the Chemin des Dames Ridge into the focus of battle.

The Aisne sector followed the northern banks of the Aisne River between the Oise River in the west and Neufchâtel in the east and extended over a length of approximately fifty miles. Rising from the top of an isolated hill close behind the front, the medieval town of Laon with its old cathedral was the sector's rear area centre. The service of supply and soldiers on leave populated Laon's streets and the picturesque cathedral was a common motive on photo postcards that were sent home by the soldiers. The sector could be divided into two parts. The northwestern part of the sector ran more or less from north to south and passed the angle formed by the rivers Oise, Aisne and Ailette between the cities of Noyon and Soissons. This part of the Aisne sector below Condé was evacuated when the German Army retreated to the "Hindenburg line" in April 1917. From that time on the frontline passed close to the western border of the St. Gobain forest which constituted a considerable barrier in this part of the sector. At the ill-famed "Laffaux angle" the frontline changed direction from south to east, forming a dangerous salient that was exposed on both flanks to French gunfire. Moreover "Laffaux angle" was the spot where the southern end of the "Hindenburg line" was connected with the Chemin des Dames Ridge. This ridge dominated the eastern part of Aisne sector and ran fifteen miles from west to east, thus separating the valleys of Aisne and Ailette. The ridge rose up to 200 metres above sea level; thus the German positions on the ridge overlooked the Aisne valley by approximately 150 metres. This naked ridge of barren soil and chalky rock got its name from the so-called Chemin des Dames road which followed the crest line between Fort Malmaison and the village of Craonne connecting just a few farms and the village of Cerny. The trenches followed the road track exactly. The sugar factory of Cerny and the farms were fought over because of their value as artificial strongpoints on the barren ridge. Wood or brush partly covered the steep slopes, which were interrupted by deep ravines. For centuries peasants had been using the chalky rock to construct cellars, cutting deep caves into it. These caves and the tunnel of the Oise-Aisne Canal, which crossed the Chemin des Dames Ridge near Braye en Laonnois, offered plenty of shellproof shelters for the troops. Thus the Chemin des Dames Ridge formed a natural fortress and an excellent observation post, from which the surrounding country could be controlled within a range of thirty miles. However, covered with trenches, dugouts, wire and shell holes it was a barren and desolate place.

**Typical views of the Western Front – The Somme. The battle of the Somme in 1916 and the systematic devastation by the German troops before their retreat to the Siegfried Line in April 1917 converted a vast area of the Somme into what was called by the German soldiers the "Somme desert".**
**Somme.**
**1918.**

**Typical views of the Western Front – The Aisne sector. The main road of the village of Neufchâtel on the Aisne River. The Aisne sector was always a critical sector because it was the part of the Western Front closest to Paris.**
**Neufchâtel, Aisne.**
**Undated.**

The hilltop at the eastern end of the Chemin des Dames Ridge was called the "Winterberg" by the Germans. This hill and its counterpart "Hill 108" were of great tactical importance. "Hill 108" rose like an isolated island from the plain that extended at the sector's eastern flank where the Aisne-Marne Canal met the Aisne River. Its extraordinary position made "Hill 108" and its quarries the objective of intensive mining. A chain of huge mine craters covered the hill. Both hills controlled the plain between Craonne and Berry au Bac which offered the only access around the eastern flank of the German Chemin des Dames Ridge position. In spite of the two pillars, "Winterberg" and "108", which guarded it, this promising option for a breakthrough at the Aisne induced the French Army's commander Nivelle to attack in 1917. This spot became the scene of the ill-fated début of the French tank force, which was the spearhead of General Nivelle's Aisne offensive on April 16, 1917, thus ending eighteen quiet months at the Aisne sector.

In October 1917 when the French Army took the "Laffaux corner" and got a firm hold on the western flank of the Chemin des Dames, the German 7th Army evacuated the ridge. In the first night of November the Germans secretly left their trenches and occupied new positions on the northern slopes of the Ailette valley. The Ailette River separated the opposing trenches. A triflingly small river, it was to become well-known by the newspaper readers of the time. Directly at the foot of the Chemin des Dames Ridge the swamps on both banks of the Ailette River formed a belt of boggy and flooded ground that was 1000 metres wide. Swamps and flooded shell holes were inhabited by thousands of noisy frogs. The reptiles performed their deafening concert undisturbed even by the shellfire. The frog's croaking successfully drowned the noise of the deploying German forces when on May 27th, 1918 the Ailette valley and the Chemin des Dames Ridge became the scene of the third German offensive in 1918. Within a few hours the German storm troopers bridged the swamps, climbed up the ridge and overran the positions that the Allies had supposed to be impenetrable. After crossing the rivers Aisne and Vesle, the offensive was finally stopped at the Marne. The Chemin des Dames Ridge was cited in army reports in the autumn of 1918 one last time. The Germans finished their second retreat from the Marne and took up positions on the ridge as they had done in 1914. But this time it was only an interlude. In the course of the general retreat, the Chemin des Dames Ridge was evacuated once and for all in October 1918.

## The Champagne Sector

The Champagne sector took shape on September 15th, 1914. After their retreat from the Marne the German Army turned round and took positions between Reims and the Argonne forest. By deliberately selecting a series of hilltops and ridges that roughly followed the course of the ancient Roman highway and overlooked the surrounding plains and valleys from a height of 30-100 metres, the Germans forced the French troops following into rather unfavourable positions at the foot of the ridges. Since the autumn of 1914 the French Army had struggled to improve their own line and to take the commanding hills. The Champagne sector was of special interest to the French Supreme Command because of its generally favourable topographic conditions. A dense network of railroads supplied the sector which was not blocked by ridges like the Aisne sector or covered with impenetrable dense woods like the Argonne sector. Moreover it formed the strategic flank of the German Western Front that offered promising prospects for a breakthrough. This induced the French Army Command to launch major offensives in the spring and autumn of 1915 and in April 1917. All attempts at a breakthrough failed however, and at the price of tremendous losses. By choosing a commanding position on Berru Hill, Moronvilliers Ridge and the northern banks of the Suippe and Py rivers, the Germans succeeded in fixing the Champagne frontline for four years. However, it was not only the French who failed to break through the Champagne sector. When Ludendorff launched his final blow, the "*Friedensturm*" (Peace Attack) offensive, on both sides of Reims on July 15th, 1918, the German Army met disaster too.

The so-called "*Champagne Pouilleuse*" was an unpleasant piece of land. Consisting of barren ground that produced only poor harvests – mainly oats – these lightly undulating plains were dotted with dispersed villages, farms, meadows and thin stripes of pinewoods under an endless horizon. Nature and villages offered only scanty cover and insufficient accommodation for the troops. Only a thin layer of vegetable mould covered the chalky ground, and each shell blast unearthed the soft white stone. In the summer heat when the little rivers were nearly dry the chalk produced asphyxiating dust, which changed after some hours of rain into a deep quagmire that covered the troops with white dirt. But the same chalky rock had the advantage of being hard enough to allow intensive tunnelling under the positions, and so it provided the troops with spacious shelters. Positions like the "*Kanonenberg*" (Gun Hill) near Massiges consisted of a network of dugouts and underground galleries that remind one of an ant-heap. The Germans improved their communications at places where they passed dangerous sectors by digging shellproof underground galleries of some hundred metres length like the renowned "*Debus Tunnel*".

A series of valleys running from east to west, like the Dormoise, the Suippe, the Py, the Retourne and the largest and northernmost of all the Aisne valley, offered a system of rearward slopes to the German defence. This was what inspired Colonel Lossberg, chief of staff of the 3rd Army at that time, when he developed the German system of deep defence. Lossberg's system, that was destined to frustrate the Allied effort in 1917, underwent its first tests on the hilly Champagne plains. In the west, the German positions were anchored on Berru Hill from where the German artillery observers overlooked Reims and the plain north of the city by 180 metres. As part of the Reims fortifications Berru Hill was improved with the works of Fort Berru and Nogent-l'Abesse, taken by the Germans in 1914. Fort de la Pompelle, which was still in French hands, was located opposite. The historic city of Reims with its famous cathedral, the traditional site of the coronation of French kings, was now directly behind the trenches that passed the city's northeastern outskirts. Directly under the German guns, the cathedral had already been set aflame in September 1914. The fortified city was covered by a circle of seven forts and some redoubts and batteries. Farther east, between Berru Hill and the Suippe valley, Moronvilliers Ridge rose up to a height of 257 metres. Together with the trenches on Cornillet Hill and the nicknamed "*Fichtelberg*" it formed the most formidable natural fortress of the Champagne sector. Occupied by the Germans, Moronvillers Ridge became the scene of intensive fighting when the French infantry tried to take this key position.

**Opposite: Typical views of the Western Front – The Champagne sector. Reims under German gunfire. As the place of the coronation of French kings the capital of the Champagne region was an important town in French history. After the German retreat from the Marne in September 1914 Reims was only two kilometres away from the German forward trench.**
**Reims, Champagne.**
**April 12, 1918.**

Cornillet Hill is particularly noteworthy for a tragedy that took place there on May 20th, 1917 when two battalions of Infantry Regiment 467 were killed in the "Cornillet tunnel". "Cornillet tunnel" was a spacious shelter and consisted of three parallel galleries, each 100 metres long and with separate exits. The tunnel was the backbone of the Cornillet defence and was heavily shelled by the French artillery. Shells had buried the exits several times. Nevertheless they had been reopened every time. On this occasion orders were issued to evacuate the tunnel but arrived too late. When three heavy shells hit the ventilation system and penetrated the cover, the garrison's fate was sealed. The exits were blocked and major parts of the galleries collapsed. The garrison of several hundreds of men were buried alive and killed by the asphyxiating gas of the exploding shells. Barrage fire blocked any German rescue operation and Cornillet Hill, robbed of its garrison, was taken by the French infantry.

On the eastern banks of the Suippe valley the German trenches clung to the ridges paralleling the valleys of Py and Dormoise; here the battle focused north of Souain on Navarin Ferme. At Tahure the frontline formed a sharp angle and projected south westerly into the French positions where it shifted to the ridge between Dormoise and Tourbe valley. This dangerous angle was nicknamed "*Wetterecke*" (storm angle) by the Germans, and it was flanked by the important hilltops of Butte de Tahure and Butte du Mesnil. At the villages of Massiges the frontline fell down to the Aisne valley, which separated the Champagne from thc Argonne forest. The eastern end of the ridges north of Massiges was the crucial point in the eastern part of the Champagne sector where the exposed "*Kanonenberg*" became a focus of combat. The "*Kanonenberg*" controlled the adjacent valleys and consequently the battlefield.

## Argonne Sector

Besides Flanders with its muddy fields and the rocks of the Vosges Mountains, the Argonne sector confronted the fighting men with the roughest terrain at the Western Front. The rugged terrain of the Argonne forest was characterized by dense wood that covered a system of isolated hilltops, steep ridges and narrow ravines that were difficult to access and to control. Flanked by the valleys of the Aisne River in the west and the Aire River in the east the Argonne forest extended from north to south at a length of twenty miles and was eight miles broad. The Argonne forest is cut into two halves by the deep valley of the small Biesme River which, like Aisne and Aire, runs from south to north before changing direction to the west. The Biesme River discharges its waters into the Aisne River near Vienne le Château. As the area was sparsely settled the troops only found a few billets and little comfort in the Biesme valley and on the outer edges of the Argonne forest. Behind the French positions the small towns of St. Menehould and Clermont en Argonne were the only major settlements. Varennes was under German control but it did not offer suitable quarters for billeting as it was too close to the front and suffered severely from the shelling. For that reason the troops began to construct a dense infrastructure of camps, communications, canteens and other installations for rest and recreation both for the men and the animals in the dense wood behind the front.

The Argonne forest, forming a veritable barrier between the Champagne and Verdun sectors, was itself an almost impregnable obstacle for any advance. The French Army and the 5th German Army hold the sector since 1914. However, in September 1914 the 5th German Army had already crossed the Argonne forest successfully when it had to bypass the fortress of Verdun in the west. They were only eight miles away from the gates of Bar le Duc when an OHL order arrived instructing them to take part in the general retreat following the Marne disaster. The 5th Army Command under the German Crown Prince although shocked by the order did obey and both sides were thus condemned to fight a difficult war of stalemate and intensive mining in the Argonne forest for four long years. In the final days of September 1914 the front between Servon and Varennes became static, crossing the Argonne forest at a total length of eight miles. Following the northern slopes of the Biesme valley in an eastern direction until Bagatelle Pavillon north of village of le Four de Paris, the frontline formed a right angle to the south to include Bolante plateau before turning east again to Boureuilles.

In 1914 and 1915 the Argonne forest was the focus of bitter combat. Under the command of *General* von Mudra, the "Argonne Corps" (the XVI. German Army Corps) was busy pushing the line some hundred metres further south. La Harazée slope, Bagatelle Pavillon, Rheinbaben Hill, Hubertus Ridge, Barricade Ridge, Bolante Plateau, la Fille Morte Ridge and Hill 285 became the scene of intensive fighting before the positions were frozen. The frontline was eventually fixed on the northern slopes of the Biesme valley between Vienne le Château and Le Four de Paris. After passing Bolante Plateau, la Fille Morte Ridge and the Hills 285 and 263 the line left the Argonne forest near Boureuilles. Under the intensive shelling the once dense forest disappeared leaving behind a strip of shell-torn ground dotted with the stumps of dead trees where the frontline passed the Argonne forest. The hilltops of Bolante, la Fille Morte and Hill 285 became the object of intensive mining operations. Engineers profited from the favourable quality of the Argonne chalk and fired dozens of mines under the enemy positions. Between la Fille Morte Ridge and Hill 285 an uninterrupted chain of mine craters separated German and French trenches at a length of 1 1/2 miles. The situation at Vauquois, an isolated hilltop on the eastern banks of the Aire River, was similar. This hilltop was severely disputed as it controlled the valley opposite the Argonne forest. When mining warfare ended in 1917 the engineers had succeeded in cutting a veritable valley of mine craters through the hill.

In the autumn of 1918, four years after the Argonne forest had became a battlefield of the Great War, this sector became the focus of major battle for the last time. The 1st U.S. Army of the American Expeditionary Forces launched their Meuse-Argonne offensive on September 26th. The Argonne sector formed the western flank of the U.S. advance. The Doughboys had to get through eighteen days of hard fighting against dense wood and German machine gun posts before they got out of the Argonne forest at its northern end near Grandpré. Twice as strong as a European division of 1914, the U.S. divisions and their service of supply became hopelessly cramped up on the few muddy forest tracks that passed the wood in a northern direction. The Argonne forest proved to be nearly impregnable yet again.

## Verdun Sector

The battle of Verdun in 1916 had as formative an influence on the French collective war memory as the Somme and Passchendale had on the British. The murderous slaughter at the Meuse River became a collective experience of the French soldiers because the French Army Command sent almost every division for a turn in the trenches at Verdun. Nearly every Poilu served and suffered there. The fortress of Verdun was called the corner pillar of the Western Front. Undoubtedly the strongest part of the Western Front the Verdun sector formed a vast salient which had been held by the French Army since 1914. After passing the Aisne and the Champagne sectors in an easterly direction, the front formed a right angle at Verdun and changed direction toward the south. This abrupt change in direction was caused by the German occupied St. Mihiel salient that projected into the fortress' hinterland south of Verdun at the Côtes Lorraines. Verdun was part of the French western border fortifications, a belt of modern fortresses constructed by the French government after the defeat in the Franco-Prussian War of 1870/71. The fortresses of Verdun, Toul, Nancy, Epinal and Belfort were connected by a chain of single forts and had effectively blocked the Franco-German border area since the late 19th century. This bulwark led the German Field Marshal von Schlieffen to hatch his ill-fated "Schlieffen Plan". He planned an invasion of France by crossing Belgium and Luxembourg to avoid a time consuming breakthrough of the ring of fortresses. The fortresses proved their worth and held firm against the German attacks in the Meuse valley and in the Lorraine in 1914. Although it had been nearly encircled by the German Crown Prince's 5th Army marching on Bar le Duc and by the V. German Corps passing the Côtes Lorraines Ridge between Verdun and St. Mihiel, the fortress was saved; on September 10th the 5th Army headquarters received an order to take part in the general retreat from the Marne. The Verdun salient took shape in the autumn of 1914 when the 5th Army retreated to a line that passed Varennes and Malancourt, crossed the Meuse River at Forges and paralleled the outer defences of Verdun between Haumont and Ornes. The south eastern flank was formed by the advance of the Armeeabt. Strantz into the St. Mihiel salient. For the French Army the loss

**Opposite: Typical views of the Western Front – The Argonne sector. German dugouts at a ravine in the Argonne forest. The rugged terrain with its dense woods separated the Champagne sector from the Meuse valley.**
**Argonne.**
**Undated.**

Lager i. d. Argonnen.

of Verdun would have meant the collapse of the ring of forts at the border. Verdun became a symbol of resistance and the fight for the fortress was as much a question of national prestige as it was of strategic importance, especially when it was stubbornly defended against the German offensive in 1916.

The situation of the fortress had been precarious from the beginning. Nearly encircled, only two railroads connected Verdun with its hinterland. One came from St. Menehould and lay in the range of the German guns. The other railroad followed the Meuse valley and was cut off by the German occupation of St. Mihiel. The French service of supply for the Verdun sector was restricted to a narrow gauge railway coming from Bar le Duc and a highway, the so-called "Holy Road", on which a never-ending column of trucks fed the battle. As a result Verdun was generally overestimated by the German OHL as a French jump-off base for offensive operations against Metz.

The German 5th Army headquarters had been making plans to take Verdun since 1914/15 but the lack of reserves meant they were never executed. For the Germans the Verdun sector was of imminent strategic importance. Any retreat at the sector of Verdun was impossible because the domination of the northern part of the Côtes Lorraines was the basic condition for the 5th German Army not to be pushed back by the French into the Woevre plain. Holding on at Verdun secured the right flank of *Armee-Abt. C* and the important mining area of Briey. But it was thought even more important to cover the railroad system Metz-Montmedy-Sedan, the supply line of the 5th, 3rd and 1st German Armies at the Western Front, considered by the German leadership to be under constant threat from the French sally-port Verdun. In actual fact the difficult French supply situation of the Verdun sector denied any such option to the French Army. It was only in the final months of the war that the idea of cutting the Metz-Montmedy-Sedan railway line began to play a role in the strategic planning of the Allies, especially with regard to the operations of the American Expeditionary Forces at the St. Mihiel salient and the U.S. Meuse-Argonne offensive in September 1918.

When the German offensive against Verdun began on February 21st, 1916, the front of the Verdun sector had a length of thirty-eight miles. The German OHL did not have enough troops at its disposal to cover the complete salient's front with attack forces for a concentric attack, so it limited the attack to a three army-corps-stripe at the north eastern front of Verdun. Falkenhayn ignored the Meuse valley as the main topographical feature, which cut the Verdun sector into a western and an eastern part. Instead of protecting the attackers' flank as expected, the river valley opened up the flank of the advancing German troops to the flanking fire of the French gunners. In position at the western banks of the Meuse River, the French artillery was out of range of the Germans and ruled the eastern banks with its fire. In March the Germans had to attack on the western banks of the Meuse to clear the German right flank. This operation increased the front of the attack to a length of fifteen miles between Malancourt and Damloup.

Verdun was the strongest and best-prepared sector of the Western Front. Something the German Command was fully aware of: It had at its disposal the "Memorandum Verdun", a detailed study and description of the permanent fortifications of Verdun. The outdated citadel of Verdun was protected by a system of modern forts, concrete infantry shelters and underground ammunition depots that were connected with trenches and wire obstacles and covered a space of sixty square miles. At the beginning of the war modern forts in Belgium and Northern France had surrendered quickly after only a few hours of heavy bombardment

**Typical views of the Western Front – The Verdun sector. Consenvoye was one of the country villages with farmhouses and barns extending along a road north of the fortress of Verdun. Such small villages billeted the German siege forces.**
**Consenvoye, Verdun.**
**Summer 1917.**

by German 42-cm-guns. As a result the French Army Command placed little value on the forts of Verdun and had reduced their guns and garrisons. But in 1916 the intensive artillery battle that was mercilessly raking the ground soon revealed how invaluable strong permanent forts and bombproof concrete shelters actually were. They were essential in fact for giving the troops a chance of survival. Even after having been half destroyed, the stonewalls and concrete shelters resisted the intensive shelling for months. After the most terrible bombardment it was possible, in the moment of attack, for some survivors to emerge from their underground shelters to frustrate the attackers' goals with the annihilating fire of their machine guns. At the northeastern front of Verdun the forts were fixed on the dominant hilltops of successive ridges. The important fort Froideterre was situated on the Froideterre Ridge, the forts Douaumont and Hardaumont on the adjacent eastern hills. Behind them was Belleville Ridge with the forts St. Michel and Souville. On its eastern extension the fort Vaux formed the second barrier. Fort Douaumont was the biggest and most important fort at Verdun. In February 1916 a few German soldiers took the fort by surprise. From a height of 395 metres the fort overlooked the complete battlefield and sheltered the German reserve troops, stores, command posts and artillery observers when the battle culminated in the summer. Though it was the object of intensive shelling and repeated French attacks the Germans held Fort Douaumont until

October 24th, when it was lost as unexpectedly as it was taken in February. Fort Vaux became renowned for the epic resistance of its garrison in June 1916. Encircled by the Germans who had already occupied the fort's surface, the men fought an underground war inside the galleries and casemates under their commander Raynal for several days. In the darkness of the underground casemates the German attackers cleared their way with hand grenades and flamethrowers and tried to break the barricades that blocked the galleries. Cut off from supply and communication the garrison eventually had to surrender. In July 1916 Fort Souville saw the high water mark of German attacks when Bavarian troops made a final attempt to break through in the Fleury-Souville sector. Some survivors reached the fort but the momentum had been lost and the German Verdun offensive stalled. While at the northeastern front the forts got involved in the battle, the German attackers never reached the forts of the Marre Ridge on the western banks of the Meuse River.

Next to the forts and concrete shelters the topography of the Verdun sector confronted the attacker with a difficult and labyrinthine system of hills and ravines. The hilltops overlooked the steep ravines by 50-150 metres. The ridges and ravines were dotted with fortified villages, quarries and impenetrable woods. The woods of Haumont, Wavrille, Fosses, Cailette and Chapitre, which were finally reduced to blackened stumps by the shelling, became ill famed battle scenes. There is no report that did not refer to the treacherous cover offered by deep ravines and muddy gullies. They turned out to be deathtraps under shellfire, like the Hassoule ravine which provided the way of access to Fort Douaumont. As most of the ridges were open to enemy observation and direct fire the troops depended on gullies and ravines for moving on the battlefield and for sheltering reserves and supplies. The artillery also depended on the limited space of the ravines for their gun pits, which made them interesting targets for enemy gunfire.

Taking into account the main battle zone, the duration of the battle and the tremendous losses of 1916, it must be admitted that Verdun is a surprisingly small battlefield. After some days of rapid advance at the northeastern front in February and March 1916, the attrition battle focused for several months on a field of nine square miles marked by the triangle of Fleury and the forts Douaumont, Vaux and Souville. Tens of thousands of men were annihilated in this microcosm of trench and crater war. The situation on the western Meuse riverbanks was similar. For months the battle was focused at Hill 304 and Dead Man's Hill, the two dominating hilltops, without bringing about a decisive victory for either side.

## St. Mihiel Sector

Pinched in between the French fortress of Verdun and the German fortress Metz-Diedenhofen (now Thionville) the St. Mihiel salient was a termed "cushy sector" despite its strategic importance. At St. Mihiel "cushy" meant that no major battle of strategic scale took place there. But intensive local fighting did take place, especially on the flanks of the salient. The German occupied St. Mihiel salient formed a nearly equilateral triangle, each side of which was twenty-six miles long. The salient had its base in the Woevre plain that extended from north to south between the ridges of the Côtes Lorraines on the eastern banks of the Meuse valley in the west and the Moselle valley in the east. The St. Mihiel salient's apex projected deep into the hinterland of Verdun in a southwesterly direction. Opposite the little town of St. Mihiel, which gave its name to the salient and lay twenty miles south of the fortress at the bottom of the Meuse valley, the Germans held a tiny bridgehead at Chauvoncourt that

**Typical views of the Western Front – The St. Mihiel salient. At the town of St. Mihiel the southern arm of the German pincer movement against Verdun crossed the Meuse river forming the St. Mihiel salient.**
**St. Mihiel.**
**Ca. 1915.**

controlled both the Meuse River and the railroad and road communications which followed the course of the river valley. From September 1914 till September 1918, when the U.S. Army cleared the salient, the bridgehead at Chauvoncourt blocked the southern approaches to Verdun. Moreover, from their positions near St. Mihiel the German artillery ruled the important railroad Revigny-Toul, which was the only west-east railway communication for the French service of supply paralleling the frontline in this sector.

The German salient was an extremely exposed position forming in its south western part a pocket that was only seven miles broad and offered open flanks for enemy pincer movements on both sides. St. Mihiel could have been the theatre for strategic battle, but it never saw more than local combat. For the German Army the St. Mihiel salient offered an opportunity to strangle the fortress of Verdun by a flanking movement. But in 1916 *General* v. Falkenhayn decided to attack Verdun directly. For the French Army the salient offered the option for a major pincer movement allowing the encirclement of the salient's garrison and an advance against the vital railroad communications at Conflans-Metz-Diedenhofen and the mining area of Briey. However, it was not until September 1918 that this idea was partly realized when, in their first independent major offensive, together with French forces, the Americans cleared the salient. Attacking from north and south the U.S. forces captured 11,000 Germans and took

hundreds of guns. The U.S. forces were already scheduled to take part in the Meuse-Argonne offensive which was to start on September 26th. As a result, far from achieving strategic relevance, the advance of the U.S. divisions was stopped on a line between Fresnes en Woevre and Pont-a-Mousson.

The southwestern apex of the St. Mihiel salient was pushed forward deep into the Côtes Lorraines ridges, heading into the Meuse valley at St. Mihiel. The Côtes Lorraines are a series of ridges and hills rising up to between 350-400 metres on the eastern banks of the Meuse River. The ridge separates the Meuse river valley from the Woevre plain in the east and overlooks both by approximately 200 metres. At its western and eastern edge the ridge is marked by abrupt slopes. As the Côtes were the only natural barrier between the fortresses of Verdun and Toul, seven French forts – Génicourt, Troyon, les Paroches, Camp du Romains, Liouville, Gironville and Jouy – were constructed there by the French government to close off access into the Meuse valley. While Fort Camp des Romains was occupied by the German Army in September 1914, the Germans failed to take Troyon and Liouville. Worse still for the Germans, the French guns of Fort des Paroches ruled the German bridgehead at Chauvoncourt and the town of St. Mihiel.

From the autumn of 1914 the salient's flanks became the target of repeated French attacks. On the northern flank the battle focused on Combres and Les Eparges Hill. At this spot the frontline entered the Woevre plain, coming from St. Mihiel and passing the Côtes Lorraines in a northeasterly direction. Combres Hill is separated from the Côtes by the tiny Longeau valley. Rising abruptly, the hill is 351 metres high and towers above the adjacent plain and valley by approximately 130 metres. The hilltop and its northeastern spur, "point x", allowed any movement in the eastern plain to be controlled. This commanding hill became the scene of intensive mine warfare which blasted more than thirty mine caters into the hill's surface. On the southern flank the fighting centred on the forests of Apremont, Ailly and Brulé, south of the important highway that connected St. Mihiel and Apremont. The possession of the highway decided who had control of St. Mihiel. In 1915 the French Army launched a series of attacks at the Apremont forest, turning the forest into shell holes and blackened stumps. At that time thousands of dead bodies in all states of decomposition made life for the survivors unbearable. Further east, the St. Mihiel salient passed the Woevre plain in an easterly direction, south of Thiaucourt, to meet the Moselle valley at Pont a Mousson. There, overlooking Pont-a-Mousson and the Moselle valley, the "*Priesterwald*" forest became the centre of the fighting in this part of the salient. At this point, a few square miles of shattered forest saw a fierce struggle for domination.

## Lorraine Sector

The Lorraine sector extended over a length of sixty-five miles between the Moselle River near Pont-a-Mousson and the foot of the western spurs of the Vosges Mountains close to the little town of Badonviller. The frontline ran mostly southeast on a course parallel to the Franco-German border as fixed by the peace treaty of 1871. As a consequence of the Battle of the Frontiers in August 1914, all the trenches were located 2-6 miles from the border on French territory. After the hot days of August-September 1914 the gentle Lothringian countryside was the theatre of four years of "cushy" war. A deep system of trenches crossed the hilly country that was dotted with villages, meadows and woods. The most extended of these woods was the Parroy forest. The frontline crossed the northern part of the forest that dominated the Marne-Rhine Canal like a natural fortress. The latter was one of the several water barriers running parallel to the border. After passing Toul and Nancy, the canal crossed the frontline between Lagarde and Parroy and cut the Lorraine sector into two halves.

**Opposite: Typical views of the Western Front – The Moselle sector. German trench north of the town of Pont a Mousson where the Western Front crossed the Moselle River.**
**Moselle River, Moselle.**
**Undated.**

The Lorraine sector was the only part of the Franco-German border that offered relatively favourable topographical conditions for an invasion compared with the rugged terrain of the Vosges Mountains or the limited space of the Belfort gap. However, with the exception of the first weeks of war in August and September 1914, the Lorraine sector was the quietest part of the Western Front, depending on the military situation in Northern France and the belt of French forts extending between Toul and Epinal. As the focus of battle was in Northern France both the German and French headquarters did not expect any major operations between the Moselle River and the Vosges Mountains. In 1915-18 the Lorraine front was held on both sides by exhausted or second-rate troops. From 1917 onwards inexperienced U.S. divisions that had recently arrived from the USA took over sectors at the Lorraine front to undergo a preliminary training for the "real war". Additionally the divisional sectors at Lorraine were much broader than those in Northern France.

Offensive operations in Northern France were a priority for the French Army because of the necessity to push back the German invader from French territory and to operate in close connection with the British Army. The main reason for the German Army's inactivity on the other hand, were the French fortifications. After the defeat in the Franco-Prussian war of 1870-71 the French government had successively closed the Franco-German border between the Grand Duchy of Luxemburg and Switzerland by constructing a belt of modern fortresses: Verdun, Toul, Nancy, Langres, Epinal and Belfort. Each fortress consisted of an ancient citadel and a circle of modern forts. Many of these were modern constructions of steel concrete. Each fortress' citadel and forts formed an extended fortified zone of, on average, seventy square miles and a diameter of ten miles. The extended construction had been intended to prevent the hostile artillery from shelling the complete fortified zone. Pre-1914 siege artillery had had an average range of 4.5 miles. The major fortresses were connected by a chain of single forts. The most famous of which, Fort de Manonviller, was at the Lorraine sector between Lunéville and Blamont, only six miles away from the border. This fort was heavily shelled by the German Krupp-made 42-cm-mortar "*Dicke Berta*" (Big Berta). 158 shots battered the fort into surrender on August 27, 1914. The heavy shells pierced the three metre thick concrete and smashed the thirty centimetre thick steel armoured cupolas.

In order to pass through this belt of fortifications it was necessary to execute a series of successive siege operations. After a successful breakthrough of this fortified belt the invader would be confronted with another obstacle forty-five miles further south, the fortress of Langres, which controlled the highland of the same name and required renewed siege. The forts of Langres and Neufchâteau – the latter halfway between Toul and Langres – blocked the vital road and railroad communications on which any invasion depended. The French government had constructed a considerable barrier between St. Mihiel and Montbéliard, consisting of more than 200 forts and permanent batteries, including Langres.

There was a broad gap in the French fortified line between Nancy and Epinal called the Trouée de Charmes. This was no accidental gap but intended by the French planners to become the battlefield of the French field army according to its favourable topographical conditions. At the Lorraine border, particularly at its eastern part in the Trouée de Charmes gap, a network of rivers, running parallel with the border and the later frontline, made the Lorraine sector much more unattractive for the German planners of major military operations. In the sector's northern part the Seille River flowed close behind the German trenches and was accompanied in wartime by swampy river banks. The eastern part of the Lorraine sector, marked by the successive obstacles of the parallel valleys of the Vezouse, Meurthe and Mortagne rivers, was much more difficult. In 1914 the German advance came to a halt on the banks of the Mortagne River. The rivers join near Lunéville to become the Meurthe River which runs into the Moselle River north of Nancy. Between Lunéville and Pont-a-Mousson both rivers cut their way through hilly countryside, forming a valley that is approximately 100 metres deep. Dominated by the adjacent hills of an average altitude of between 200-400 metres, the river valley was an additional considerable obstacle between the French frontline positions and the fortified zone of Toul-Nancy that lay 3-4 miles behind.

German strategic planning depended on a quick victory in the west. Therefore Schlieffen and the German General Staff were deterred from the time consuming exercise of bombing their way through the Lorraine network of fortresses and preferred the invasion of Belgium. However, the Lorraine sector did see major action in August and September when the French Army launched its Lorraine offensive. According to "Plan 17" an "offensive a outrance" should fight its way into the centre of Germany, passing between Metz and the Vosges. But the plan failed. After a twenty-five mile advance into German territory, the French infantry was repulsed by the German 6th and 7th Armies in the battles of Morhange and Saarebourg on August 20-22, 1914. Crown Prince Rupprecht, commanding the 6th Army, and the German Supreme Command could not resist the tempting opportunity to launch an attack against the retreating enemy. This operation was contradictory to the "Schlieffen Plan" and resulted in an "ordinary frontal assault", as it was called in German General Staff terminology. After inflicting a serious defeat on the French, the 6th Army was not strong enough to achieve more than slightly pushing back the enemy. Breaking through the fortresses of Toul-Nancy was beyond the 6th Army's capacity. This was far from a decisive victory but the French offensive was stalled and finally the crisis in Northern France called for both German and French reinforcements to be shifted northwards. Later the German forces evacuated some of the conquered ground and retreated to the border. The Lorraine sector then became a "cushy sector".

## Vosges Sector

The Vosges sector passed the Vosges Mountains on a length of fifty miles between the valley of the Plain River in the north and the medieval town of Thann at the southern end of the mountains. Proceeding mostly from north to south, the trenches ran parallel to the course of the frontier between France and Germany, which was fixed on the mountains' main ridge. But

**Typical views of the Western Front – The Lorraine sector. Rear area of the village of Maderich in the quiet Lorraine sector. This village was a rest area and the site of an NCO training school. Maderich, Lorraine. December 19, 1917.**

here in the Vosges Mountains, at the Bonhomme Pass, the Western Front crossed the border and entered Germany. On its final fifty-five miles to the Swiss border the Western Front was on German territory, 6-15 miles east of the Franco-German border of 1871.

Although only a secondary chain of mountains and classed as a "cushy sector", the Vosges confronted French and German infantry with the hardest climatic and topographical conditions at the Western Front. As they were entrenched on barren hills and precipitous slopes, the infantry was exposed to thunderstorms in the summer and to snowstorms and frostbite in the winter. Both thunderstorms and snowstorms came relentlessly from the west, giving the crippled trees and bushes their characteristic bend towards the east. In the winter several metres of snow buried the trenches, and icy rain could make each step in the rocky trenches dangerous. Sudden thaw melted snow and ice, converting trenches into torrents, flooding caves and dugouts. While the peaks of the main ridge were barren and rocky, the lower mountains were covered with dense pine forest and dispersed rocks. But the extreme climatic conditions accelerated the erosion of the hills and slopes that had been shattered and stripped of their vegetation by the shelling. The battle zone was converted into a moving mass of rock and debris scattered with the burned stumps of the torn up timber forest.

The topography made conditions for trench war in the Vosges mountains even worse. The course of the frontline was characterized by a permanent change between exposed hilltops rising up to 1200 metres altitude and deep valleys falling abruptly to 700 metres. Running from north to south, the Vosges are marked by a gentle rise in the west that culminates in the main ridge, an uninterrupted chain of peaks with an average altitude of 1200-1300 metres. The highest peak of the main ridge is Hohneck Mountain, near the important Schlucht Pass, which rises to an altitude of 1361 metres. But the highest mountain is the Grand Ballon; with an altitude of 1423 metres, it crowns a major spur that turns away from the main ridge in a southeasterly direction. Both were under French control and offered valuable observation posts. The eastern slopes of the main ridge are abrupt, in most places forming a perpendicular wall of rock, which dominates a ten-miles-broad belt of wooded mountains and gentle valleys descending to the plain of the River Rhine valley in the east. Elevated by the adjacent hills by between 600-800 metres, the valleys offered the only useful road and railroad communications. These communications normally came to an end at the head of the valleys in difficult and narrow mountain roads that crossed the main ridge of the Vosges on half a dozen pass routes. On the mountains the fighting infantry and the service of supply had to cope with considerable altitude differences and the problems caused by a thin network of roads and mountain tracks. A serious disadvantage in the Vosges Mountains was the lack of communications running from north to south, parallel to the front. On the German side the moving of troops from one part of the sector to the other usually required extended detours along the valley of the River Rhine. The French Army solved this problem with the construction of a road along the reverse slope of the main ridge, the Route des Crêtes, which today serves as a road for tourists.

The topographic features described above inevitably had a deep influence on the military situation and the fighting in the Vosges sector. The course of the frontline was the result of the military operations in autumn 1914 and some local battles in 1915 and the winter of 1915/16. In an attempt to liberate the Alsace the French Army launched a general invasion heading to Mulhouse in August 1914. Several flank detachments crossed the Vosges at Ventron, Schlucht and Bussang passes and advanced downhill. But the French attack failed. After having been repulsed by the German 7th Army's counterattack, the French mountain troops got a hold in

**Typical views of the Western Front – The Vosges sector. The German Haicot position carefully improved with timber. Plenty of building material for the trenches was offered by the dense forests of the Vosges Mountains. But the high mountain range confronted the soldiers with extreme weather and terrain conditions.**
**Brigade-Ersatz-Bataillon 84 Offenburg.**
**Haicot, upper Liepvre valley, Vosges.**
**Summer 1916.**

the southern Vosges when the 7th Army changed its focus of battle to the northern Vosges, in accordance with OHL orders, leaving behind only secondary Landwehr forces. In the north the Germans retook Donon Hill and advanced up the Breusch valley towards Senones and Saint Dié. After the Germans had pushed their front forward into French territory, the frontline became static between the Celles and St. Marie passes, taking a southeasterly course between the Meurthe River and the border. Entering the southern Vosges, the frontline crossed the border and the main ridge at the Bonhomme Pass. Climbing up the dominating hilltop of Tête des Faux, the trenches passed the Weiss valley near Orbey and descended to the Fecht valley west of Munster. The front followed the upper Fecht valley for several miles before it climbed Hilsenfirst Hill and upper Lauch valley up to the Grand Ballon spur, from where the frontline descended step by step along the southeastern peaks of this spur – Sudelkopf, Hartmannsweilerkopf – to the Rhine valley.

In 1914/15 the front at the Vosges sector did not consist of an uninterrupted line of trenches, as it already did further north at the Western Front. Dominating peaks and rocks had been converted into strongpoints by the infantry which controlled adjacent valleys and slopes with guns only. Spots of military importance were severely contested in the phase where the Vosges front was developing. In autumn 1914 the fighting focused on important hills like Hartmannsweilerkopf and Hill 425 where the frontline left the southern Vosges and entered the plain of the River Rhine. The Hartmannsweilerkopf became one of the most contested mountains at the Vosges sector in the following year. In the winter of 1914/15, there was still enough room for patrols and movement. At Hilsenfirst Hill, which controlled the upper Guebweiler valley, German mountain troops successfully attacked on skis. In the following winter newly constructed trenches and continuous wire confronted ski runners with insurmountable obstacles, and classical mountain warfare was finished. To gain control of the valleys, the French mountain troops attacked the adjacent mountains. One of these operations, in the summer of 1915, consisted of a series of bloody assaults against the peaks of Reichackerkopf, Lingekopf and Schratzmaennele which were launched to open up access to the Munster valley. The defiles of the main ridge were hot spots at all times. The peak of Tête des Faux Hill, guarding the Bonhomme Pass, which was one of the vital communications through the Vosges, was converted into a fortress of reinforced concrete by German infantry. The situation was similar at the Tête de Violu near the Markirch defile. December 1915 saw the last major battle at Hartmannsweilerkopf. The Germans retook the hill one last time. After this the Vosges sector fell silent and became a "cushy sector".

## Alsace Sector

The Alsace sector was the southernmost sector of the Western Front. The frontline passed between the south eastern spurs of the Vosges Mountains near Sennheim (Cerny) and the Swiss border at Pfetterhausen over a length of twenty-six miles through the picturesque countryside of Upper Alsace. Medieval framework houses and dispersed woods were scattered over the hilly country. Hills rising up to 300 metres and super-elevating the adjacent valleys by 20-50 metres mark the topography. South of Mulhouse, the only bigger industrial town and capital of this area, the Sundgau forms a triangle of remarkably elevated land. This elevation points with its tip to Mulhouse and rises up to 450 metres. Its steep slopes control the Rhine-Rhone-Canal in the west, which passes the Alsace in a north easterly direction, and the Rhine valley in the east. North and east of Mulhouse is the plain of the Rhine valley, limited only by the Vosges and Black Forest mountains.

Despite being considered the "cushiest" sector in the war in August 1914 the Alsace was nevertheless the scene where the first soldiers were killed in action and where the first large-scale battle was fought. In the morning of August 2nd, 1914 the German 3rd *Jaeger-Regiment zu Pferd* (mounted riflemen) garrisoned at Mulhouse, sent out a scouting party to reconnoitre the dislocation of the French forces behind the Franco-German border. This happened thirty hours before war had been declared but at a time when general mobilisation was already in progress in both camps. Eight riders under the command of Lieutenant Meyer met a French piquet at the exit of the tiny village of Jonchery. In a sudden exchange of fire Coporal Peugot (who commanded the French post) and Meyer were killed, becoming the first soldiers killed in action at the Western Front. One week later the French VII. Army Corps entered Mulhouse on its mission to liberate the Alsace from the German occupation that had lasted since 1871. The German 7th Army bound for battle in Lorraine took the opportunity to achieve a victory by its superior forces and attacked on the evening of August 9th. On the next morning Mulhouse was retaken, and the beaten French divisions were in full retreat towards the border. A second battle followed on August 19th. This time the French Army won the battle but – for the meantime – was nearly losing the war in Northern France. Mulhouse had to be evacuated a second time by the French Army, which had to send all available forces northwards. What followed were fours years of trench war.

Although, next to Lorraine, only the Alsatian part of the Franco-German border offered passable terrain, a battle there could never be more than a sideshow due to the strategic outset, the topographical conditions and the border fortifications. For the French Army the attack in 1914 was more a political than a strategic question because the liberation of Alsace-Lorraine from German rule was regarded as a national mission. The Germans seized the opportunity to hurt the enemy but they never envisaged a major battle on the upper Rhine. Southern Alsace is the crossroads where the Belfort Gap meets the upper Rhine valley, forming a pass that connects eastern France with western Germany. But this pass is in fact only a narrow tube. No broader than ten miles at Belfort, it widens up to twenty miles on the upper Rhine down-stream, and narrows to a gorge of 1-2 miles in width up-stream. It is surrounded by the Vosges, Jura and Black Forest mountains which are inaccessible for a major military invasion.

The Belfort Gap was blocked by the French government in the late 1880s when the old fortress of Belfort, ten miles away from the border of 1871 and well known for its stiff resistance under siege in the Franco-Prussian war, was considerably improved. Schlieffen allotted a role to Alsace and southern Germany that was similar to that of eastern Prussia; accepting, if unavoidable, even an enemy occupation in order to concentrate all available forces for a decisive victory in Belgium and Northern France. As it happened, the battle in the north eventually freed the southern German territory from the threat of a French invasion by attracting the enemy divisions to the point of crisis. But the idea of ceding own territory to the enemy, even if only temporarily, had never been popular in the eyes of German generals. In 1911 General von Mudra, then inspector of the German fortresses, altered the strategic planning at the upper Rhine. He limited the territory that was left open for an enemy invasion to southern Alsace by improving the German fortifications and bridgeheads of Mutzig, Strassburg, Neubreisach, Eichwald, Istein, Hueningen and St. Ludwig. These fortifications formed a right angle along the Rhine with its tip at Strassburg, blocking the Rhine crossings and the exit to the north between this city and the Vosges. According to the military rule that river defence is most effective on the far banks, the German fortifications formed bridgeheads on the western Rhine banks ready to attack the open flanks of any French invasion or to deliver sudden counterstrokes, as was so successfully done against the VII. French Corps at Mulhouse in August 1914.

In the autumn of 1914 mostly Landwehr brigades – over aged secondary troops – took up the line and fixed the front in a series of minor combats against their French antagonists. As it was a secondary sector, only secondary troops served at the Alsace sector which became a rest and recreation area. In the forest of Habsheim large camps offered billets for divisions undergoing reorganisation and retraining. The frontline between Sennheim and the Swiss

**Opposite: Typical views of the Western Front – The Alsace sector. Alsatian timber framed houses in the shelled village of Ammerzweiler. Between the Vosges Mountains and the Swiss border Upper Alsace offered the only passable access to the Rhine valley.**
**Landwehr-Infantry-Regiment 123.**
**Ammerzweiler, Alsace.**
**January 1916.**

border ran generally from north to south. At Sennheim Hill 425, originally covered with vineyards before trenches printed a new pattern onto the slopes, was severely contested. Here the frontline left the Vosges Mountains and entered the plain, thus allotting local importance to the tiny hill. South of Sennheim the front crossed the Ochsenfeld plain and climbed up a number of low hills on both banks of the Doller River to turn slightly east, where at Ammerzweiler the two southernmost mine craters of the Western Front were exploded in 1915. After crossing the Rhine-Rhone-Canal, which follows the course of the valley of the Larg River, the frontline passed the little town of Altkirch and the Hirzbach forest. Running on its last miles directly south, the Western Front met the Swiss border one mile west of the village of Pfetterhausen. This was the end of the Western Front.

**Opposite: Typical views of the Western Front – The southern end of the Western Front. German and Swiss soldiers guarding the southern end of the Western Front. Three kilometres east of the village of Pfetterhausen the Western Front reached the Swiss Border.**
**German-Swiss border.**
**Undated.**

During the war the German military administration constructed the so-called "southern fence", a wired and strictly guarded border fence between the southern end of the Western Front and the River Rhine near the St. Ludwig bridgehead. The fence was intended to prohibit all illegal traffic across this wooded and hilly section of the border between the Alsace and Switzerland. Following roughly the course of the German-Swiss border, it excluded parts of the Alsatian border territory to economize border control. This brought additional hardships for the people living there because men liable for military service or soldiers on leave were not allowed to enter the zone even if their families lived there. The German military administration suspected the Alsatian people of having pro-French sympathies and feared that soldiers of Alsatian origin would desert and pass across the nearby Swiss border. Moreover, the area so close to the Franco-Swiss border was perfectly suited for the purposes of enemy espionage. Forty-five years after the Alsace had become part of the German Empire the German Army still behaved like a force of occupation.

Chapter One

# War in the Trenches -
## Impressions of the Western Front

In the final months of 1914 a battle zone arose at the Western Front that had never been seen in military history. A strip of total destruction that was several hundred miles long and 30-50 miles deep passed through Belgium and France from the channel coast to the Swiss border. This strip of ruined land was covered by a spider's web of trenches, shell holes, wire belts and pillboxes. Millions of men and their machines of destruction inhabited this artificial desert. The desert's hostile population was split up by a network of wire and a zone called no-man's-land where friend and foe opposed each other like mirror images. The daily life of these men equipped with steel helmets, rifles and stick bombs was an underground existence in trenches, shell holes and dugouts. In the daylight the surface was empty. Enemy artillery observers and air reconnaissance aircraft looked out for targets and the men were forced under the cover of dugouts or tarpaulins in order not to attract enemy shelling. Darkness was the time for all major activities like relief, construction work or the transport of supplies. The infantrymen's perception of the surrounding cratered country was reduced to the narrow scope of their loophole or the little window of a periscope. Their world was restricted to some dozen square metres of trench and shell holes. At some spots snipers made even a peep over the edge of a shell hole a suicidal undertaking. Day and night the air more or less vibrated from the noise of bursting shells and rattling machine guns. Dirt covered the soldier's damp uniforms, boots and skin. Their lungs were filled with the smell of decomposition and burning material that evaporated from the battlefield and ruined villages. The ground was strewn with the remains of killed human beings and animals and – much more prosaically – littered with the rubbish produced by modern mass societies such as empty tins and boxes, rotten blankets and old boots. The hardened faces of dirty infantrymen coming back from the trenches; sentries observing no-men's land with bundles of stick bombs ready to throw; the labyrinth of trenches; lonely runners passing a ruined village; houses blown half away by hostile artillery; craters; mud – the Western Front produced millions of impressions which burnt themselves deeply into the minds of a generation of men who were forced to fight each other in Belgium and France from 1914-1918. The photographic camera caught these impressions and preserved for our eyes what has been levelled by the flow of time, reconstruction and more than eighty years of farming since the war. These were the infantryman's impressions of the Western Front.

**Opposite: "Back from the trenches. Much dirt." – In the confusing labyrinth of the trenches sections became the basic form of combat organization. To survive these, groups of men had to count on each other and on their guns.**
**Northern France.**
**December 1916-January 1917.**

**Opposite**
**Top left: Deep belts of wire separated the hostile lines from 1915 onwards, making no-man's-land inaccessible and protecting the trenches against surprise attacks. Empty tins often hung on the wire and worked as alarm bells.**
**France.**
**Undated.**

**Bottom left: Heavily shelled wood in the Argonne forest. Gunfire turned even dense timber forest into an area of charred stumps and shell holes.**
**III. battalion, Grenadier-Regiment 123.**
**Argonne.**
**January 1916.**

**Right: Sentry in front of his post. The trenches had to be supervised day and night by sentries to alarm the trench garrison in case of an enemy attack. These sentries had to spend many hours alone at their posts, observing no-man's-land.**
**France.**
**Winter 1916/17.**

**Below: German trench cut through a devastated landscape. The sentry is observing the quiet line, which could be woken up at any moment by gunfire or the rattling of machine guns.**
**France.**
**Summer 1917.**

**Right: A quiet afternoon in the trenches. The mood is quiet but not careless. The sentry is observing the hostile line. Ladders are available for exiting the trench in the case of a counterattack.**
**France.**
**1915.**

Kirchhofstellung St. Quent

**Opposite: Trenches between graves and tombstones. Deserted German positions at the cemetery of the town of St. Quentin a few days after the German offensive had overran the British lines in March 1918. Cemetery position, St. Quentin, Somme. March 1918.**

**Right: A bulwark position at the Lorraine sector. In swampy areas the ground water made the digging of trenches impossible and forced the troops to rely on bulwarks. Near Château-Salins, Lorraine. Winter 1915/16.**

**German trench in the Vosges sector improved with trunks, sandbags and loopholes. A box with rifle ammunition is fixed between the sandbags. The wire netting was to protect the trench against hand grenades.**
**Brigade-Ersatz-Bataillon 84 Offenburg.**
**Liepvre valley, Vosges.**
**Summer 1916.**

**Flooded trench of 52. Infantry-Division at the Somme. Apart from the enemy mud and rain were the most hostile force soldiers had to face and at times made the underground world of the Western Front a nearly uninhabitable place.**
**52. Infantry-Division.**
**Somme.**
**1915/16.**

**Communication trench at the Somme. Relieving forces, runners, food and ammunition bearers depended on these covered pass ways which were often turned into hazardous paths by mud and rain.**
**52. Infantry-Division.**
**Somme.**
**1915/16.**

**Opposite**
**Top left: Men of a machine gun company waiting for orders to go forward while resting at the reserve position near Douaumont in the Verdun offensive in 1916. The machine gun is fixed in a portable pack which can be carried by one man. Smoke from firing German guns can be seen in the background.**
**Machine Gun Company, Reserve-Infantry-Regiment 120.**
**Douaumont, Verdun.**
**May 28, 1916.**

**Top right: Smoke cloud from a bursting shell at the French line in the Argonne forest seen from the German trench. From their observation posts in the trenches artillery observers directed shellfire on nearby enemy trenches.**
**Argonne.**
**Ca. 1915.**

**Bottom left: Cratered battlefield. The intensity of gunfire turned vast parts of Belgium and France into a veritable moonscape.**
**6th Battery, Reserve-Field-Artillery-Regiment 28.**
**France.**
**August 1917.**

**Bottom right: Deep wire belt at St. Laurent near Arras. During the course of the war the German Army constructed a deep system of defensive positions in the rear area.**
**St. Laurent, Artois.**
**1917.**

**Below: Exploded tower of an industrial plant in Northern France. The artillery used church towers and chimneys as observation posts. At the same time however such exposed landmarks attracted shellfire. Most were exploded to deny any use to the enemy.**
**Northern France.**
**1916.**

**Right: A vice-sergeant-major of Infantry-Regiment 165 entering the line at Liévin. In 1915 the appearance of the trench soldiers changed. Gas mask, stick and raincoat completed their equipment.**
**10th company, Infantry-Regiment 165.**
**Liévin, Artois.**
**October 1915.**

**Above: Blocked main road of the damaged village St. Mard near Roye. The German troops constructed a barricade of stone and timber to prevent the enemy from gaining a view or access,
St. Mard, Somme.
June 15, 1918.**

**Top right: Half-blown up house at a frontline village. Many villages at the Western Front disappeared after months of intensive shelling.
France.
1917/18.**

**Right: Lonely runner walking along the main road of a destroyed village directly behind the lines. When telephone communication broke runners had the dangerous job of delivering orders and reports. In front, a fresh shell crater.
France.
1916.**

**Opposite: Relieving troops resting on their way into battle. In the summer of 1915 the French Army failed in their attempt to break the Vosges front on both sides of the Muenster valley.
Fecht valley, Vosges.
Summer 1915.**

Chapter Two

# DAILY LIFE AND COMBAT

Trench war at the Western Front constituted the daily life of millions of German soldiers from 1914-1918. Infantry and engineers inhabited wet trenches and crowded narrow dugouts that were only a few hundred metres away from the enemy positions. Dirt, dust and mud shaped their environment. Under bad weather conditions boots, clothes, blankets, food and shelters were wet, muddy and stinking for weeks on end. Personal hygiene was only possible at the rest areas behind the front. In the line even shaving was a luxury. The men in the trenches were deprived of any privacy and had to share bunkbeds and blankets. For years the German soldiers lived in the close community of their section and platoon under the strict supervision of their NCOs and the platoon leader. The men's liberty to move was restricted. At the front they were not allowed to move freely in the trenches but had to stay in their respective sector, even when off duty. Behind the front the men's radius was limited to the village or the rear area camp where the troops were billeted. Special permission was needed if they wanted to visit a nearby city. These strict military rules guaranteed the troops' functioning as a military body, ready for action at all times. In addition the close-knit social life they led and the strict rules they had to adhere to produced a form of military social control that ensured good conduct and discipline without depending on the strict enforcement of martial law. In the Imperial German Army military justice was surprisingly liberal and capital punishment was rarely imposed. The few cases of desertion that occurred were not punished with the firing squad. Good social cohesion was the core reason for the German army's effectiveness and the small number of offences against military discipline.

From autumn 1914 onwards the infantrymen's life was organized by a schedule of frontline service, reserve line service and rest and recreation behind the front. The men in the trenches were occupied with sentry duty, construction work and serving as bearers. Sentry duty to control no-man's land and their own trench system took up most of their time. Off duty the infantrymen spent their time sleeping in their damp holes and musty dugouts. In a letter to his family later published in the journal "*Taegliche Rundschau*", the soldier Fidus Sohnrey wrote in October 1914 from the Aisne that immobility in the trenches and the darkness of their stuffy underground shelters caused them to feel tired all the time. It was hard to resist the temptation simply to sleep hour after hour. When the weather was particularly bad the trench garrisons were confined to their boring underground world for days on end, interrupted only by the hours of sentry duty. Tallow-candles emitted barely enough light for reading newspapers or writing letters. Others killed time by playing skat (cit: *Von Flandern bis Polen*, p.223-229). The soldier's dull underground existence was nevertheless a dangerous one. Life in the trenches was ruled by a permanent atmosphere of more or less small-scale warfare. Enemy patrols or raids were a never-ending threat. Even so-called "quiet" days were characterized by artillery or mortar fire, nervous machine gun rattling and rifle fire, patrols and sniper activities. Parts of the forward trench garrison were occupied with construction work to improve trenches and dugouts. Most of the work had to be done at night. The fight against the destructive impact of artillery and mortar fire together with the influence of weather conditions on trenches and dugouts was a never-ending job. Combat and life required a permanent influx of ammunition, food and building materials into the forward positions. Service in the fatigue parties transporting equipment and materials was the third main occupation of infantrymen. Working under such difficult conditions and the careless use of dangerous equipment and arms caused many accidents. Stick grenades were a particular problem because their explosive load was often used for cooking, or for other non-authorized purposes. The improved lethal power of arms and ammunition, as well as technical defects, was also often responsible for accidents. The problem was so serious that for example in August 1915, at a quiet sector near Reims in the Champagne, the Fuesilier-Regiment 40 received an order from the brigade headquarters that urged for more prudence in the handling of arms and ammunition because there were more injuries caused by accidents than by enemy fire.

Lice became a symbol of daily and social life in the trenches. Lice were permanent companions in the trenches and in the crowded billets of the rest area camps behind the frontline. Despite the permanent health checks carried out by medical officers, personal hygiene was low for men and officers when they were serving their turn in the trenches. At the frontline it was impossible for the soldier to wash and clean or change his dress and underwear, sometimes even for weeks. The exceedingly poor hygienic conditions granted excellent living conditions for vermin. Troops infested with lice left behind dugouts and trenches completely contaminated with lice when they had finished their turn, thus making the infection of the relieving unit unavoidable. The families at home sent their boys at the front plenty of chemical agents against lice, but these turned out to be inefficient. The only effective way of delousing was the officers' and soldiers' daily search for lice on uniforms and underwear. This became a typical aspect of daily social life in the trenches. Plenty of photos show trench fighters sitting together half naked and checking their clothes for the small insects. Lice surpassed social barriers and infected officers and simple soldiers in the same way. The daily delousing was a quiet moment of privacy, allowing a personal chat, when officers and men talked about home and private affairs. Newcomers from the home country were totally integrated into the trench fighter community only when dirt and lice covered all their rear area cleanliness. The famous World War I author Walter Bloem wrote in his book "*Sturmsignal*" about the social aspects of lice and delousing and how it improved the feeling of solidarity in military bodies. When he served as a battalion commander he had the impression that his men accepted him as a real frontline soldier only when he was sitting half naked together with his men hunting lice. Bloem called lice "the glue of comradeship", referring to the democratic aspects of the lice problem bringing together officers and men fighting a common problem in a daily private war. His battalion, including himself, was full of lice "from top to toe" (cit. Bloem: *Sturmsignal*, p.308-309). For inexperienced newcomers like Hans Kuhn who entered the Western Front as a young draft in April 1918, discovering lice on his body was a real and embarrassing shock. In his war memoirs he vividly describes how, as he was carefully checking his uniform, he found his clothes crawling with brown dots inhabiting every part of his underwear and trousers. In his first shock he thought "that he would die of disgust or that the lice would eat him alive." At the front he had expected to find dirt, hunger, fear, injustice, fatigue, gas and to be wounded or killed. He had been prepared to bear all this with "heroic magnanimity" and was thoroughly disappointed that he had to cope with such "disgusting trivia". An older comrade told Hans Kuhn to bear this plague with philosophical equanimity and that fighting lice was a waste of time and energy (cit. Kuhn: *Das Leben im Tode*, p.35-37).

Living and fighting in the trenches the soldiers depended on each other and comradeship between the men had to bridge social barriers and, to some degree, even ranks. The experience of the daily living conditions at the front and of the common work and dangers shared by the men who came from all social classes and professions to serve their country exerted a deep and lasting influence on the social system. Germany was, as all other European countries, a class society with clearly defined groups. The economic prosperity of the pre-war period and a general increase of income, even amongst the lower classes, helped to improve social permeability. However, class-barriers still existed even if wealth and education could bridge them. Remarkable inconsistencies in the country showed that a form of social development was in progress. For example all German men were liable for military service and the German army was declared a symbol of German social unity. However, higher educated young men had the privilege of reducing their service time and serving as one-year volunteers. Jews held important positions in politics and business but were not allowed to become reserve officers. Walther Rathenau the famous Jewish leader of the AEG enterprises regretted this fact all his life. On the other hand, the active officer's rank was originally reserved for the nobility in Germany. But the ever-increasing army depended on officers of middle class origin. Thus the middle class officers had to be accepted and the guard regiments became the nobility's exclusive right. Reserve officers, who generally originated from the middle classes, were considered inferior by the noble active officers. These inconsistencies and the slow pace of social development produced a form of social unrest in the young, pre-war generation that was also a protest against technological progress. This "*Wandervogel*" (ramblers) movement represented young and well-educated people of the middle class who tried to escape the stiff social order in place by hiking in the countryside and who dreamed about reviving the traditional forms of old Germany's country life. Many of the famous World War I veteran writers were linked to the "*Wandervogel*" movement and they experienced the outbreak of war in August 1914 as a liberation from social tightness. Of course they could not have known that the same social inconsistencies and the rule of technology were awaiting them in the trenches. There the depressing social order and the pre-war mental state were confronted with the Western Front living conditions already described. This resulted in disillusionment and a brutalization of the young soldiers. The experience of the new social order of the trenches, marked by comradeship, community and social control, took root in the perception of the war generation as what was later called war socialism. With the exception of Russia the Great War produced no new society but it provoked deep mental changes that influenced post-war societies. In Germany the right wing and nationalistic part of the war generation, who not only experienced the war in the trenches but also took part in the ensuing civil war and its cruelties against their own people as "*Freikorps*" fighters who suppressed the revolutionary uprising in Germany, embarked on a combination of nationalism and socialism that would later culminate in the NS period. National Socialism had its roots in the trenches and tried to establish a new society according to these principles.

**Two infantrymen in close combat at a forward sap on the famous Chemin des Dames Ridge. Advanced posts were often involved in close combat with rifle and hand grenades. Helmets, steel plates and armour were introduced to reduce losses. But the armour proved to be unsuitable.**
**52. Infantry-Division.**
**"Winterberg", Aisne.**
**Autumn 1917.**

**Reserve forces waiting in the second line at Juvincourt. The second line troops were prepared to counterattack if the forward trench would be attacked. Rifles and hand grenades are ready.**
**52. Infantry-Division.**
**Juvincourt, Aisne.**
**Autumn 1917.**

German trench at Gommecourt. From 1915 trench life was well organized and trenches were carefully prepared and deep enough to allow safe traffic. Special steps were constructed for sentries and combat.
52. Infantry-Division.
Gommecourt, Somme.
Summer 1915.

**Left: Infantrymen playing cards under their shelter in the forward line near Ville aux Bois. This position was called the "Poteau Werk".**
**5th Company, Infantry-Regiment 192.**
**"Poteau Werk", Ville aux Bois, Aisne.**
**December 1915/January 1916.**

**Bottom left: German dugout with signs for the aviators.**
**France.**
**1917.**

**Below: Two German soldiers enjoying a few moments in the sun in front of their dugout. Bad ventilation and dampness were a permanent problem in the dugouts. Such small entries led down a narrow staircase into the underground shelter. To avoid the inhabitants being buried alive by shellfire, dugouts normally had two separate entries.**
**France.**
**1917.**

**German infantrymen holding the enemy position under rifle fire at the shattered Priesterwald wood. Orders for active trench war prescribed as much combat activity as possible. Because of the expected retaliation, trench garrisons often tended to avoid too much activity.**
**Priesterwald, Moselle.**
**1916.**

**Bursting shells. Gun and mortar fire was a daily ritual to harass the enemy. The bureaucratic administration of the trench war counted all impacts and reported them back to the higher commands daily.
France.
1916.**

**Before and after: Well-prepared German trench on the north side of Thiepval village. In the background the ruins of the village are visible. This area became the scene of bitter fighting when the British Somme offensive started on July 1st, 1916.**
**Thiepval, Somme.**
**Spring 1916.**

**Before and after: The same spot north of Thiepval after being shelled by the British artillery. The trench has collapsed. A 28-cm-shell has blocked the entire trench and prevents the view of Thiepval.**
**Thiepval, Somme.**
**Spring 1916.**

**Opposite**
**Top left: German officer firing his sniper rifle on Hill 60. Sniping was a feature of active trench warfare, keeping the enemy under permanent pressure in order to cause a feeling of insecurity.**
**Infantry-Regiment 126.**
**Hill 60, Ypres, Flanders.**
**March 1915.**

**Right: Snipers observing the enemy line with a periscope. Successful sniping depended on careful observation. Sniper rifles were provided with telescopic sights.**
**52. Infantry-Division.**
**Somme.**
**1916.**

**Bottom left: View from the loophole over no-man's-land and the French position at Biache as the sniper saw it.**
**Biache, Artois.**
**September 1915.**

**Right: Sentry observing the access to a forward sap. If enemy patrols raided forward saps the communication trenches granted them free access into the position.**
**5. Bay. Reserve-Division.**
**Artois.**
**July 1915.**

**Left: Company officer supervising the work of his men at the quarry near Fort Vaux one month after the capture of the fort in the Verdun offensive. Stones and debris were piled up to improve the position. Vaux Hill was bitterly disputed.**
**Infantry-Regiment 126.**
**Fort Vaux, Verdun.**
**July 1916.**

**Opposite: Men of Infantry-Regiment 126 doing salvage work at the quarry near Fort Vaux. The quarry provided dugouts for the headquarters of the K.T.K. (Kampftruppenkommandeur) and the reserve company. The K.T.K. was the responsible officer in this sector. In the summer of 1916 the battle zone around Fort Vaux was reduced to a heap of litter and debris.**
**Infantry-Regiment 126.**
**Fort Vaux, Verdun.**
**August 1916.**

**Below: No-man's-land at Verdun as the men of Infantry-Regiment 126 saw it from their position at the railway embankment near Fort Vaux in the first few days of August 1916. The drumfire at Verdun left nothing that you could call a trench.**
**Infantry-Regiment 126.**
**Fort Vaux, Verdun.**
**August 1916.**

**Top left: The Western Front at night. British night attack near Ypres. A lightning of flares has turned night into day. Night time at the Western Front was a never-ending display of fireworks. Between Zillebecke and Hooge, Flanders. July 5, 1916.**

**Above: Rising flares during a night attack near Neuville. Flares were used to light the battlefield and as signals for asking for artillery support or counterattack forces. The signals were fired in different colours. Neuville, Artois. September 30, 1915.**

**Left: In the trench of Infantry-Regiment 170 near Gommecourt after a British attack had been repulsed the night before. The attacking Highlanders left behind the dead body of a killed comrade. Infantry-Regiment 170. Gommecourt, Somme. August 1916.**

**Opposite: Company leader dugout at "Winterberg" Hill. Company leaders had their own small staffs consisting of vice-sergeant-majors, NCOs, orderlies and runners. 52. Infantry-Division. "Winterberg", Aisne. Summer 1917.**

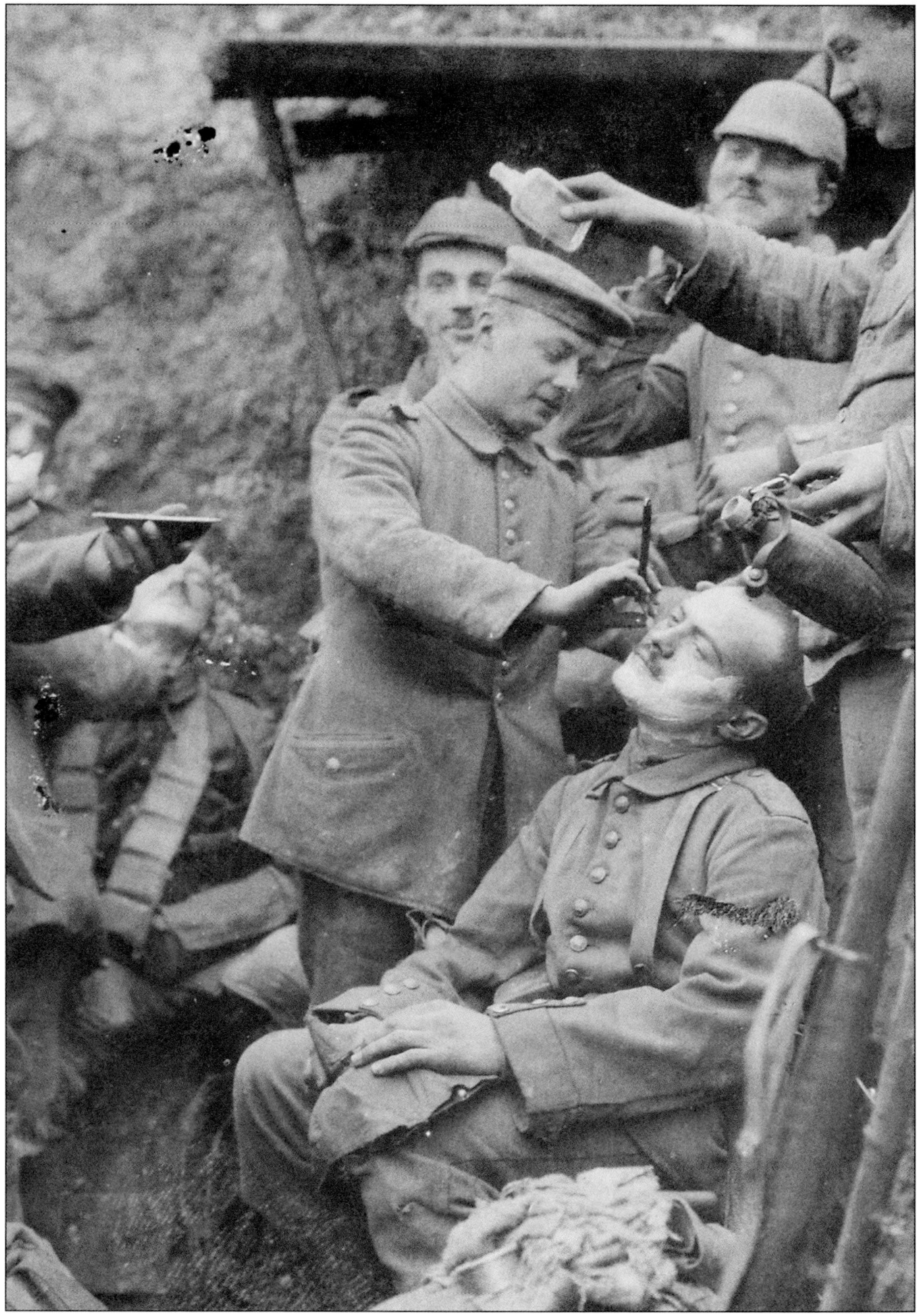

**Opposite**
**Left: Men of the 52. Infantry-Division cut their sleeping place into the parapet. When there were not enough dugouts available, primitive holes had to serve as a place for sleeping and cover.**
**52. Infantry-Division.**
**Near Hébuterne, Somme.**
**1915.**

**Right: A barber in the ranks of the 52. Infantry-Division shaving his comrades. Short beards were not only a question of hygiene but necessary for fixing gas masks appropriately.**
**52. Infantry-Division.**
**Somme.**
**Summer 1916.**

**Above**
**Left: Infantrymen clearing their underwear from lice. As a result of the poor hygienic conditions and the crowded life in the trenches lice were a common plague that nobody could escape.**
**52. Infantry-Division.**
**Somme.**
**Summer 1916.**

**Center: A toilet in the ruins of a destroyed village in the line at the Somme. Because of the crowded living conditions in the trenches medical officers put a lot of emphasis on the construction of toilets to maintain a basic level of hygiene.**
**52. Infantry-Division.**
**Somme.**
**Summer 1916.**

**Right: Company leader dugout at the Ypres salient. The company leader had to live and work in his small shelter. A stove, chair, table, lamp and some pictures made the place somewhat comfortable. The tarpaulin on the ceiling is draining the dugout.**
**Infantry-Regiment 126.**
**Hooge, Flanders.**
**February-May 1915.**

**Right: Holiday in the shelter with a barrel of beer. Beer and other types of alcohol were important for the soldier's morale on both sides of the line. The living conditions at the front were full of stress and frustration. The separation from their families at home had a depressing effect on the men at the front.**
**Western Front.**
**Undated.**

**Left: Two battalion officers having their meal in their dugout. While they are eating reports come in by telephone and their gas masks are always ready on the table.**
**France.**
**1917.**

**Bottom left: Before and after: Dugout "Hockenheimer Hut" of Ersatz-Bataillon 84 in the Vosges Mountains. Most dugouts had names, which were marked on signs.**
**Brigade-Ersatz-Bataillon 84 Offenburg.**
**Upper Liepvre valley, Vosges.**
**Summer 1916.**

**Below: Before and after: The same dugout a few days later smashed by a French mine. The sign survived the blast.**
**Brigade-Ersatz-Bataillon 84 Offenburg.**
**Upper Liepvre valley, Vosges.**
**Summer 1916.**

**Opposite**
**Left: Fatigue party repairing a trench that has collapsed because of the rain and melting snow. Maintenance work in the positions consumed most of the labour force, a constant battle against the elements.**
**52. Infantry-Division.**
**Somme.**
**Autumn 1915.**

**Right: Infantrymen at the Somme improving a communication trench with wickerwork and duckboards to secure the passage against erosion and mud.**
**52. Infantry-Division.**
**Gommecourt, Somme.**
**Summer 1916.**

Above: Soldiers of Infantry-Regiment 126 passing Equancourt on their way to relieve a Bavarian regiment at Sailly-Saillisel at the Somme. The village is under fire.
Infantry-Regiment 126.
Equancourt, Somme.
October 1916.

Above right: Attack forces waiting for the order to move forward at the artillery positions in the Verdun offensive. Waiting for the right moment of action was often not only a nerve-racking but also a dangerous business because reserve positions were often shelled heavily.
Verdun.
Spring 1916.

Right: German infantry accommodated at an unfinished camp on Hill 300 near Verdun before the offensive. Inside the unfinished shelters the soldiers put up tents using their tarpaulins to have some cover against the weather.
Hill 300, Verdun.
Spring 1916.

Opposite: Fatigue party carrying shells on a muddy track to a battery position behind the trenches. When not busy with sentry service or construction work the infantrymen had to bring equipment and ammunition to the forward line.
Northern France.
Winter 1916/17.

**Christmas Eve at a rear area billet behind the front. These soldiers have a gramophone that they possibly found somewhere in the deserted houses.**
**Western Front.**
**Christmas 1917.**

**Opposite: Happy faces after coming back from the trenches. Infantrymen of the 52. Infantry-Division after finishing their term at Gommecourt.**
**52. Infantry-Division.**
**Gommecourt, Somme.**
**Summer 1916.**

**NCOs and company-sergeant-majors picking out their lice at the rear area quarters at Hooglede. Lice were not only the privilege of the rank and file.**
**Hooglede, Flanders.**
**November 17, 1917.**

Chapter Three

# TRENCHES AND DUGOUTS

The first trenches and dugouts appeared at the Western Front as early as September 1914. In stationary sectors of the front the intensive small arms fire forced the infantrymen to take cover by digging holes in the ground. Groups, platoons and sometimes even whole companies constructed the first unconnected trenches. The deteriorating weather conditions in the autumn of 1914 led the troops to furnish these first trenches with a cover against the rain and the cold; thus the first makeshift dugouts appeared. Parts of the trenches were covered with shutters or the wings of gates and doors from nearby farm buildings and barns which were packed with a thin layer of soil. On both sides of the trench benches were carved out of the earth and bolstered with straw to provide the inhabitants with a certain degree of comfort. Shelter halves closed the entries. In the night passing sentries who had to walk over the sleeping comrades disturbed the comfort of these first dugouts. The Germans called this early form of dugout a "covered trench" (*Deckungsgraben*). But these covered trenches only offered cover against bad weather and enemy observation. To expect any protection against splinters of bursting shells or direct hits would have been naive. Other variants of early dugouts were little caves, the British soldiers called them "funk holes", simply cut into the trench wall and closed with a shelter half. Often these little caves collapsed and buried their inhabitants alive, or rain flooded them. But clever infantrymen found a solution by improving the caves with wooden supports and digging the caves above the level of the bottom of trench.

At the end of October 1914 whole systems of connected trenches appeared at the Western Front making covered traffic possible all along the line between companies and battalions. The armies in France and Belgium had realized that the stalemate would last and the approaching winter required weatherproof and heatable dugouts. Busy construction work was starting all along the frontline and various types of improvised dugouts were built. Each NCO turned into an architect of some sort. In front of the trenches or behind them, rectangular pits were excavated and covered by layers of wooden girders and earth. In the coal region of Northern France the German soldiers stripped the mines of their pit-wood when pillaging for construction material. The principles of construction were often erroneous and the dugouts were therefore not bombproof. But the important progress of this period of dugout construction was that the dugout became a separate construction outside of the trench and was no longer just a covered part of the trench. At this time dugouts became comfortable places to live in; they received individual names like "Villa Erna" or "Hockenheimer Hut". Fixed under the dugout's roof of wooden girders or pieces of corrugated iron, shelter halves were placed to protect the inhabitants against the permanent trickling in of water and the water was collected in empty tins. The dugouts were equipped with furniture picked up from half destroyed houses in the deserted villages or directly behind the lines. Some dugouts were furnished with sofas and armchairs, mirrors and wall-clocks; even pianos could be found in some underground shelters. But the deserted villages and towns at the front were soon robbed of all usable furniture and equipment, and as a consequence the decor in the dugouts became simpler, being reduced to bunk beds. Finally those first dugouts were replaced by well-constructed shelters in the line; and the anarchic underground lifestyle that had been possible at first was transformed into something more like that of a typical military barracks.

From January 1915 onwards, trench construction became more systematic in the German Army. The German High Command began to lay more emphasis on the construction and maintenance of a sophisticated trench system. Well-organized trench systems allowed an effective defence, reduced the number of troops necessary to occupy the line and offered healthier living conditions for the trench garrison. General Falkenhayn, Chief of the German Supreme Command, outlined this programme in two memoranda issued to the armies at the Western Front on January 7th and 25th, 1915. These memoranda demanded the construction of a strong forward trench which would be the main line of resistance and was to be held at all costs. The forward trench had to be fortified and organized to resist at length even a superior enemy using a minimum of ones own forces. As soon as the forward trench was overrun by the enemy it had to be immediately retaken in a counterattack. Behind the forward trench a second trench had to be constructed, providing bombproof shelters and covered communications for the garrison. Anticipating the danger of hostile breakthroughs, Falkenhayn directed the construction of a rearward position outside of the range of the enemy artillery. This rearward line was to be occupied in the case of an enemy attack. While all available forces of the German Army were sent to the Eastern Front to seek a decisive victory there in 1915, the garrison at the Western Front was left back busy with an overwhelming construction programme. The lack of labour force and different local conditions prohibited a homogenous execution of the construction work, but by autumn the work was nevertheless more or less completed. However, this construction programme was only a first step. From 1915 onwards the German positions were in a permanent process of construction, building a deep defensive zone of successive lines and deep wire entanglements step by step.

While still under construction the new German defence system underwent its first test in battle when the French Army attacked in the winter of 1915. The use of heavy drumfire by the French in the winter battle in the Champagne made it clear that really shellproof shelters were of vital importance. From March/April 1915 manuals were issued to battalion commanders describing the experience gathered in the winter battle and stating how necessary it was to improve the construction of deep dugouts with wooden frameworks similar to that used in the mining industry. Initially these deep dugouts were only an underground stair, 120 centimetres high and eighty centimetres broad, dug four metres into the earth. Four metres of earth above it and the wooden frames turned these narrow dugouts into bombproof shelters for four or five inhabitants crowded on the stairs. The German infantryman called these narrow dugouts "rabbit-burrows" (*Karnickelloecher*). Later two deep dugouts of this kind were always connected by an underground gallery. They eventually became spacious shelters, twenty or more steps underground, and provided room for 25-40 men. In 1915 and 1916 these "rabbit-burrows" in the Champagne and at the Somme saved the lives of the German trench garrisons and confronted the slowly advancing Allied armies with considerable German resistance even after days of devastating preparatory shellfire. But at Vimy Ridge on April 9th, 1917 the unexpected quick advance of the Canadian infantry turned the deep dugouts into death-traps. After several days of intensive shelling and a never-ending struggle to clear the dugout entrances from falling debris the Germans were surprised by the Canadians. They appeared suddenly at the entrances of the dugouts before the Germans had had time to climb up the twenty or more steps to the surface. Many Germans were caught in their shelters and forced to surrender or they were finished off with Mills bombs thrown down the stairs by the Canadians.

The two main problems faced by trench and dugout construction were shellfire and the weather. Rain and melting snow had an equally destructive effect on positions as bursting shells. The trench garrisons had a tremendous job to ensure that a position offered a strong as possible defence against both the enemy and erosion. Plenty of construction material was used for this purpose. The most commonly used materials were wood, wickerwork, concrete, steel girders, wire, sandbags and corrugated iron. By 1916, especially at so-called "cushy sectors", the German soldiers had developed a sophisticated trench system. An example of the elaborate work that was accomplished was found at the Somme on the eve of the 1st of July 1916. As it had been a quiet sector since the autumn of 1914 the Germans had had plenty of time to convert the Somme area into a veritable fortress. Behind two successive belts of barbed wire, each thirty yards broad, lay the forward line with three successive trenches. The first trench harboured the sentry groups, the second included the bombproof shelters where the trench garrison was comfortably billeted and the third trench served as the support trench. The trenches were intersected with thick traverses to contain the burst of direct hits, and to stop flanking fire in the case that hostile raiders entered the trench. Sentry posts and machine gun pits were constructed in concrete and the trenches were reinforced with wooden frames and wickerwork. There were dugouts with two entrances and a depth of 20-30 feet every fifty yards which offered space for approximately twenty-five men each. Wooden steps led into the interior where the soldiers slept on bunk beds. Wooden casings and tarboard were used to keep the interior dry. The intermediate line of strongpoints, including veritable over- and underground fortresses, like the "Schwaben Redoubt" at Thiepval, extended 1000 yards behind the forward position. The second line, out of the range of the enemy artillery, was constructed similarly to the principles of the forward line. A third line 3000 yards farther back was nearly finished. Communication trenches and a system of telephone lines connected trenches, strongpoints and artillery.

In 1916/17 the construction of trenches and dugouts by the German Army reached its peak. Dugouts and trenches were reinforced with concrete. Networks of concrete bunkers and pillboxes appeared in considerable numbers at the Western Front, each of them a mini-fortress resisting even direct hits of heavy calibres. As they were camouflaged with earth the concrete boxes were difficult to locate and they successfully protected the machine guns and their crews even under bombardment. Consequently, the machine guns survived even the heaviest shelling and were ready to repulse any attack with their deadly fire. As a result most pillboxes had to be cleared in close combat. At Passchendale concrete pillboxes, dispersed in the flooded shell holes, were the backbone of the German resistance in 1917. However, in some places the sophisticated constructions turned out to be negative. For example, wire entanglements were so deep that they blocked the German Army's own patrol activities. Trenches improved with timber, wickerwork and wire netting were weatherproof but they could also become deathtraps for the soldiers buried by shellfire in the debris of such well-constructed trenches. It was impossible to excavate a man from an impregnable mixture of earth, splintered timbers and torn wire. When ordered to take over such a well-constructed trench in 1918, the German infantry joked that the supreme headquarters had supplied them generously with plenty of wood for their coffins. The men preferred to occupy a few shell holes nearby. The permanent improvement of trenches and dugouts was the German response to the growing use of artillery ammunition by the Allies. Strong and deep defensive zones, deep dugouts and concrete shelters were able to bear much more shelling then the two successive trenches of 1915. In the end however, the experience at the Western Front showed that well-aimed heavy shelling could destroy even the strongest shelter. A few dispersed shell-holes, although often uncomfortable, proved to be much safer places for the infantry.

**Bulwark of the Groenenburg position between Zillebecke and Zandvoorde in May 1915. This primitive position is still far from the sophisticated architecture of later trench warfare.**
**Infantry-Regiment 126.**
**Groenenburg, Ypres salient, Flanders.**
**April 1915.**

**Communication trench to the forward line near Hooge. The condition of the trees riddled by shell splinters bear evidence of the heavy shelling in this sector.**
**Infantry-Regiment 126.**
**Hooge, Ypres salient, Flanders.**
**Summer 1915.**

**Some officers and men in front of their dugout. Next to the dugout entrance is a wooden box for the rifles. In the case of alarm the soldiers leaving the dugout could pick up their guns easily.**
**France.**
**Summer 1915.**

**Forward trench at the Lorraine sector in October 1915. The access from no-man's-land is already blocked by wire entanglement and movable wooden knife rests.**
**Lorraine.**
**October 1915.**

**German trench position completely constructed out of sandbags. Sandbags were used to improve trenches, especially in soft ground. At many spots in Belgium the level of ground water was so high that the digging of trenches was impossible. 1915.**

A "perfect" trench of a rearward position with a complete wooden covering. Such trenches were part of rearward defence lines which where built by private construction companies behind the front in 1916/17. This trench was the best defence against weather and erosion but in combat it was useless and dangerous. Trench fighters called this wooden planking ironically "coffin planks".
Western Front.
Ca. 1916/17.

German communication trench in the muddy pulp of the famous Twin Hill 60. Hill 60 was one of the few elevations around the Ypres salient but even these hills offered only a surface of soft ground for trench construction.
Twin Hill 60, Ypres salient, Flanders.
Ca. 1915/16.

**Concrete shelter in a German trench somewhere in France. Next to wickerwork and sandbags, the use of concrete for the construction of pillboxes and shelters became popular in 1915. Note the large periscope used by the sentry to observe the enemy line.
France.
1915.**

**A concrete pillbox on Hill 60 at the Ypres salient. From 1916 onwards the Germans constructed increasing numbers of concrete pillboxes at the frontline. Even infantry officers attended courses to learn how to use concrete.
II. battalion, Infantry-Regiment 127.
Hill 60, Ypres, Flanders.
May 1916.**

**Well constructed forward trench at Chilly-Fouquescourt. This trench is fully fortified with wickerwork, sandbags and wooden planks to protect against the destructive influence of bad weather. Under fire such trenches became an impenetrable chaos of debris.**
**III. Battalion, Grenadier-Regiment 128.**
**Chilly-Fouquescourt, Somme.**
**June 1916.**

**Position of Brigade-Ersatz-Bataillon 84 at the "Waldhaus" in the upper Liepvre valley. The Vosges Mountains were classed as a quiet sector which meant there was time to improve the trenches with wood and wire netting.**
**Brigade-Ersatz-Bataillon 84 Offenburg.**
**Waldhaus, upper Liepvre valley, Vosges.**
**Summer 1916.**

**Left: A German trench after heavy shelling. The debris is already cleared. This trench was improved with concrete which bears the traces of the bursting shells.**
**Western Front.**
**Ca. 1916/17.**

**Bottom left: Ravine at the St. Mihiel salient near Flirey blocked with a barricade of sandbags. At some spots veritable fortifications were constructed with sandbags. This barricade is two-storied.**
**1st Ersatz-Battery, Fuss-Artillery-Regiment 8.**
**Flirey, St. Mihiel salient.**
**April 1915.**

**Below: Communication trench leading into the sector of the 25. Reserve-Division in the Argonne forest. The wood of the Argonne forest offered enough material for the improvement of the trenches.**
**25. Reserve-Division.**
**Argonne.**
**1916.**

Members of the 1st Company Infantry-Regiment 170 at Gommecourt after heavy rain flooded the trench. The soldiers are busy trying to drain the trench in order to avoid the dugout also being flooded.
1st Company, Infantry-Regiment 170.
Gommecourt, Somme.
August 1916.

Duckboards in a trench of the 52. Infantry-Division's sector near Pusieux after heavy rain. Duckboards make the flooded trench passable. Sophisticated systems of drainage channels under the duckboards kept the trench dry.
52. Infantry-Division.
Pusieux, Somme.
Summer 1916.

**A German water pump at Hooge. Thousands of water pumps were in use at the Western Front for draining dugouts in sectors with high ground water or for when rain flooded the shelters. The Flanders sector was particularly renowned for this problem.**
**II. Battalion, Grenadier-Regiment 123.**
**Hooge, Flanders.**
**April 1916.**

**Flooded communication trench near Pusieux at the Somme. Heavy rain often converted the trenches into rivers.**
**52. Infantry-Division.**
**Pusieux, Somme.**
**Summer 1916.**

Concrete entrance of an underground tunnel at the so-called "Kanonenberg" (Gun Mountain). The "Kanonenberg" was a seriously disputed hilltop at the eastern part of the Champagne sector. The steep northern slopes of the hill offered space enough for the construction of tunnels to house reserve forces, kitchens and supplies.
52. Infantry-Division.
Kanonenberg, Massiges, Champagne.
1917.

Construction company of Reserve-Infantry-Regiment 111 driving a tunnel into the chalky underground of the Champagne. Some regiments formed their own construction companies. The soldiers are using an electric drill.
Bau-Kompanie, Reserve-Infantry, Regiment 111.
Cernay en Dormoise, Champagne.
November 1917.

**Officers of Ersatz-Infantry-Regiment 51 at the entry of the Ist Battalion's headquarters near Bouchavesnes. The shelter is still under construction. The piles of strong timber in front of the dugout were used to strengthen the shelter with dugout frames.**
**Ersatz-Infantry-Regiment 51.**
**Bouchavesnes, Somme.**
**October-November 1916.**

Engineers and members of Infantry-Regiment 13 in their underground shelter at La Bassée. Berths fitted into the sides of the shelter served as sleeping places for the inhabitants. Such underground shelters were often several floors deep in the earth and could resist even the impact of heavy shells.
Infantry-Regiment 13
La Bassée, Artois.
November 1915.

A so-called "Karnickelloch" (rabbit hole) dug into the railway embankment at Loivre. From the summer of 1915 such small, deep dugouts, improved with frames, became very important against the increasing gunfire.
Infantry-Regiment 113.
Loivre, Champagne.
July-October 1915.

**Above: Officer's shelter at the Vosges Mountains in the spring of 1916. This shelter was called "Wilhelmsburg". The sign on the right shows the way to the forward line.**
**Vosges.**
**Spring 1916.**

**Top right: Shellproof shelters at a reserve position in the Argonne forest. Reserve positions often became the target of enemy shelling because the artillery knew that reserve forces were concentrated there.**
**Argonne.**
**Ca. 1915/16.**

**Right: Interior of a comfortable officer's dugout. At quiet sectors shelters and dugouts were well furnished with pictures, carpets and furniture. Two of the pictures show the Emperor Wilhelm II and the Crown Prince.**
**Western Front.**
**Ca. 1915/16.**

**Left: Battalion staff shelter at the Vosges Mountains. The shelter was constructed by covering prefabricated vaulted corrugated iron with stone, earth or concrete. The furniture and the stove were taken from the evacuated villages of the battle zone.**
**Brigade-Ersatz-Bataillon 84 Offenburg.**
**Upper Liepvre valley, Vosges.**
**Summer 1916.**

**Opposite: Reserve forces spent their free time at their shelter behind the front. The shelters for the rank and file were furnished like barracks: Bunk beds, table and benches.**
**France.**
**1916.**

CHAPTER FOUR

# WEAPONS AND EQUIPMENT - A WAR OF SPECIALISTS

Trench war at the Western Front was a war of specialists. Combat in a confusing system of trenches, craters, underground shelters and obstacles confronted the infantrymen with new tactical challenges and technical tasks. In their daily struggle to survive in a hostile underground world the infantrymen had to introduce tools and technical devices that had originally been engineer's equipment. Engineers took over the role of technical advisers for the infantry, assisting in solving the technical and static problems of trench, dugout and blockhouse construction. The inventive genius of the trench fighters and the modern technology of the industrial age provided the armies with a broad variety of special equipment to cope with the challenges of trench warfare. However, technical equipment was not always helpful. The new technical devices for the trench war often turned out to be defective or had design faults. Wire cutters that could not cut the wire, hand grenades that did not explode or exploded prematurely, low quality small arms ammunition that jammed rifles and machine guns, flares that exploded in the face of the signaller or ignited ammunition dumps were often an unpleasant surprise for the fighting infantrymen in both camps.

The personal equipment of the infantrymen was stripped of all superfluous belongings before they entered the trenches. Luggage was left back in the rear area camps. In the confined world of the trenches the infantryman's combat pack was reduced to a field bag and a tent section. His main equipment was a rifle, a revolver, a steel helmet (weighing 1865 grams), a gas mask, bags filled with stick grenades, sandbags and the inevitable wire cutter. Fatigue parties had to follow close behind the shock battalions to bring ammunition, tools and rations into the captured trenches. In the spring of 1918 when the German Army was preparing for the coming war of movement the infantryman's equipment consisted of his rifle, his bayonet, rifle ammunition in his pockets and field pack, a steel helmet, a few stick grenades, a spade and a wire cutter. The bayonet was fixed on the right side of the man to avoid any rattling with the spade and wire cutter. Personal belongings were put into the field pack: Coat, mess kit, rations, underwear, foot-wear, lace boots, field service cap, rifle kit and tent section. Combat in the trenches required a flexible and lightly equipped fighter but technical equipment loaded the infantryman with a heavy burden.

Machine guns and hand grenades became the typical weapons of trench warfare. Special machine gun crews and bomber squads were trained for their respective tasks. The German machine gun was the water-cooled Maxim 08/15 which was served by a crew of two men. The crew was responsible for its maintenance and minor repair works. Belt-loading gave the machine gunners plenty of work. In combat one man of the crew fired the gun; the other had to insert the ammunition belt. The cotton belts were affected by weather conditions and caused many problems. Each machine gun crew was assisted by a few men who had to carry the ammunition boxes and water for the cooler. The machine gun was a formidable weapon firing with a maximum cadence of 500 rounds per minute. To economize ammunition this was normally reduced to 100 rounds per minute – still enough to slaughter entire enemy battalions within minutes. Initially a special weapon handled by specialists, the number of machine gun companies per regiment was considerably increased during the course of the war. In addition, even the infantry companies received a few machine guns to increase their firepower. In response to the effective British Lewis guns the German Army issued the light machine gun 08/15 to the infantry in the final phase of war. Most infantrymen were trained in handling these guns. The light machine gun increased the mobile firepower of the infantry considerably. Although tens of thousands of machine guns were used at the Western Front it was still a valuable weapon and every loss of a gun had to be reported in detail. The capture of enemy machine guns was rewarded with prize money. Captured enemy machine guns like the valuable light Lewis gun were often used by the German infantry when ammunition was available.

The German Army equipped their bomber squads with stick grenades to bomb their way through hostile trenches. The design was completely different from the egg-shaped hand-grenade (the Mills bomb) used by the British and French infantry. It was inspired by the first hand grenades improvised by the forces in the field in 1914/15. German infantrymen simply used wire to fix a charge of high explosives to a stick and ignited the charges with a fuse cord. The final design of the stick grenade saw an explosive charge fixed in a cylindrical tin at the end of a thirty centimetre long wooden stick. The opposite end of the stick was closed with a metal cap, keeping the fuse cord inside the hollow stick. To charge the stick grenade the infantryman had to take off the metal cap and pull the fuse cord. The stick grenade exploded after five seconds. Its shape inspired the British soldiers to call the German stick grenade a "potato masher". Stick grenades were responsible for many deadly accidents. To have stick grenades ready at disposal, soldiers took off the metal cap. This was quite risky because in the crowded conditions of trenches and dugouts the fuse cord often became entangled with equipment or wire and caused accidental explosions. There were careless infantrymen who opened the tin that contained the explosive charge and they used the charge as fuel for heating their meals. Sometimes it turned out to be their last. As well as the stick grenades the German infantry also used several types of ball grenades.

Other important items of the trench fighter's equipment were a spade, a wire cutter and a gas mask. The spade was not only a tool for digging, it also proved to be a quite deadly weapon in hand-to-hand fighting. Sometimes even steel rods or iron or wooden cudgels were used. The wire cutter became a prerequisite for any move in no-man's land. Wire obstacles of considerable depth blocked the space between the trenches, and each patrol or raiding party had to cut its way through the impenetrable networks. From April 1915 onwards, when the German Army used poison gas for the first time to break the British positions at Ypres, a gas mask became part of the soldier's personal equipment. Gas masks had to be fitted to each man personally to guarantee its tightness, and gas drills secured the correct and quick handling of the mask. After some improvised experiments with cotton the industry supplied the armies at the Western Front with workable gas masks. The successive introduction of new kinds of poison gas required the technical improvement of the gas masks. In 1918 the mixed firing of chemical and high explosive shells was common practice in both camps, and the gas mask could cope with different chemical agents and protected the infantry successfully. However, fighting or working while breathing through a gas mask was a serious physical strain and reduced the field of vision considerably. When in March and May 1918 the German artillery preparation fired a large number of gas shells against the Allied artillery at the Somme and the Chemin des Dames, the main purpose was to suppress their firing activity to a minimum by forcing the gunners to wear their gas masks. The wearing of gas masks was also a burden for the assaulting troops. Bloem reports that when leading his battalion across the St. Quentin Canal on March 21st, 1918 he refused to order his men to put on their gas masks to allow a quicker advance and a better orientation. But, as a result, many of them suffered badly when passing the dissolving gas clouds that caused the men to vomit or feel sick (Bloem: *Das Ganze halt!*, p.531-532).

Another item of the German Army's equipment at the Western Front was the so-called "Grabenpanzer", a kind of infantryman's armour. This armour protected the body and a special shield fixed to the steel helmet made the front side of the helmet bulletproof. This armour was designed for sentries who were often prey to infantry or sniper fire. But the heavy weight of the armour considerably reduced the mobility of the armoured soldiers and made the equipment unsuitable for trench warfare. In hand-to-hand combat in the trenches the weighty armour would have left the soldier no chance of survival. The armour was often photographed as an old-fashioned curiosity but it was never accepted as equipment by the infantry.

The flamethrower that was introduced in 1916 by the German Army at Verdun to mop up the French positions was, on the other hand, a deadly and terrifying weapon. Two soldiers, one loaded with a tank of combustible liquid, the other using the sprayer, poured a jet of burning masud into the enemy trenches and dugouts, thus spreading shock and terror in the French forces. The flamethrowers' victims were burned alive. But the flamethrower crews had a dangerous job. A single bullet piercing the tank of combustible liquid sufficed to set the crew aflame, burning them alive like their victims. The flamethrower's job was so perilous that nearly no amateur photos of flamethrowers in action exist.

Communications at the Western Front also required an increasing number of specialists and new equipment. In the autumn of 1914 even larger units, like regiments or brigades, were commanded by direct orders from their officers on the battlefield or by bugle calls. Under the chaotic and confusing conditions of trenches, craters and deafening gunfire of the 1915 battlefield the job of a company leader became an even more complicated business. Where communication ceased – and even the telephone communications usually collapsed in the first few minutes of combat under the impact of exploding shells – officers and NCOs depended on prefixed orders, timetables, trench maps, aerial photographs, and on their wrist-watches to handle their dispersed men. To comply with prefixed timetables on the battlefield officers and NCOs had to know where they were and the correct time, at all times. For this the wristwatch was an essential requisite. The first wristwatches in the trenches were pocket watches fixed in leather watchbands; these went on to become the modern wristwatches of our times.

But prefixed orders and timetables turned out to be inflexible tools for battle command, often hindering and slowing down the forces on the battlefield. Cooperation between the respective units, particularly between the infantry and the artillery, was indispensable. The trenches at the Western Front and the rearward command posts were connected by a network of telephone communications. Telephone exchanges and specially trained telephone operators maintained these networks and repair squads patrolled the telephone lines to repair the wires cut by shells or careless infantry. When the vulnerable telephone communications collapsed the infantry in the trenches fired flares to maintain communications with the observation posts behind the frontline. Very light pistols could fire signal cartridges with different colours to ask for artillery support or counterattacks. Every night, together with the Very lights that were used to light up no-man's land in the dark, signal rockets produced an impressive show of fireworks over the opposing trenches at the Western Front. Signal-lamp communication allowed an even more detailed communication on the battlefield. The German Army profited from blinker-signal stations and mobile blinker squads, particularly in the offensive operations in 1918. Specially trained lamp-signallers exchanged messages and orders with their lamps at long distances, quickly and undisturbed by shellfire.

Sturmtrupp de Niem
Weihnachten 1916.

Opposite: Group portrait of "Storm Troop de Niem" behind the front, Christmas 1916. In 1916 storm troopers were organized by the infantry-divisions. These elite forces received special training and equipment and were intended for special attack or counterattack operations. The storm troopers were equipped with pistols, hand grenades and wire cutters for hand-to-hand combat in the trenches.
"Sturmtrupp de Niem".
France.
December 1916.

Above: Machine gun position near Hooge at the Ypres salient in 1915. The fixed gun carriage and optical device allowed no-man's land to be ruled with deadly and accurate bursts of fire.
Infantry-Regiment 126.
Hooge, Ypres salient, Flanders.
June-August 1915.

Top right: Machine gun fit into a dugout in the positions of Infantry-Regiment 126 at the Ypres salient. The mechanism and cooler of the machine gun were vulnerable to dirt and shell splinters.
Infantry-Regiment 126.
Hooge, Ypres salient, Flanders.
June-August 1915.

Right: German machine gun post with a captured French machine gun in the winter of 1917/18. When ammunition was available, captured guns were used in the trenches. The infantry received rewards for captured guns.
France.
Winter 1917/18.

**Training of a machine gun crew behind the front. Effective handling of machine guns and its technical devices required intensive training.
Western Front.
Ca. 1916/17.**

**Group portrait of Machine Gun Company 114 at Verdun. In the first half of the war machine gunners were specialists organized in special machine gun companies. In the final phase of war the machine gun became a standard weapon for all infantrymen. The machine gun carriages are a special design of this unit.**
**Machine Gun Company 114.**
**Verdun.**
**Summer 1916.**

**Left: Trench garrison on stand-by. The soldiers are equipped with self-produced makeshift hand grenades and the first generation of provisional gas masks. High explosives fixed to wooden sticks and a few layers of wool and cotton represented the first generation of hand grenades and gas masks.**
**Priesterwald, Moselle.**
**Spring 1915.**

**Below: Officers and men of Infantry-Regiment 126 attending an initial training course for the use of hand grenades behind the Ypres salient. The first stick grenades arrived at the front in the spring of 1915, to replace the makeshift hand grenades manufactured by the soldiers. These officers are using both types for the training.**
**Infantry-Regiment 126.**
**Chapelle d'Epines, Ypres salient, Flanders.**
**May 1915**

**Opposite: A group of German infantrymen entering the trenches somewhere in France in 1917. Each man had to carry a few stick grenades and plenty of infantry ammunition in his pockets.**
**France.**
**1917.**

**Left: The storm trooper of 1917/18. Two sandbags filled with stick grenades were his most important and most frequently used weapon in the trenches.
France.
Ca. 1917/18.**

**Below: Men of Brigade-Ersatz-Bataillon 84 Offenburg behind the cover of loophole shields from where they could observe the French positions in the Liepvre valley. The intensity of infantry fire and the omnipresent snipers required bullet-proof loopholes. Together with sandbags or concrete, metal loophole shields could be installed quickly to construct armoured observation posts.
Brigade-Ersatz-Bataillon 84 Offenburg.
Liepvre valley, Vosges.
Summer 1916.**

**Opposite
Left: Two German soldiers busy with screwing fuses into hand grenades. The infantry used hand grenades in large numbers and had to get them ready before using them in the trenches. For safety reasons the hand grenades arrived at the front without fuse.
Lingekopf, Vosges.
Summer 1915.**

**Right: Sentry in the sector of the 52. Infantry-Division observing the enemy position with a periscope. Snipers made observation from trenches or loopholes a dangerous business for the sentries. Periscopes were used in the trenches from 1915 onwards.
52. Infantry-Division.
Somme.
1915/16.**

**Left: German light mortar position in the forward trench. The close distance between their own trenches and enemy ones often prohibited the use of artillery as it seemed to be too risky for their own infantry. From 1915 onwards the German infantry received different types of light mortars to shell nearby enemy trenches.**
**Western Front.**
**Ca. 1915/16.**

**Below: Sentry with trench armour in the sector of the 52. Infantry-Division at "Winterberg Hill". Hand grenades at the ready.**
**52. Infantry-Division.**
**"Winterberg", Aisne.**
**Autumn 1917.**

**Opposite: German machine gun crew equipped with trench armour. Trench armour was intended to reduce losses. But even in immobile trench war the armour was too heavy and cumbersome and thus never became popular.**
**Western Front.**
**Ca. 1917.**

Above: Gas alarm bell in front of a dugout entrance at Schratzmaennele Hill. Metal plates and hammers were fixed in the trenches as alarm bells. Any soldier who smelt gas had to alarm his comrades.
Schratzmaennele, Vosges.
Summer 1915.

Right: Fitting of gasmasks by Brigade-Ersatz-Bataillon 84 Offenburg at the Liepvre valley. Gas masks to protect the infantry against poison gas were issued to the troops from 1915 onwards. It was imperative that the mask was properly fitted if it was to be effective.
Brigade-Ersatz-Bataillon 84 Offenburg.
Liepvre valley, Vosges.
Summer 1916.

**Opposite**
**Top left: German flame-thrower in action at the Verdun sector. Flame-throwers used a high-pressure spray with burning liquid against soldiers and positions to burn the enemy to death.**
**Verdun.**
**1917.**

**Top right: Flame-thrower crew of the 52. Infantry-Division burning enemy positions at the Aisne sector. Flame-throwers had to be operated by two men each. One man handled the tube; the other bore the tank with burning liquid. The flame-thrower crew operated at very high risk to themselves as bullets or shell splinters could hit the tank.**
**52. Infantry-Division.**
**Aisne.**
**1917.**

**Bottom left: Fatigue party bringing prefabricated knife rests to the positions.**
**France.**
**1915.**

**Bottom right: Electric wire. Wire did not suffice to stop enemy patrols. At Bois du Four in the Argonne forest the wire was electrically charged with 1750 volts.**
**Batterie 279.**
**Bois du Four, Argonne.**
**April 24, 1916.**

Flammenwerfer

**Opposite**
**Top left: Infantrymen cutting trees to make stakes for the wire entanglements. Much of the construction material for the trenches and dugouts had to be produced by the troops themselves.**
**Lorraine.**
**1915.**

**Top right: Reserve line camps with dumps of engineer supplies at Flirey. The knife rests have been prepared for the transport to the forward line. Such transports took place under the cover of darkness.**
**Fuss-Artillery-Regiment 8, 10. Ersatz-Division.**
**Flirey, St. Mihiel salient.**
**May 1915.**

**Bottom left: The most frequently used "weapon" of trench warfare: The shovel. Infantrymen at the Western Front dug and maintained tens of thousands of kilometres of trenches, accomplishing a level of work never before seen in military history.**
**52. Infantry-Division.**
**Aisne.**
**1917.**

**Bottom right: An infantryman at rest sleeping on his field pack and equipment: Rifle, bayonet, mess kit, water bottle and spade.**
**Machine gun company, Infantry-Regiment 150.**
**Laon, Aisne.**
**February 1918.**

**Right: German officer with a 30.5-cm-dud which was used to blow up the church tower of Prouvais village at the Aisne. On his wrist the officer is wearing a small but important piece of equipment: A wristwatch. Wristwatches came into fashion in the First World War and were crucial for timing the operations in the trenches.**
**Prouvais, Aisne.**
**1917.**

**Above: Members of the German signal service with their equipment. Communication at the Western Front depended mainly on the telephone. The signal service had the dangerous job of constructing telephone lines between the trenches and command posts and of repairing these vulnerable lines under shellfire.**
**Western Front.**
**Ca. 1915/16.**

**Top right: Blinker-squad with their signal equipment. As a result of the vulnerability of the telephone lines and runners to shellfire contact between the trenches and the command posts was often held by signal-lamp communication. Signal-lamp communication used special blinker-lamps to send their messages. Incoming signals were observed with telescopes.**
**Western Front.**
**Ca. 1917/18.**

**Right: Lamp-signallers at their blinker-signal station in France in the summer of 1918. The signallers found camouflage and shelter under bushes and pieces of corrugated iron and called their station "Blinker Heim" (Blinker's Home).**
**France.**
**Summer 1918.**

# CHAPTER FIVE

# DEATH IN THE TRENCHES

In the trenches at the Western Front death was an integral part of the soldier's everyday life. Even on quiet days at the "cushy sectors" the trench garrisons had to pay their death toll to snipers or bursting shells. The experience of death in major operations was much more intensive when in a small sector one's own comrades and enemy soldiers were killed by the thousand within a matter of days. The regimental history of the *Hohenzollernfusiliers* describes just such a terrible scene of carnage when the regiment took over the trenches at Loos during the last few days of May 1915. The French had occupied Loos two and a half weeks before in their offensive of May 1915. One day later, on May 10th, 1915, the German Infantry Regiment 114 retook the town. The *Hohenzollernfusiliers* relieved the exhausted 114th Regiment in the darkness of the night. When the sun came up it shed light on a scene of utter destruction. The battlefield was littered with military equipment and hundreds of unburied corpses of both friend and foe. Parts of the trenches were completely filled with heaps of dead bodies. The fluid of decomposing bodies infiltrated the trenches and the smell made the position nearly uninhabitable. Many fusiliers felt sick under such horrendous conditions. Fatigue parties had to be organized to bury the corpses in trenches and shell holes. Chlorine was used to disinfect the ground. The regimental staff ordered new trenches to be dug in order to give the living a space apart from the dead. However, dead soldiers remained co-inhabitants in the underground world of the Loos sector from this time on (Fuehren: *Hohenzollernfuesiliere*, p.200).

It was often impossible to recover killed soldiers from the battlefield at the Western Front. Many of them were buried in their trenches or dugouts by gunfire; others simply disappeared in the cratered landscape. Dead bodies in various stages of decomposition polluted the air in no-man's-land. Wherever possible, collapsed dugouts or shell holes filled with corpses were marked with crosses indicating that these places were graves. Even today remains of missed soldiers are still being found in France and Belgium whenever any construction work or excavations take place on the former battlefields. In the 1970s, when Lingekopf Hill in the Vosges Mountains was transformed into an open-air museum, the excavations of collapsed trenches disclosed more than a dozen corpses of German and French soldiers who had been killed in the terrible fighting on this tiny hilltop in the summer of 1915. The Vosges Mountains were only a "cushy sector" however. At the Somme, at Verdun or in Flanders tens of thousands of men found their unknown graves on the shell-torn fields. Although the collective experience of death quickly became a normal part of life in the trenches and despite the fact that soldiers often opened old graves when they were digging new trenches, the dead comrades – friend and foe – were generally honoured. Wherever possible the bodies of killed soldiers were recovered from the battlefield and buried at military cemeteries behind the front – often under personal risk to the rescue teams. Some regiments constructed their own cemeteries with monuments and artificial doorways behind their respective sectors. The burial was an official ceremony including a service held by the divisionary chaplain and music played by the regimental band. The First World War was the first war in Europe where all ranks received individual graves. In the wars of the 19th century and before only officers were honoured with individual graves. The rank and file were buried in mass graves without any markings. In the Great War the fate of each soldier became the subject of research and documentation. The families back at home were informed by the company leader of the death, and the circumstances that led to it, of their loved one. This information was also recorded in the military passport of the killed soldier. When somebody was reported as being missed in action the company-sergeant-major interrogated the surviving comrades about what happened. For the purpose of individual identification of mutilated or already decomposed bodies each German soldier had to wear an individual identity disk, a small metal sign hanging from a chain around the neck, which contained data with his name, home address, birth date, depot unit and combat unit together with his individual regimental number. From 1916 onwards the "dog tag" bore two identical sets of data and was perforated in the middle so it could be broken into two halves when the bearer was killed in action. One half was sent to his company to report the loss while the other half was left on the body to allow later identification.

What was a personal tragedy for the infantrymen in the trenches and for their families at home was merely a question of statistics for the army staffs of both camps. The processing of own losses – killed, wounded, missed and POWs – consisted of a system of sophisticated statistics, evaluation and analysis. By comparing these data with the number of expected new drafts they produced a constantly up to date picture of their available human resources. Information about the strength of the enemy was of equal importance to them. The amount of enemy killed also became an important figure in the war of attrition and thus the subject of intensive research. The respective intelligence departments focussed much attention on the number of enemy losses. For the troops in the trenches this meant establishing the number of enemy corpses in no-man's land and reporting it, together with the number of captured POWs.

The number of soldiers killed at the Western Front was tremendous: 1,493,000 German soldiers, 1,432,000 French and 684,000 British soldiers lost their lives there. The figures were published by the belligerents after the war. In Germany the data was collected and published by the Zentralnachweiseamt and the Reichsarchiv. The British data could be found in the official publication "The Military Effort" and the French published their losses in the official parliamentary report in 1920. A careful analysis of the figures shows some surprising results. In spite of serious losses the armies at the Western Front were constantly increasing in number up until 1917. Plenty of manpower was available to prodigally feed the battles in France and Belgium. Kitchener's new armies and Commonwealth troops brought the tiny British Army up to the strength of a million men. Germany fielded new army corps and divisions to cope with the manpower demand at the Western Front. The French Army fell back upon her colonial empire to fill up the ranks with colonial troops from Africa. But in both camps this increase was paid for with intensive exploitation of their manpower. Killed or disabled, the middle generation of soldiers disappeared and younger and older soldiers filled the gaps in the ranks. After ruthless offensive operations against well-prepared German positions the French and the British met the limit of their manpower in 1917; the German side did not face their manpower crisis until the summer of 1918. Attrition war and stalemate ate up the manpower at the Western Front. However, this process depended more on the duration of the war than on the intensity of the killing. On the German side, the battles at Verdun, at the Somme, in the Champagne/Artois and in Flanders had each claimed a death toll of between 60,000 and 100,000 men. But the war of movement in the autumn of 1914 and in the spring of 1918 was much more costly, killing 115,000 German soldiers each. The French losses confirm this observation. August-September 1914 claimed the incredible death toll of 313,000 men from the French Army. Both offensive battles in 1915 resulted in 121,000 and 115,000 killed soldiers each. At Verdun 156,000 French soldiers lost their lives. The Allied war of attrition wore down French and British manpower much more than German manpower.

Victory at the Eastern Front increased the German Army in the west considerably. On March 21st, 1918 139,213 officers and 3,590,378 men were ready to attack. The successful breakthrough battles in the spring of 1918 were ultimately fatal for the German Army. Ludendorff's experiment of fighting a decisive battle by ending the costly stalemate and re-opening the war of movement resulted in the greatest losses since 1914. In spite of the sophisticated system of loss processing and analysis the German OHL underestimated the losses in offensive battle and the resulting war of movement. In 1918 the German Army had an average monthly loss rate of 160,000 killed, wounded and missed. Within thirteen weeks of offensive battle 700,000 men, including 115,000 killed soldiers were lost. At the same time Ludendorff was confronted with insufficient numbers of new draftees in the summer of 1918. The class of 1900 produced only 250,000 recruits, which corresponded to an average of 20,000 per month. Additionally 60,000 recovered soldiers reported back from hospitals and a maximum of 150,000 could be made available from industry, thus totalling approximately 90,000 men to replace losses of 160,000 each month. This in itself was a very optimistic calculation as the war industry could not spare the valuable workers and Ludendorff hesitated to send the youngest into battle. This imbalance resulted in a reduction of the German fighting power at the Western Front by approximately 550,000 men. It was the fighting infantry that had to bear the brunt of the losses. Many companies had only forty rifles, most divisions were not stronger than 3000 men and Ludendorff had to break up his first divisions (Volkmann: *Der Grosse Krieg*, p.157, 181).

In spite of intensive wartime research and analysis, the figures of losses cited in the available literature are often unreliable. For some battles completely exaggerated figures were reported where the author obviously put much more stress on the importance of the respective battle than on a careful analysis of the available loss lists. Much confusion still reigns regarding the meaning of "losses" which includes all cases of killed, wounded and missed. In many war books the amount of losses is confused with the number of killed. Death figures should still be treated carefully and they should always be seen in the context of the traditional ratio between killed and wounded, which was 1:4 in World War I as in most other wars. The battle of Verdun in 1916 provides us with an example of the problem of loss figures. The numbers of soldiers killed cited in the literature range from between 100,000 to 500,000 for each side, producing the fantastic figure of one million killed and four million wounded French and German soldiers within ten months at a front of twenty-five kilometres. However, a more realistic number would be 160,000 French killed and 100,000 Germans killed.

**Above: British howitzer and its killed crew. This artillery position was captured by the Germans near Gibercourt south of St. Quentin in the course of the German offensive in March 1918.**
**Gibercourt, Somme.**
**March 1918.**

**Top right: Captured French trench. The position of the dead bodies and the dispersed equipment show that the trench was taken by violent hand-to-hand combat.**
**France.**
**Ca. 1917/18.**

**Right: Dead body of a French soldier in the no-man's-land in front of the 52. Infantry-Division at the Somme in 1915. No-man's land became the unknown grave for many soldiers at the Western Front.**
**52. Infantry-Division.**
**Somme.**
**1915.**

**Top left: Killed Highlanders of the British Army in Flanders. Tactical requirements turned insignificant places like this farm into scenes of bitter fighting.**
**Flanders.**
**1915.**

**Above: German soldier's grave somewhere in the Vosges Mountains.**
**Vosges.**
**Ca. Winter 1917/18.**

**Left: Dead body waiting for burial at the German military cemetery at Bezonvaux at the beginning of the German Verdun offensive in the spring of 1916. If it were possible dead bodies were recovered from the battlefield and buried at cemeteries behind the frontline.**
**Bezonvaux, Verdun.**
**Spring 1916.**

**Opposite: Burial of a fallen comrade behind the 52. Infantry-Division's sector at Gommecourt. The divisional chaplain is giving the sermon.**
**52. Infantry-Division.**
**Gommecourt, Somme.**
**October 28, 1916.**

**Opposite**
**Top left: Mass grave at the German military cemetery at Lens. The ditch would be filled step by step with coffins depending on the amount of incoming corpses.**
**Lens, Artois.**
**Ca. 1915.**

**Bottom left: British rearward position somewhere between St. Quentin and Noyon at the Somme taken by storm in the German March offensive in 1918.**
**1st Machine Gun Company, Infantry-Regiment 150.**
**Between St. Quentin and Noyon, Somme.**
**March 1918.**

**Right: German trench after a repulsed attack. French soldiers penetrated the German position and the trench became the scene of severe hand-to-hand combat. The corpse of a killed French officer lies under the tarpaulin.**
**France.**
**Undated.**

**Right: Boots of two unknown killed soldiers. Their dead bodies are sticking in the parapet of a German trench somewhere at the Western Front. Artillery fire caused trenches and dugouts to collapse and bury the corpses. When German soldiers dug new trenches they would often unearth corpses.**
**Western Front.**
**Undated.**

**Below: Decomposed corpses of two French soldiers killed in no-man's-land. After attacks, raids or nightly patrols dead bodies were often left back unburied between the lines. In some sectors the putrid smell emanating from unburied corpses made it unbearable for the living to stay in the trenches.**
**Western Front.**
**Undated.**

**Left: Grave of five German soldiers buried alive by their collapsing dugout in trench "A1" near St. Soulpet. For many soldiers their dugouts became their graves after receiving a direct hit.
5th Company, Reserve-Infantry-Regiment 3.
West of St. Soulpet, Champagne.
Winter 1917/18.**

**Opposite
Top left: German forward position at St. Georges, southeast of Nieuwport at the channel coast. Within the German trenches and dugouts is the grave of several Belgian soldiers, marked by the Germans with a cross bearing the inscription: "Hier ruhen tapfere belgische Soldaten" (Brave Belgian soldiers are resting here).
St. Georges, Flanders.
1915.**

**Top right: Members of the medical service holding a commemoration for their fallen comrades somewhere in the Vosges Mountains.
Vosges.
Ca. Winter 1917/18.**

**Bottom left: Military cemetery behind the damaged mansion of Aveluy. At that time the village was directly behind the frontline and still under fire.
Aveluy, Somme.
Spring 1918.**

**Bottom right: Gateway of a German military cemetery in France. Outside inhabited areas the military cemeteries were decorated with wooden gates and fences. At the gate there is the inscription: "Krieger-Friedhof" (Soldiers' Cemetery).
France.
Undated.**

tapfere belg. Soldaten

Krieger-Friedhof.

**Left: Grave of the pilot Lieutenant Walter Utermann killed on April 16th, 1917 near Juvincourt. The burial places of pilots received special attention. The cross was often made out of damaged propellers.**
**Flieger-Abt. 228.**
**Juvincourt, Aisne.**
**April 1917.**

**Below: Individual graves at the German military cemetery at Vilosnes north of Verdun. If known, the name, date of birth, day of death and the unit of the buried soldier were recorded on the crosses.**
**Vilosnes, Verdun.**
**Undated.**

Chapter Six

# STAFF -
## Planning the Battle

Battle command and control were the unsolved problems at the Western Front from 1914-1918. Staff organization and communication proved to be unable to cope satisfactorily with the challenge of leading mass armies and controlling the use of unprecedented amounts of technical equipment and modern weapons on a nearly unlimited battlefield. The army command and control system was much closer to the principles of the Napoleonic epoch than to the 20th century and the age of technical warfare. It usually collapsed, together with the communication system, the moment battle began. Lessons taught by the Civil War of 1861-1865 or by the Russo-Japanese War in 1905 had been misunderstood or ignored by the European general staffs. Although they were living in an age of technical progress and in spite of the fact that many new weapons and technical devices (like the machine gun, the telephone, the wireless and the aircraft) had already been introduced into the armed forces, most generals and officers entered the war mentally unprepared. Even in 1914 some artillery officers still ignored the "technical toys" of telephone communication. They preferred direct fire from open firing positions instead of sending forward an artillery observer to direct the shelling of the hidden guns by telephone. Within a few minutes these ignorant officers lost entire batteries that were annihilated by well-observed enemy fire. Lessons were learnt but the Great War was nevertheless a never-ending bloody lecture about how to command in modern war.

The German military leadership was organized into the "Great General Staff" and the "Troops General Staff". The departments of the Great General Staff assisted the "Chief of General Staff of the Field Army" in commanding the German Army in the field. According to the mobilization orders, the Chief of Staff was authorized to issue orders on behalf of the Emperor who was titular Commander in Chief of the German Army. The Chief of Staff and his staff organization – the Great General Staff – formed the German Supreme Command "*Oberste Heeresleitung*" (OHL) and were responsible for guiding land warfare. The troops' General Staff provided the staff officers with army groups, armies, corps and divisions. General staff officers formed a military and social elite within the German officer's corps and were selected from the best graduates of a three-year course at the military academy in Berlin. The percentage of aristocrats and officers from the guards' regiments in the ranks of the war academy's graduates was remarkably high and surpassed 50% in 1913. This was far beyond their numerical share within the German Army. After three years only 30% of a class of 100 students passed the final test successfully and were ordered to do two years training duty in the Great General Staff. But of these approximately thirty officers only four or five were finally incorporated into the General Staff, holding the rank of a captain The rest were sent back to their regiments or served as teachers at military schools. Altogether they formed a reserve of officers already trained for staff duty, something which was so urgently needed when the German Army grew from its peace time strength of 800,000 men to the 8,200,000 of its war strength in 1916. Marked with the General Staff officer's badge – red stripes on both sides of his trousers – the young staff officer normally took over the post as the youngest staff officer of an army corps' staff and assisted the corps' Chief of Staff. To avoid any alienation between General Staff officers and the combat forces, the officers had regular breaks in their staff career where they had to take over the command of troops as company, battalion, regimental, brigade or division commander. The first really independent position of a staff officer was the post of the Chief of Staff of a division. In 1914 the Great General Staff consisted of 120 officers, while 650 officers served in the staff organization of the armed forces of 800,000 men.

In the Great War the German staff officer's education and ideas were deeply influenced by the famous pre-war Chief of General Staff, Alfred Graf von Schlieffen, who had held the post for the long period of 1891-1906. Schlieffen was responsible for designing the "Schlieffen Plan" which determined the opening moves of the German Army in August 1914. His successor, from 1906-1914, was *General* v. Moltke who had to bear responsibility for the failure of the "Schlieffen Plan" in the disaster at the Marne. After the Marne battle *General*

Erich v. Falkenhayn took over. However, the impressive German victories in the East in 1915 could not outweigh the fact that Falkenhayn had twice – at Ypres in 1914 and at Verdun in 1916 – failed to win the war at the Western Front. The crisis reached its peak in August 1916 when the team Hindenburg-Ludendorff formed the third OHL. Nevertheless, all Allied thrusts were finally repulsed and the defence and war economy both successfully reorganized. Ludendorff's new doctrine for a deep defensive battle allowed the German Army to prevail against Allied pressure in 1917. But when in March 1918 Ludendorff launched his final blow at the Western Front it was already too late. The Allied superiority was overwhelming and defeat was imminent.

The German OHL realized very early on in the war that there was a conflict between a nearly unlimited battlefield, the primitive network of communications and an inflexible chain of command. In the battle of the Marne in September 1914 Moltke, commanding his troops by direct orders from his headquarters in Luxembourg, 200 miles behind the advancing armies, lost control of the battle. Insufficient communication left him without updated situation reports and an adequate estimation of the situation. Battle and tactical command faced the same problems: Communication and reconnaissance were slow and unreliable. Situation reports were already out of date when they arrived at the respective headquarters and gave the higher command an entirely false impression of the situation. Orders issued from the rearward corps or division headquarters reached the battlefield too late and asked the troops to execute missions which were inadequate and often suicidal because the situation had already changed. The chain of command was too long and too slow, especially as each level of command had to work out reports and orders in detail. Direct communication was substituted by written communication and the trench war at the Western Front became more and more bureaucratic. The engineer officer Ulrich Sander refers to this situation as a "writing and telephone war" (cit. Sander: *Pioniere*, p.229). The typewriter was the most important weapon in this war producing a never-ending flow of reports, statistics and orders. These documents, along with maps and aerial photographs, were the main source of information for headquarters behind the front. Many staff officers never left their headquarters and avoided risky and time-consuming trips to the battlefield. Thus their perspective of the trench war remained relatively theoretical. This aroused plenty of criticism at the front. The British infantrymen ridiculed the shortcomings of general staff work as "Château General Ship" but the attitude in the German Army was comparable. The historian Rosinski even argues that the commanding generals, who had time to visit the troops at the front, were better informed about the conditions of their soldiers than the staff officers who spent all their time at their desks busy dealing with military bureaucracy (cit. Rosinski: *Die deutsche Armee*, p.145). There were exceptions, like the German colonel v. Lossberg, a well-known specialist of defensive battle at the Western Front. As corps and army Chief of Staff he spent plenty of his time reconnoitring the battlefield. However, in spite of the shortcomings of general staff work in the Great War, staff officers' work was the inevitable basis of battle organization.

In 1914 the German OHL sent liaison officers to the battlefield in order to improve battle command. *Oberstleutnant* Hentsch, on his fateful mission at the Marne, was one of them. Another provisional arrangement was that armies were temporarily under the command of the senior army commander at the respective theatre of war. This was intended to improve coordination at the supreme command level. Later, in 1916, this led to the formation of army groups in order to establish a level of command that would link the OHL with the armies on the battlefield. The tactical command had to cope with similar command problems directly on the battlefield, where enemy fire, bad weather conditions and the cratered ground influenced the movement and the supply of troops in the trenches. Telephones, wireless, runners and carrier pigeons were used to maintain the command system which was often paralysed by impenetrable artillery fire. When this happened the infantry was cut off from all communications and fought an isolated battle in the trenches. As a result, the coordination of infantry movements and artillery support fire was a problem that could never be solved satisfactorily. The German Army improved the situation by altering tactical organization and establishing a "Combat Forces Commander" (*Kampftruppenkommandeur* or KTK). He was stationary in the combat zone of his sector, well acquainted with the local conditions and had the freedom to take direct decisions regarding the battle. This reduced his dependence on the rearward headquarters and allowed him to fight independently from collapsing communication systems. This organization secured adequate tactical command for the KTK and freed him from the inflexible and slow procedures of the chain of command. The rearward headquarters were reduced to supplying the frontline with men, ammunition and material while the KTK conducted the infantry battle.

The complexity of mass armies and technical warfare in the trenches at the Western Front led to a considerable increase in divisions, corps and army staff personnel. Specialists for machine guns, artillery, communication services, transport, the air force and chemical warfare were attached to the pre-war staff organization. As a result of the general increase of the staff organization, the build-up of additional armies, corps and divisions and an inevitable rate of losses, the demand for staff officers increased during the course of war. Filling the reserve corps staffs with trained staff officers became a particular problem. At Sedan a general staff officers' school was established where officers attended a six-week course before taking over a staff officer's post at a division or corps headquarters. Before the war staff officers had had to pass a three year course. Staff officers criticized this development and complained about a general decrease in quality in the staff's work. In his war memoirs General v. Moser refers to the increasing influence exerted in the German army by young general staff officers who were often not older than thirty years old and held only the rank of captain. The artillery commander of Moser's 27. Infantry-Division nicknamed these young officers "general staff boys" and claimed they aroused tensions in the officers' corps by their arrogant behaviour (cit. Moser: *Feldzugsaufzeichnungen*, p.240).

The army corps was a typical branch of the German Staff Organization. The corps' Commander in Chief was assisted and advised by his Chief of Staff. The Staff was organized in sections; each of them was responsible for its respective field of work. Section I was the General Staff Division or Plans and Operations Division (Ia). Together with section Ib (Field Trains) and Ic (Intelligence). These sections constituted the tactical group of the General Staff responsible for battle command. Section II consisted of division IIa (Officers Personnel Management), IIb (Aide-de-Camp) and IIc (Enlisted Personnel Management and Horses). The Office of the Judge Advocate was designated as Section III, the Department of the Quartermaster General as Section IVa, the Medical Service as Section IVb, the Veterinary Service as Section IVc and the Chaplaincy as Section IVd. The military postal service, the commander of the headquarters and the headquarters company, the military police and trains were also part of the General Staff Organization but were not designated by separate Latin numbers. A corps' staff had considerable strength. In March 1917, the staff of the XIV.

German Reserve Corps consisted of fifty officers when the corps was holding a sector of eleven kilometres. In comparison, a division's headquarters' staff personnel was surprisingly weak at the outbreak of war. The divisional commander was assisted by only one staff officer, two aide-de-camps, one special-missions staff officer, two judge advocates, a chief of the division supply services and two medical officers. As a result, the division Chief of Staff was overburdened with staff work. In the following years the divisional headquarters were reinforced with a quartermaster, two additional special-missions staff officers, an intelligence officer and a veterinary officer. From 1915 onwards a map office and technical officers were gradually added.

A peculiarity of the German Staff Organization was the role of the Chief of Staff. The Commanders in Chief of an army corps, of an army or of an army group were mainly titular heads, spending their time inspecting the troops and with ceremonial duties, while the Chief of Staff was responsible for the battle command. This typical feature of the German Staff Organisation gained special weight in the stalemate at the Western Front where the necessity for quick decision making decreased whilst administrative staff work increased considerably (cit. Rosinski: *Die deutsche Armee*, p.144). Usually all staff officers reported to their commanding general daily or weekly. However, every matter had to be discussed with the Chief of Staff first. He decided how important or not a matter was and filtered persons and information before they were given access to the commander. The telephone allowed the higher commands' Chiefs of Staff to remain in permanent contact and enabled them to discuss all-important matters of command personally and directly. Originally only thought of as a means of quick exchanges of information this system of close and direct communication between the Chiefs of Staff resulted in the development of a Chief of Staff network that excluded the commanding generals from the daily business of command and from the decision-making process. Some Chief of Staff even secretly overruled their commanding general's will by approaching their colleagues at the respective superior commands by telephone, promoting the decision that they thought would be the best. In the German Army the duties of the Commanding Generals and their Chiefs of Staff were not clearly defined. As a result the command's efficiency depended heavily on the personal relationship between the Commanding General and his Chief. Members of royal houses in particular, like the German Crown Prince Wilhelm who commanded the 5th Army at the Western Front from 1914, were assisted and controlled by a professional Chief of Staff. This unclear division of responsibilities sometimes created serious conflicts. For example, the Crown Prince and his Chief of Staff, *General* v. Knobelsdorf had very different views on the battle for Verdun: While the former believed in the mission to take Verdun, the latter fought a bloody battle of attrition without informing his royal Commander in Chief openly. The third OHL of Hindenburg and Ludendorff is another typical, but harmonious, example of the divided German command system. Hindenburg and Ludendorff met for a regular briefing everyday and Hindenburg was involved in all-important decisions. However, the daily planning, decision-making and battle command were handled independently by Ludendorff. As was common practice in the German Army Hindenburg, ostensibly at least, backed Ludendorff's decisions with his authority. Representing his commanding general, the Chief of Staff could give orders even to generals superior in rank to himself. The Chief of Staff system reached its climax in the German Army in 1917/18. Important strategic planning conferences were attended only by the army groups and the armies' Chiefs of Staff, under the direct guidance of Ludendorff, while the Commanding Generals and Hindenburg were excluded. In the later phase of war this system was generally accepted. As a result, in the case of failure, the officially responsible Commanding General was not dismissed but his Chief of Staff, or alternatively a specially selected Chief of Staff was sent to influence the situation at a respective theatre of war. While the ideal was trustful cooperation and joint decision-making between the Commanding General and his Chief of Staff, the latter was often the real leader in battle in the German Army during the Great War.

**Left: Briefing of the 1st Battalion's staff of Infantry Regiment 126 at the rear area camp "Litzmann-Lager" before entering the line at Fort Vaux. Updated trench maps and aerial photographs were used to prepare the mission behind the front.**
**Infantry-Regiment 126.**
**"Litzman" camp, Verdun.**
**June 1916.**

**Opposite**
**Top left: Group of German officers reconnoitring the positions. Before taking over a new part of the line officer patrols were sent out to find out about the conditions of the new positions from the relieving troops.**
**Western Front.**
**1916/17.**

**Bottom left: Inspection of the line by officers of the 52. Infantry-Division at Amifontaine. Only the sentry is present but rifles and helmets show that the garrison is under cover nearby.**
**52. Infantry-Division.**
**Amifontaine, Aisne.**
**Summer 1917.**

**Right: Staff officers of the 52. Infantry-Division in the German trenches at Juvincourt on the first day of the German push to the Marne in 1918. The first enemy line has already been taken. Weeks of careful and secret planning and preparation preceded the successful breakthrough.**
**52. Infantry-Division.**
**Juvincourt, Aisne.**
**May 27, 1918.**

Right: Artillery staff office at the Verdun sector. The maps on the walls show the dislocation of guns and their fire range. Artillery in particular demanded plenty of administrative work.
Verdun.
Spring 1916.

Opposite
Top left: Staff officer receiving reports from the front line forces by telephone. The telephone was the main form of communication and battle command at the Western Front. Its vulnerability to shellfire often resulted in a complete collapse of communications. This was the moment for the runners to take over.
Western Front.
1917/18.

Top right: Lunchtime at a battalion staff's dugout somewhere at the Western Front. The telephone connects the staff with the forward trench and the regimental or divisional headquarters behind the line.
Western Front.
1916/17.

Bottom left: German Army administration office somewhere in France. Control and provision of a modern army at the Western Front was a large-scale administrative business.
Western Front.
Summer 1918.

Bottom right: Regimental staff office near Ripont. Topographical and geological surveys came to be an important part of staff work at the Western Front. The typewriter became an indispensable tool.
Infantry-Regiment 111.
Ripont, Champagne.
November 1917.

Right: Artillery and naval staff officers reconnoitring at the Verdun sector in spring 1916. At the battle of Verdun the German Army tried to break the French resistance by using an unprecedented amount of gunfire including heavy naval guns.
Verdun.
Spring 1916.

CHAPTER SEVEN

# SUBSISTENCE AND FOOD

In military life food plays an important role in a soldier's well-being and morale. The growing food shortages in Germany from 1914-1918 also affected the fighting forces. In his book "*Kriegfuehrung und Politik*" General Ludendorff gives a short but unequivocal comment on the problem: "The food supply for the men and horses was often inadequate. Food was scarce and not balanced. (...) The capabilities of the men and the horses decreased" (Ludendorff: *Kriegfuehrung und Politik*, p.159). The German leaders realized that the food supply situation was deteriorating; already in January 1915 food ration cards for bread were issued to the German population and bread consumption for civilians was reduced to 2000 grams per week. In the following years more and more foodstuffs were only available with ration cards and rations were also reduced little by little. From 1916 onwards subsistence and food for the German World War I trench fighter were marked by shortages and low quality. The food shortages increased seriously in 1917 and 1918. Food shortages and bad quality food were especially hard to bear for the men at the front considering the strenuous living conditions there, and resulted in a permanent state of malnutrition.

After arriving at his field unit the German infantryman was entitled to receive the field ration. The field ration consisted of a daily portion of bread, meat, vegetable and various groceries. At the beginning of the war the soldier received a daily bread ration of 750 grams. This was reduced to 700 grams in 1918. In the meantime bread rations were anyway subject to considerable variations depending on the general food situation. In 1915 and in April 1917 the bread ration was generally fixed at 500 grams. The daily ration of fresh meat was reduced from 375 to 300 grams and a "meatless day" was introduced in April 1916. However, the forces were allowed to decide themselves whether they wanted to accept the "meatless day" or to have a smaller meat ration every day instead. "Meatless days" were limited to the forces behind the lines. Later, the meat ration was decreased down to 250 grams per day and then to 200. Next to bread and meat the field ration included 1500 grams of potatoes, rice, barley and vegetables, twenty-five grams of salt, twenty-five grams of coffee, three grams of tea and seventeen grams of sugar. These were issued to the troops daily. Coffee and tea could be replaced by a daily ration of fifty grams of cocoa together with thirty-four grams of sugar. The cocoa ration was reduced to twenty-five grams of cocoa and twenty-five grams of sugar in 1916. In the course of the war the necessity of maintaining the level of fitness of the combat troops required a considerable improvement in the ingredients of the field ration. Additional foodstuffs like tobacco, butter, lard, jam, spices, tinned and salted vegetables, vinegar, cooking oil, fish, citric acid, mustard and honey were added to the daily rations. The daily ration of butter or lard was fixed at sixty-five grams. If not available 200 grams of jam or 125 grams of liver sausage or seventyfive grams of honey could be handed out. But this did not mean that the rations the German soldiers received at the Western Front contained all the foodstuffs they were entitled to every day. If a sufficient ration of fat was not available, butter or lard was issued to the troops only on special days, or distribution was limited to the fighting troops. Army commands were authorized to increase the ration in urgent cases and to issue up to 1000 grams of bread when the meat ration could not be provided in full. Mountain troops, when serving at altitudes above 1000 metres, could receive a maximum bread ration of 1000 grams and combat troops fighting hard days or coming back from major battles were entitled to 750 grams bread. If supplies were available, such troops could additionally receive twenty-five grams of sugar, seventy-five grams of sausage-meat, or one salted herring, or one egg, or forty-five grams of tinned meat. Nevertheless the amount of food the soldiers received was insufficient.

From 1917 onwards hunger and malnutrition were a permanent condition for most of the soldiers. The rations were not sufficient for the hard labour in the trenches. After three years of war only soldiers from rural areas still received parcels with food from home. For the others the flow of parcels had ceased. The families at home had nothing left to send to their boys. Malnutrition in the civil population in Germany was far worse than at the front. Meat became a rare delicacy for the frontline soldiers. Sausage-meat sandwiches or bread and butter were replaced by thin jam. Butter, milk and fresh vegetables were seldom. Dried vegetables, the so-called "*Doerrgemuese*", boiled in pure water without potatoes, bread or meat became an infamous and much hated staple at the front. Soldiers called this unhealthy food "*Drahtverhau*" (tangled wire), expressing how the soldiers felt after consuming this diet. There is no war memoir that does not refer to this frontline diet without irony. *Major* Bloem's orderly remarked for example, that the "*Doerrgemuese*" could be cooked and eaten or smoked in a pipe. When crushed with the fingers into powder, it was even excellent snuff (cit. Bloem: *Das Ganze halt!,* p.520). On the eve of major battles the troops received better food – if available of course. Such moments were often recorded as extraordinary events in war diaries and post war memoirs. Some of the German regiments which were called to stop the Allied breakthrough at Villers-Bretonneux on August 10th, 1918 east of Amiens, were very fed well before entering the line. Hans Kuhn remembers how he and his comrades received a "fantastic" thick soup of barley, vegetables, potatoes and big heaps of tinned meat from the company's rolling kitchen as they were leaving the trains at Ham where they had been sent by an emergency order (cit. Kuhn: *Das Leben im Tode*, p.58).

At the Western Front the food was usually cooked behind the line by the company's rolling kitchen. Army bakeries produced the bread behind the front. At dusk the rolling kitchens moved as close as possible to the frontline, often under shellfire. At meeting places food carriers, loaded with mess kits and cans, waited for the rolling kitchens to pick up the hot food and the bread rations and bring them into the trenches. Gunfire often killed the food carriers on their way or hit the rolling kitchen and infantrymen would then wait in vain for their drinks and their meal. At other times, the food that arrived was already cold. Solidified alcohol was issued to the troops in the trenches to heat up their cold food. Where solidified alcohol was not available the hardened infantrymen used the charges of their stick grenades as fuel for heating their meals in the dugouts. This method was both risky and forbidden but certainly effective. The situation for the infantrymen in the line was very hard when intensive shelling blocked the supply of tea, coffee and water. The army physician Wilhelm His refers in his memoirs to the supply problems of the XV. Army Corps in the battle at Verdun. Of the thousand water bottles that had been sent to Fort Douaumont only thirty passed the French artillery barrage unbroken. The thirsty men had to depend instead on the water in the shell holes that was contaminated with decomposing bodies and poison gas (cit. His: *Die Front der Aerzte*, p.115-118). In some sectors, if spacious dugouts were available, the kitchens were constructed directly within the positions. In this way the daily losses of killed food carriers could be reduced considerably and the frontline troops received their rations hot and on time.

Food shortages were sometimes a cause of motivation for combat for the German soldiers. Raids at the enemy's positions often offered the opportunity to improve their own rations with captured British or French food. The regimental history of Fuesilier-Regiment 40 recalls such an episode when in position at Verdun. On March 4th, 1917 the Hohenzollernfusiliers attacked the French position at "Vaux Kreuz Hill" to improve their own line on this important hilltop. After tremendous shelling by heavy mortars the French trench was captured and fatigue parties prepared the position for permanent occupation. In the meantime storm troopers raided the dugouts of the second French line. The storm troopers found sandbags filled with white bread, canned sardines, tinned meat, chocolate and other delicacies that had been missed for a long time. After blowing up the French dugouts they retired to their new trench where the fusiliers enjoyed this welcome booty with much pleasure during the days that followed (cit. Fuehren: *Hohenzollernfusiliere im Weltkrieg 1914-1918*, p.372-375).

Trenches, saps, shell craters and dugouts were always clammy places to reside in, particularly during the cold seasons. As a result, hot drinks were very important both for the troops' physical well-being as well as for their morale. Next to coffee and hot chocolate, sweet tea became the best-liked drink in the German Army. Hot sweet tea was an integral part of the soldier's diet at the front. Tea was especially new for most German soldiers from the lower classes; it had been unknown to them to this extent before the war. Relieved troops coming back from the trenches were received with hot chocolate or coffee from the rolling kitchen at the billets. However, tea, coffee, and hot chocolate were all products from the colonies and had to be imported via the neutral neighbouring countries. From 1917 onwards, when Great Britain intensified the blockade policy against Germany and the neutrals, these colonial products also became rare in Germany. Next to hot drinks, alcohol had an important influence on the morale of officers and men. The consummation of alcohol was not reserved to special events or the rear area but was often consumed to reduce stress levels. The consumption of alcohol, especially in the officers' ranks, reached such an extent that it often came close to alcoholism. Many officers' war memoirs refer to the regular consumption of wine and other alcoholic beverages at little get-togethers at the front. Responsibility for their men, the permanent danger and the influence of heavy shellfire had a deep impact on the nervous system. Alcohol helped them to feel relaxed. For the better-paid officers alcohol was more easily available than for the rank and file. Before assault operations and raids, alcohol was served to the rank and file to reduce nervousness and stress. Ironically, some German war memoirs refer disparagingly to captured "drunken" British assault troops. However, the same observation – that the Germans drank too – was surely made by the British. And alcohol captured in the French or British trenches was certainly not rejected by the German troops.

**Right: German engineers preparing beans in their kitchen in France. Fresh food meant plenty of manual work for the soldiers.**
**Pionier-Ersatz-Bataillon I 2, Landwehr-Pionier-Company 13.**
**France.**
**August 1918.**

**Opposite**
**Left: Lunchtime in the trenches of Infantry-Regiment 169 at the Somme. Hot meals served in mess kits.**
**Infantry-Regiment 169.**
**Somme.**
**1916.**

**Top right: German kitchen shelter somewhere in France. Runners usually had the dangerous job of picking up hot food from the rolling kitchens under the cover of the night. Where possible shellproof kitchens were constructed in the line to improve the supply of the trench garrison with hot meals and drinks.**
**France.**
**1915/16.**

**Bottom right: Peeling potatoes at an improvised field kitchen at the railroad embankment near Martinsart after the German Somme offensive had finally been stopped in the last few days of March 1918. The newly occupied territory of the Somme lacked all infrastructure and accommodation possibilities.**
**Martinsart, Somme.**
**March 1918.**

**Right: Chow line at the kitchen of the 1st Machine Gun Company, Landwehr-Infantry-Regiment 110 at Manheulles. Food carriers waiting to pick up the hot rations for their comrades.**
**1st Machine Gun Company, Landwehr-Infantry-Regiment 110.**
**Manheulles, Woevre plain.**
**May 26, 1917.**

**Left: NCOs' lunchtime at the Somme. At quiet sectors lunchtime could be quite a comfortable affair at a table and with a bottle of wine.**
**52. Infantry-Division.**
**Somme.**
**1916.**

**Opposite**
**Top left: Typical lunchtime in the German trenches at the Western Front: Mess kits, army-bread and tinned meat.**
**France.**
**1917.**

**Top right: Infantrymen of the 52. Infantry-Division back from the trenches at Gommecourt. The rolling kitchen is serving hot drinks.**
**52. Infantry-Division.**
**Gommecourt, Somme.**
**Summer 1916.**

**Bottom left: Drawing rations at the rolling kitchen somewhere in France in May 1916. The rolling kitchen was invented only some years before the Great War and was a decisive improvement in supplying infantrymen with hot food.**
**May 1916.**

**Bottom right: Food carriers with the mess kits of their comrades waiting to pick up the hot rations at a rear area camp kitchen in France. The day's menu consists of potatoes, carrots and beef. However, in 1918 German food rations were often quite meagre.**
**France.**
**February 21, 1918.**

**Above: Lunchtime chow line at the kitchen in a rear area camp somewhere at the Western Front. This kitchen is offering meatballs at midday and hot coffee in the morning and evening.**
**Western Front.**
**1916/17.**

21.2.18.

**Top left: Canteen of Infantry-Regiment 113 at the railway embankment at Loivre. The infantrymen could buy additional food, alcohol or cigarettes at the canteens.**
**Infantry-Regiment 113.**
**Loivre, Aisne.**
**July-October 1915.**

**Above: Butchers of the 3rd Battalion killing a pig at the 126. Infantry-Regiment's rear area camp near Rouvres. Before taking part in the attack at Verdun, good food and celebrations were intended to improve morale.**
**3rd battalion, Infantry-Regiment 126.**
**Rouvres, Woevre plain.**
**May 1916.**

**Left: Distribution of meat at the supply depot at St. Etienne. Behind the front the quartermaster's organization was responsible for supplying the frontline forces with food and equipment.**
**Infantry-Regiment 113.**
**St. Etienne, Champagne.**
**September-October 1915.**

**Opposite: Drawing hot rations and coffee at a kitchen somewhere at the Western Front. This kitchen is fitted into a truck.**
**Western Front.**
**1917/18.**

X
16

Chapter Eight

# POWs

From 1914-1918, 182,000 British, 506,000 French and 740,000 German officers and men became prisoners of war at the Western Front. For the hard core of the fighting men and for the professional soldiers this was a depressing experience, excluded from the heroic fight for their country's victory by an unfortunate twist of fate. For the others, sobered up by the reality of trench war, it was a personal chance to escape the fighting and the war. Nevertheless, it meant years of captivity for all of them and often enough a life under very frustrating conditions in enemy POW camps. Not all of the prisoners returned. 18,900 French and 5500 British POWs died in German prisoner of war camps; equivalent to a mortality rate of 4% and 3%. German POWs at French POW camps lived under much harsher conditions than their comrades who had been taken prisoner by the British Army. In the French camps 9% of the German prisoners died, in comparison with only 3% who lost their lives in British captivity. The survival of the prisoners of war depended on the accommodation, health care and food supply. In German captivity the Allied POWs suffered the same levels of malnutrition as the German civilian population and the German soldiers at the front. The food supply for the French and British POWs in Germany was improved considerably by gifts sent to Germany from their home countries. The Russian POWs however received no help and had to face the full consequences of the general food scarcity in Germany. They had much more difficult living conditions and a considerably higher death toll – especially under the conditions of forced labour – than the captured western Allies. Thousands of half starved and poorly dressed Russian prisoners of war were used by the German Supreme Command for salvage work, road construction and building the system of rearward defensive positions, like the "Hindenburg Line", behind the Western Front.

For the fighting community of the trenches and in post-war publications captivity was closely linked with morale. Nearly every German regimental history refers with an undertone of contempt to captured enemy soldiers passing the line on their way to the nearby prisoners' collecting point crying and laughing in pidgin French; "La guerre fini, la guerre fini!" – The war is over. Such stories are not only told to demonstrate the supposed low level of morale of the enemy in comparison with the pretended determined attitude of the German infantry. These stories reflect more than anything else the astonishment and silent shock felt by the hard core of the fighting men and the professional soldiers, who eventually wrote most of the war books, when they realized the extent of the collapse in morale that had taken place in the enemy ranks after the defeat. They knew that no army or regiment was spared from moments of a breakdown in morale in battle. For the fighting men however it was sometimes quite difficult to tell if they were succumbing to a crisis of morale or if they just had to accept a totally hopeless situation, when for example ammunition ran out and superior enemy forces turned further resistance into unreasonable suicide. In the eyes of the army commanders and staff officers, the trench garrisons – officers as much as the rank and file – that were captured in considerable numbers were generally suspected of a failure of morale. With this in mind General Ludendorff refers in his memoirs to the German defeats at Verdun in November 1917 and at Villers-Brettonneux in August 1918 when the German resistance quickly collapsed and thousands of Germans were taken prisoners within a short space of time. For Ludendorff these defeats were caused by a breakdown in the soldiers' morale. The British Army showed the same attitude towards this problem after the war when it investigated the circumstances of the capture of each British officer who was taken by the Germans when Gough's 5th Army disintegrated in March 1918. The suspicious commanders often did their troops an injustice. The men were simply overwhelmed and had met their point of exhaustion; a situation that was too often not taken into account at the staff offices behind the front.

In the stalemate at the Western Front most POWs came from the infantry that had fought in close contact with the enemy. Members of the artillery, the cavalry and the service of supply were only captured in the 1914 war of movement and later on the occasion of major breakthroughs, like that at Vimy in April 1917 or at the Somme in March 1918, when members of all branches of the service were taken prisoner. The infantrymen in the forward trenches and the pilots who crossed the line with their vulnerable aircraft were those at most risk of becoming prisoners of war. The positions were carefully guarded day and night by sentries in the forward trenches and separated by deep obstacles of barbed wire, often hung with empty tins that made a noise when touched by careless patrols crawling in no-man's land. Despite these precautions there were plenty of occasions for the infantrymen at the Western Front to become POWs. The infantry executed raids against the enemy trenches and took prisoners in order to strengthen combat morale and to ascertain the identity of the enemy troops holding the trenches opposite. According to Keegan, the first raid at the Western Front was carried out in the night of November 9/10, 1914 by Indian troops, who thereby introduced tactics of tribal warfare from India's north-western frontier to the European battlefield (Keegan: *The First World War*, p.182). While the Indians left the Western Front for warmer theatres of war, raiding refined the tactics of trench war. Raiding ranged from actions of small groups crawling by night silently into the enemy trench to pick up an incautious sentry to major operations involving several companies that were covered by the artillery's barrage fire. Major battles, like the Anglo-French offensives or the German attack at Verdun in 1916 and the offensive in 1918, produced the other tremendous sudden influx of POWs, when enemy trenches were captured and the survivors of close combat surrendered. Detached infantry moped up the captured enemy positions to pick up all enemy soldiers who were still hidden in their dugouts and shell holes that had already been passed by the rearward waves of attacking troops. However, the attacking infantry was also liable to be captured. Storming infantry, depleted by losses and exhausted by the strain of battle, sometimes advanced too far and found themselves isolated in small groups somewhere in the occupied enemy trenches when they were hit by a deliberate counter-attack. Cut off from reinforcements and supplies such forces were overwhelmed and forced to surrender. Exactly this took place on 1st of July 1916 when a considerable number of British soldiers were captured by the Germans at the Somme even though they had been battered by seven days of drumfire.

Captured enemy officers and infantrymen were checked for valuable documents like trench maps, orders or diaries and were then immediately sent back to the nearby prisoners' collecting point, often without an escort because the forward infantry could not spare any men for this purpose. Before being marched off to the next railhead, where cattle wagons awaited the prisoners for their rail trip to a POW camp in Germany, the prisoners were subjected to a detailed interrogation and investigation at the prisoners' collecting points. POWs were a valuable source for information about the forces holding the opposite trenches, for details about the enemy trench system and about intended military operations. Most imminent major military operations at the Western Front were either betrayed by captured soldiers or they were learnt about from captured documents. The effect of this leaked information sometimes had catastrophic consequences for the other side. In April 1917 for example the French at the Chemin des Dames were received by the well-prepared defence of the alerted enemy and in July 1918 the Germans in the Champagne experienced the same. Having access to information about the identity and the location of enemy troops made it possible to derive a relatively detailed picture of the organisation and dislocation of the hostile army and its military preparations. This source of information did however have its limits; it required a steady inflow of POWs, which meant active combat. In 1917 German intelligence completely missed the French mutinies taking place. Specially trained intelligence officers at the divisional headquarters were responsible for POW interrogation. While some prisoners gave information quite freely, in the hope of receiving better treatment, others refused any cooperation beyond giving their name and unit. Some also gave false information. The more audacious responded with cheek, as the German lieutenant Heinrich Palmus reported in a letter written at Givenchy on October 10th, 1915. In response to an intelligence officer asking for the British artillery positions a British prisoner told him to: "Go and look yourself" (cit. Hoffmann: *Der deutsche Soldat*, p.194).

Although being captured was one way to escape the murderous bloodshed at the Western Front it was not without its dangers. Many surrendering soldiers were not taken prisoners but shot or bayoneted in the heat of battle, or they were killed on the way back by shells from their own artillery bombarding the rearward enemy communications. The killing of POWs was reported in both camps. German war memoirs or regimental histories generally blame British soldiers and French colonial infantry for "murdering" POWs. In the German infantry the French colonial infantry had a bad reputation for never taking prisoners. However, this stemmed from the racist attitude of the German Army which cursed the Allied governments for leading "inferior" African or Asian soldiers against white men. They argued beyond the trenches for a white brotherhood between Germany, France and Britain that should not be violated. POWs were mostly killed in the heat and stress of battle. But there was deliberate killing also; trench garrisons fighting desperately to the end and machine gunners who could slaughter complete battalions with their guns, pouring deadly fire into the attackers right up until the last moment before surrender. They frequently found no mercy under the bayonets of the surviving assailants. This produced the myth that German machine gunners were chained to their guns and ordered to fire until they were killed. This myth was well propagated amongst the men of the American Expeditionary Forces in 1918 who saw plenty of German machine gunners lying killed beside their guns. However, the truth was that most machine gunners did not survive because they had to be killed by the attacking infantry in order for them to overwhelm the gun position, or they were finished off when surrendering.

After several days on the train POWs arrived at their designated POW camps somewhere in Germany. There the prisoners were billeted in barracks secured by fences and guard turrets. Guard-duty at the camps was carried out by Landsturm soldiers, the oldest men liable for military service up to the age of forty-five. The old guards usually wore the pre-war blue uniform with high leather caps. Allied prisoners in Germany got a number which was fixed to the uniform, while the letters "PG" (prisonier de guerre) were marked with black paint on the uniforms of German prisoners in France. One of the camps in Germany was Muenster in Westphalen which had the capacity to billet 25,000 men. It was originally designated to house British and French prisoners but never-ending conflicts between the two nationalities caused the Germans to evacuate the British. A combination of Russian and French POWs proved to be more successful because the latter were relatively "rich" prisoners and thus able to pay the Russians for minor services with cigarettes. Food shortages forced the German administration to limit bread production to brown bread, for which the French had an insurmountable disgust. The French government assisted their captured countrymen by sending weekly food packages via Switzerland that included five pounds of white bread, chocolate and cigarettes. Most POWs slept at the camp but spent the day working at the adjacent farms.

The living conditions of the prisoners depended very much on the goodwill of the camp's commander. Both sides accused each other of treating their POWs badly and of violating international law. The German government claimed that the German soldiers captured by the French Army suffered bad living conditions, cruelties, insufficient food and forced labour in the fire zone. To deter France from the alleged maltreatment of German POWs the German Army concentrated specially selected French POWs at so called reprisal camps behind the front. Just such a reprisal camp was situated in the engineer depot at Monchecourt in the sector of group Quéant. There, captured French soldiers from the educated classes were forced to live and work under the same bad conditions that the German government claimed German POWs did in France.

**Column of British POWs captured on the second day of the battle at the Somme. A German officer is speaking with the leading British officer to gather preliminary information. POWs were an important source for gaining information about the enemy.
Somme.
June 2, 1916.**

**German hussars guarding a column of French POWs captured at Neuville. The time of the cavalry was running out, even as guard forces.
Neuville, Champagne.
1915.**

**Opposite
Top left: Gathering of French POWs captured in the Vosges Mountains. Some of the French soldiers belong to the mountain troops.
Alsace.
September 1915.**

**Top right: Collecting point for British POWs captured in the attack on Guillemont in the morning of August 8th, 1916. In a courtyard at Sailly German officers of the 27. Infantry-Division are interrogating the British soldiers and checking if they have any valuable documents or maps.
27. Infantry-Division.
Sailly, Somme.
August 8, 1916.**

**Opposite
Bottom left: Interrogation of captured Highlanders by German officers. After the registration of the POW's personal data the interrogation officers tried to get as much information as possible from the POWs.
France.
1916/17.**

**Bottom right: French mountain soldiers captured by Brigade-Ersatz-Bataillon 58 who had raided the enemy trenches in the Vosges Mountains near Markirch. For these prisoners the war is now finished.
Brigade-Ersatz-Bataillon 58.
Markirch sector, Vosges.
Summer 1916.**

**Left: Wounded POWs of the French Infantry-Regiment 63 captured at "Winterberg Hill". The German soldier who shot this photo as a souvenir noted on the picture: "My booty at Winterberg."**
**"Winterberg", Aisne.**
**Summer 1917.**

**Above: German cavalry escort passing the village of Esnes with a column of British POWs captured in the German offensive at the Somme in March 1918. German soldiers resting next to the road looking curiously on at the beaten enemy.**
**Esnes, Somme.**
**March 1918.**

**Opposite**
**Left: British soldiers taken prisoner at the Aisne near Juvincourt on the first day of the German offensive to the Marne. Some British divisions which had already been shattered at the Somme by the German March offensive were sent to the supposedly quiet Aisne sector in April 1918 where they were hit by the next German push on May 27.**
**52. Infantry-Division.**
**Juvincourt, Aisne.**
**May 27, 1918.**

**Top right: Transport of French POWs at a railroad station behind the front. The POWs were gathered at railheads for the transport to the POW camps in Germany.**
**France.**
**1916/17.**

**Bottom right: Columns of French POWs assembled at the railhead before entering the transport wagons. The German Army used goods wagons or rail stock cars for the transport of POWs.**
**France.**
**1916/17.**

**Top left: German soldiers guarding captured French colonial soldiers at the Aisne in May 1918. French colonial troops had a bad reputation in the German ranks because they were suspected of killing prisoners.**
**Aisne.**
**May 1918.**

**Above: Captured French colonial troops arriving in Germany. On their march from the railway station to the prisoner of war camp a crowd of spectators has lined up along the road, attracted by the picturesque uniforms of the Zouaves.**
**Germany.**
**Summer 1915.**

**Left: French POWs assembled in front of their barracks at the prisoner of war camp Immendingen. Each prisoner received an individual number worn on a badge on his arm.**
**Immendingen, Germany.**
**July 1915.**

**Opposite: Fatigue party of French POWs improving the embankment at a railhead somewhere in France. The situation looks relatively relaxed.**
**France.**
**Summer 1916.**

**Top left: French prisoners leaving their POW camp for fatigue duty. POWs had to work on farms or carry out construction work in Germany. Note the 1914-style field uniform of the French POWs.**
**Germany.**
**Undated.**

**Above: Distribution of mail at the POW camp for French prisoners at Muehlheim.**
**Muehlheim/Rhein, Germany.**
**1917.**

**Left: German prisoners of war at a camp somewhere in France. The prisoners' uniforms were marked with a painted "PG – prisonier de guerre" and an individual number.**
**France.**
**Undated.**

**Opposite: German war prisoners in their barracks in the British POW camp on the Isle of Jersey. POWs were allowed to send such photos home to stay in contact with their families.**
**Isle of Jersey, Britain.**
**Undated.**

Chapter Nine

# Mining Warfare

It was modern technology that caused the deadlock at the Western Front. Modern artillery and effective machine guns resulted in a stalemate and forced the troops to dig in. Nearly impregnable positions appeared on the battlefield shortly after the beginning of the trench war in 1914/15 and both sides fell back on one of the oldest forms of siege warfare: Mining warfare. Engineers excavated underground galleries that led under the enemy positions. Spacious chambers at the end of the galleries were loaded with tons of high explosives and then the entire enemy position would be blown up. Complete company sectors disappeared in huge craters together with the garrison. Even at a distance of 150 metres from the crater men were buried alive by the debris that rained from the sky for several minutes. The mining provoked counter mining. To stop hostile mining activities there was only one option: To detect and destroy the enemy gallery with one's own mining operations before the opponent's preparations were finished. From 1915 onwards engineers fought a desperate and nerve-racking underground war of mining and countermining all along the Western Front. There was a permanent danger of being buried alive in one's own gallery by enemy countermining and asphyxiating gases threatened the lives of the mining engineers. Even days after a mine explosion toxic gases would still be evaporating from the earth and could fill the tunnels. Careful ventilation of the underground galleries was an important part of the tunnelling engineer's business.

Geological conditions also had a deep influence on mining warfare. The stone of the Argonne forest for example was very suitable for mining. The chalky earth in the Champagne was however so worn out that only wooden mining frames could stabilize the tunnels. Initially, mining warfare did not take place any deeper than fifteen metres under the surface. Later, the engineers constructed their galleries between fifteen and thirty metres under no-man's land and the enemy positions. In the end, improved technical equipment and methods allowed successful mining at a depth of fifty metres. The engineers used pickaxes or a hammer and chisel to drive the galleries further into the rock. The work had to be done silently to avoid enemy detection. If the stone was very hard electrical drills were operated and sometimes high explosives had to do the job. However, this destroyed all secrecy and was the best way to provoke countermining. Mining warfare demanded a huge amount of labour. At Vauquois Hill for example two engineers and one mining company worked in a sector of 1700 metres; altogether 1400 men. Fatigue parties worked shifts of six hours tunnelling. To drive a gallery of a length of seventy metres in a depth of forty metres a fatigue party of eleven men was needed: Two men to drill and two men to fill the debris into sandbags. An additional seven men transported the earth to the surface. In certain cases, another two men were needed to operate a water pump when ground water infiltrated a gallery. Two more men were needed for ventilation. Pumps and ventilators were operated by hand and produced insufficient results. Later on electric pumps and ventilators were used with more success, and electric light replaced the candles.

The work of the tunnelling engineers was a physically and morally exhausting job. The tunnels were uncomfortable places to work in. Eighty centimetres broad and 120 centimetres high, the size of the galleries meant the men had to work in a stooping position. When the galleries and the chamber were finished the charge of high explosives had to be loaded. Fatigue parties, consisting of dozens of men, transported tons of high explosives in boxes or sandbags to the end of the tunnel. They then blocked the charge with twenty metres of sandbags. This work took between five and thirty hours, depending on the size of the charge. Before blowing up the mine one's own infantry would have to secretly evacuate their nearby position. Storm troopers would be ready to occupy the new crater. Immediately after exploding the mine – the debris would be still raining from the sky – both sides would try to occupy the crater and convert the position into a strong fortress. Often stiff hand-to-hand combat followed such a manoeuvre in an attempt to gain control of the new crater. An explosion produced a deep and wide crater, surrounded by a wall of debris several metres high. Crater slopes offered excellent steep rearward positions for dugout construction and the debris around the crater formed a circular fortress.

Up until the end of 1917 several thousands of miners were busy on both sides at the Western Front. From 1915-1917 complete hills were cut by a series of mine craters. Messines Ridge at Flanders, Vimy Ridge at Artois, la Boisselle at the Somme, Hill 108 in the Aisne valley, Vauquois Hill at the Argonne sector and Eparges Hill at the Côtes Lorraines all became renowned for the mining warfare that took place there. One of the most well known mining operations was the British attack at Messines Ridge in June 1917. The high ground of Messines Ridge dominated the southern flank of the Ypres salient and was found to be the key for any British offensive operation at the Flanders sector in 1917. On June 7th, 1917, after months of intensive tunnelling, the British 2nd Army exploded 500 tons of high explosives under the German positions. The explosions transformed the German trenches into a chaos of craters and destruction and silenced all German resistance. However, mining was not limited to major offensive operations. Mining was a permanent feature of daily trench war. Dominant hill positions and strong points became the favourite objectives of the engineers' tunnelling activities. Positions such as these were held by the infantry under the permanent nerve-racking threat of being blown away by underground mines.

**Right: German soldiers constructing dugouts and defences in a new mine crater. Dispersed equipment of the former British occupants who were buried by the mine explosion is visible between the soldiers: Rubber boots, an English sign and the hat of the German soldier on the right.**
**Hooge, Flanders.**
**1916.**

**Below: Exploding mine. In the moment of the mine explosion a huge cloud of earth and debris is being blown up into the sky. For several minutes earth and debris were raining from the sky. This photo was taken from the frontline trench. In front of the mine explosion, an older crater is visible together with the typical wall of debris.**
**Somme.**
**1916.**

**Bottom right: Mining pit under construction. The crank on the right side was used to tow small vehicles transporting mining debris out of the gallery.**
**Western Front.**
**Undated.**

**Left: Fortified mine crater on Hill 60. Hill 60 was one of the few important hills in the flat country of Flanders. The mine crater is part of the first line and the fire trench has been dug into the far lip together with boxes full of hand grenades. On the ground of the crater a dugout is already finished. The blanket in front of the entrance was used as gas protection.**
**Hill 60, Flanders.**
**1917.**

**Opposite: Mine crater directly in front of the German frontline trench. This crater is only some hours old. The shattered earth is fresh and shows no signs of erosion. Soldiers brought tools and wire into the crater to construct entanglements and fire trenches. Despite its size, this crater was levelled within some days by gun and mortar fire.**
**Vimy Ridge, Artois.**
**Undated.**

**Below: Mine crater position on Hill 60 at winter time. As one of the few important hills in the flat country of Flanders Hill 60 was severly contested.**
**Hill 60, Flanders.**
**1917.**

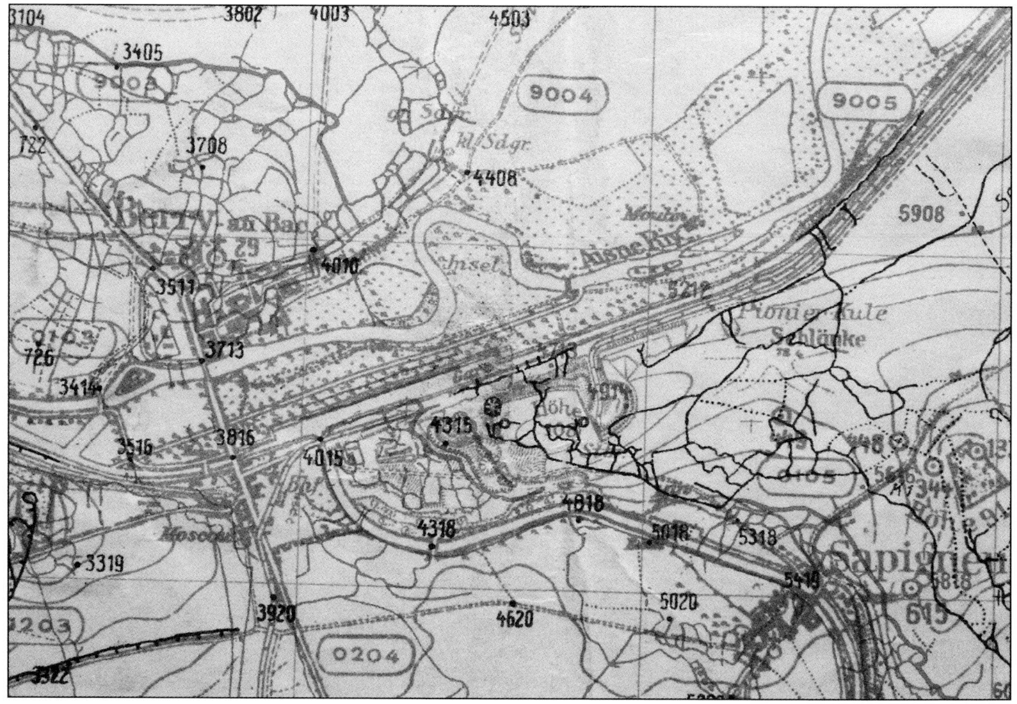

**Top left: Aerial photograph of the mine craters on Hill 108. Hill 108 was a severely disputed position dominating the Aisne valley. Holding Hill 108 meant control of this part of Aisne sector.**
**Hill 108, Aisne.**
**December 27, 1917.**

**Above: Trench map showing the same position as the aerial photograph: Hill 108. Detailed maps of the battlefield were compiled by ground and air reconnaissance to guide trench fighters and staff.**
**Gruppe Sisonne.**
**Hill 108, Aisne.**
**September 16, 1917.**

**Left: Mine crater position. Several connected mine craters form a bastion with a lot of dugouts cut deep into the crater slopes.**
**Western Front.**
**Undated.**

**Opposite: German soldiers visiting a mine crater at the old frontline near Broodseinde. The area was captured by the Germans in the 2nd Ypres battle in April 1915 and is now far behind the frontline. Underground water has flooded the crater's bottom.**
**Broodseinde, Flanders.**
**Summer 1915.**

Minentrichter bei Broodseinde

Above: Mine crater at Hooge blown up by British engineers on July 19th, 1915. Diameter fifty-five metres, depth twelve metres. The crater has been occupied by German soldiers. Sandbags have been used to improve the fire trench at the crater lip.
Infantry-Regiment 126.
Hooge, Flanders.
July 1915.

Top right: Improved mine crater position. Wickerwork, wood and sandbags have transformed the shattered earth slopes of the crater into a permanent position with trenches and dugouts capable of resisting gunfire and bad weather.
Infantry-Regiment 120.
Somme.
November 1916.

Right: Mine crater at the Argonne forest. The wooden ridges of the Argonne forest became the scene of intense mining warfare. The impressive view of the site prompted two officers to visit the crater with their camera to shoot some photos.
Argonne.
Undated.

# CHAPTER TEN

# ARTILLERY - MASTER OF THE BATTLEFIELD

Artillery was the master of the Western Front battlefields. Guns were responsible for the bulk of destruction and most of the losses in men and material. Gunnery at the Western Front developed into a sophisticated system that performed and guided an intensive artillery fire. Tens of thousands of guns poured nearly unlimited amounts of ammunition into the enemy, unprecedented in military history. The artillery battle increased tremendously between 1914 and 1918. For example, in the first three months of 1918 German factories produced more guns than the German Army had had at its disposal in August 1914. When the French artillery developed "drumfire", gunnery on the battlefield was transformed into industrial work, performed by soldiers who became workers of war, delivering as much destructive power as their machines could produce.

Since the 1880s, artillery techniques had undergone decisive developments. The invention of smokeless powder and the use of high explosives improved the destructive effect of shellfire and extended the range and firepower of guns. Extended fire ranges and a high firing sequence of field and heavy guns allowed the artillery to deliver intensive fire indirectly from remote and camouflaged positions. Forward observers commanded the firing of the batteries by telephone. The invention of hydraulic recoil systems considerably improved targeting. The recoil system held the gun at its exact position in the moment of firing. Only the barrel moved backwards to absorb the pressure of the launching shell. France had already introduced the hydraulic recoil system with the 7.5-cm-field gun, the M 97, back in the 1890s. However, Germany had not kept pace with this development and did not improve the field gun 96 until 1906. This 7.7-cm-field gun had a maximum range of 7800 metres and became the counterpart to the renowned French "soixante quinze". This, along with scientific methods of calculating the trajectory, allowed accurate and intensive firing. The intensive fire capacity had devastating effects and strengthened the effectiveness of defence by clearing the open ground of all military activity. The permanent threat and deadly effects of gunfire forced the infantry to the ground to look for shelter in trenches and dugouts. At the same time however impregnable trenches, dugouts and the deep zone of wire entanglements were the reason that there was more and more focus on heavy guns which were powerful enough to destroy the obstacles.

Already in the late 1890s technical inventions and the support of Emperor Wilhelm II and the General staff, under the command of Count Schlieffen, had furthered the reorganization of the heavy artillery in Germany. Originally only used for defending fortresses or as siege guns that were fired from specially constructed permanent positions, heavy guns were now destined for mobile service in the field, together with infantry and field artillery. From 1914-15 the German heavy artillery at the Western Front was vastly superior in number. This allowed the field artillery to focus the fire on the hostile infantry while the heavy guns battered enemy artillery and entrenched positions. "Fuss-Artillery", as the heavy artillery was called in the German forces, took the field with several different types of heavy guns in the beginning of the Great War. The 21-cm-steel-mortar had a maximum range of 7700 metres, but it was already a relatively old fashioned model in 1914 because of its lack of a recoil system. In 1902 the German artillery introduced the heavy field howitzer 02. It fired the "shell 04" which had a very sensitive fuse and burst into a large number of small splinters at a maximum range of 7400 metres. By firing the "shell 04", one single howitzer 02 battery could, under favourable conditions, annihilate an artillery force three times bigger than itself within twenty minutes, relying only on the ammunition from its transport wagons. An improved version – the heavy field howitzer 13 – appeared in 1913. Firing at a maximum range of 8500 metres it was the best gun of this class in the Great War. In 1906 the 10-cm-gun 04 was introduced. The gun had been constructed to fire from a flat angle and achieved a maximum range of 10.200 metres. This gun was originally destined for use as a siege gun but experience at the Western Front taught how useful this type of gun was for artillery battle. Only a short time before the war the German artillery had received an updated version of this gun. Called the 10-cm-gun 14 it had an improved fire range of 11,400 metres. In 1909 the backbone of heavy artillery, the 21-cm-mortar, was introduced. The mortar had a maximum fire range of 9.400 metres and was renowned for its firing accuracy. As it was very heavy the gun had to be disassembled for transport. The barrel, the carriage and the chain wheels of each gun had to be transported on three separate wagons. Mobility was nevertheless excellent. At the outbreak of the war the German heavy artillery had 256 21-cm mortars at its disposal. The heaviest gun of the German heavy artillery was the "*Dicke Berta*" (fat Berta). This 42-cm-howitzer was constructed with close cooperation between the General Staff, the Artillery Commission and Krupp factory. They managed to keep it a secret until the beginning of the war. The first model was introduced in 1911 but it turned out to be too heavy for transport and employment in the field; the gun thus depended on railroad transport. Thirty-six hours were needed to get the gun ready to fire. The later model L/12 (M-Geraet) was much lighter and could be transported by four vehicles on the road. The gun could be assembled within the surprisingly short time of four hours and it could fire a shell of 800kg at a range of 9300 metres. The "*Dicke Berta*", together with the 21-cm-mortars, knocked out the Belgian fortresses in 1914 and opened the way for the German invasion into Belgium and France.

The French, who had relied on their famous 7.5-cm-field gun M 97 as a universal gun, turned out to be mistaken. The French and the British learnt their lesson however and an arms race of artillery power became a significant feature of the war at the Western Front. Both the British and French armies considerably increased their number of heavy guns and soon caught up with German heavy artillery. After that, each offensive exceeded the preceding one in the amount of guns used, the intensity of fire concentration and the duration of the preparatory fire. Preparation for offensive operations developed into an overwhelming logistical undertaking that lasted several weeks. Thousands of guns had to be brought into position and millions of shells had to be dumped near the frontline. Trenches, dugouts, concrete shelters and deep obstacles made an intensive artillery preparation necessary in order to clear the way for the attacking infantry. The Somme offensive on July 1st, 1916 was prepared with a week's shellfire that was intended to pulverize the German defences and to kill the garrison. However, the disastrous result of the failed attack demonstrated that even a whole week of shelling was not sufficient. The third battle of Ypres, beginning on July 31, 1917, was prepared by two weeks of continued gunfire. At the Champagne, Verdun and the Somme, the infantry had to endure the first climax of "drumfire". Firing a combination of high explosive shells and gas had been a normal procedure in the never-ending artillery battle at the Western Front since 1915. However, the daily gunfire also caused many losses and much destruction at the "cushy sectors". When guns failed to clear the infantry's way at the Western Front artillery became the main weapon of attrition warfare, aimed at destroying the enemy's material resources and manpower. Nevertheless, in spite of its overwhelming destructive power, artillery only contributed to the consolidation of the stalemate. It was not until March 21st, 1918 that artillery regained its role as an offensive weapon at the Western Front. The early morning of that day brought a change in artillery tactics. To regain the momentum of surprise the German Army refrained from several days of treacherous "drumfire" and prepared "Operation Michael" at the Somme with a hurricane bombardment of unprecedented intensity that lasted only three hours. 6500 guns and 3500 mortars poured more than a million shells into the British lines and crushed the resistance. The way was now open for the German storm troopers.

Several different kinds of gunfire were used in the trench war at the Western Front: Preparatory, creeping barrage, barrage, counter battery and retaliation fire.

Preparatory fire preceded every military operation and was directed to clear a way for the attacking infantry through to the enemy position. Wire, trenches and dugouts formed a nearly impregnable barrier that had to be pulverized before the infantry could attack.

The creeping barrage was used to protect the attacking infantry from 1916 onwards. The advancing infantry followed closely behind a curtain of shell impacts designed to keep the defender down until the moment the attacker could jump into the enemy trenches. Sophisticated coordination and accurate firing were an indispensable condition for this artillery tactic.

The defender used barrage fire to protect his positions against attacking hostile infantry. In the moment of alarm, the artillery observers or the infantry called for barrage fire by firing flares. Alerted by the flares the artillery would open up fire and cover their own positions with a curtain of blasting shells that hit the attacking forces even before they could reach the forward defensive trench.

When one's own artillery was shelling the hostile gun positions it was called counter battery fire. This fire was meant to paralyze or destroy the enemy artillery. Suppression of the enemy artillery was a prerequisite to gaining superiority on the battlefield.

Refusing the domination of the battlefield by the enemy, the artillery responded with retaliation fire to each hostile activity. Enemy raids and artillery fire were carefully registered and retaliated with strafing fire. The gunning of pre-registered targets immediately paid back every destroyed part of a trench or crashed dugouts. To a certain extent retaliation fire contributed to the development of "cushy sectors" where both sides refrained from aggressive activities to avoid the enemy reaction.

Even at quiet sectors gunfire was a daily experience. Gunfire formed the trench war. The permanent threat of gunfire resulted in the "emptiness of the battle field" that is often cited. This meant that even strongly garrisoned positions looked empty in the daylight. Gunfire turned the battlefield at the Western Front into a moon landscape where all traces of former cultivation were wiped out by shell holes and destruction. The infantry suffered badly under the heavy gunfire but the men learned to hold out. In 1914, the impact of a few 42-cm shells fired by heavy guns, like those used in the "*Dicke Berta*" Krupp gun, was sufficient to force the garrison of an armoured fortress to surrender. Fort de Manonviller at Lorraine and the forts of Antwerp were taken by German troops although they were far from being seriously damaged. The mental effect of 42-cm shells was strong enough to break the resistance. In 1916 heavy German navy guns even shelled French trenches and dugouts at Verdun but the infantry was able to endure it if they were not directly hit or killed by the blast. The famous forts Douaumont and Vaux at Verdun were under heavy shellfire for many months. Even when the forts had finally been reduced to shattered blocks of concrete there were still some usable galleries and casemates that offered welcome protection to the garrison holding out in a sea of destruction and death. At the same time however the infantry did suffer seriously from the effects of the permanent heavy gunfire. The blast and concussion of high explosive shells had a deep impact on the men's nervous systems. This form of stress became known as "shell shock". Shell-shocked soldiers were unable to move or to speak for hours or days, many were also completely paralysed for longer periods of time and had to be treated in hospitals.

**Above: Firing heavy field howitzer 02 (15cm). This howitzer had a maximum range of 7400 metres.
Flanders.
August 1916.**

**Top right: Before the infantry attack. The artillery had to pulverize the enemy trenches and shelters.
German positions under British artillery bombardment.
Somme.
1916.**

**Right: The eye of the artillery. Camouflaged forward artillery observer position. Forward artillery observers had their observation posts in the frontline trenches and were in close contact with the infantry, sharing their life and dangers.
Fuss-Artillery-Regiment 8.
Flirey, Côtes Lorraines.
April 1915.**

**Top left: Camouflaged battery position. Type field gun 96. Counter battery forced the artillery into camouflaged positions. Some trees next to the road offer good protection against enemy artillery spotters.**
**3rd Battery, Field-Artillery-Regiment 103.**
**Pusieux, Somme.**
**Autumn 1916.**

**Above: The backbone of the German heavy artillery. 21-cm howitzer at its fire position hidden under trees in an orchard. The 21-cm howitzer launched heavy projectiles to hammer enemy positions but it was still transportable even on difficult terrain.**
**52. Infantry-Division.**
**Pusieux, Somme.**
**Summer 1916.**

**Left: Krupp 10-cm-gun 04 immediately after being fired. Smokeless powder produced only a short flash when the gun was fired. The hydraulic recoil system is in its most backward position at this moment, being pressed by the concussion of the parting shell. Note the revolving gun position.**
**Verdun.**
**1916.**

**Opposite: Gun position at the Flanders sector. Insufficient industrial capacities forced the German Army to use old-fashioned gun models without a hydraulic recoil system to compete in the intensifying artillery battle. Soft Flanders ground made it necessary to plank this gun position.**
**Blankaart Lake, Flanders**
**May 1917.**

Villa
zur
guten
Hoffnung
Villa
10cm
Kanone

**Above: Firing 10-cm-gun 14 next to the Menin-Ypres road in the Flanders battle in 1917. Ammunition, ready to fire, is dumped next to the gun. Behind the piece the gunners have constructed a makeshift shelter, using branches and tarpaulin, against the wet Flanders weather.**
**Flanders.**
**Autumn 1917.**

**Top right: 10-cm-gun 04 before loading. The gunner on the right is operating the breechblock.**
**Vic, Lorraine.**
**1915.**

**Right: Captured French gun position at Verdun. The 15,5-cm-guns were the backbone of the heavy French artillery. A direct hit removed the track from the wheel of the gun in the foreground.**
**Verdun.**
**Spring 1916.**

**Opposite: Quiet moments at the gun position. The crew of this 10-cm-gun 04 converted the cellars of a farm building into dugouts and named them "Villa zur guten Hoffnung" (Villa of Good Hope) and "Villa 10cm Kanone" (Villa 10-cm Gun). Furniture picked up from the deserted houses made life at the front more comfortable.**
**Northern France.**
**1915.**

**Opposite**
**Top left: Artillery observer sitting in the trench with binoculars.**
**52. Infantry-Division.**
**Alsace.**
**Spring 1917.**

**Bottom left: Fatigue party transporting shell boxes to the gun position. Shell supply was a tremendous logistical challenge and a never ending task for the gunners. Note the gas alarm bell made of a piece of rail.**
**France.**
**1917.**

**Right: Splinter proof artillery ammunition dump near the artillery position. To avoid the catastrophic consequences of accidental hits only a limited amount of shells was dumped directly at the guns. Shells were transported in wicker baskets.**
**Champagne.**
**1915.**

**Above: 21-cm-howitzer in position between the farmhouses of Ornes village during the early phase of the battle of Verdun. In February there was still snow and plenty of mud at Verdun. The tarpaulins protected the muzzles and breechblocks of the howitzers against bad weather. Ammunition is dumped in wicker baskets all along the buildings. Later on the village was destroyed completely.**
**Ornes, Verdun.**
**February 1916.**

**Opposite**
**Top left: This 21-cm-howitzer in a forest north of Verdun is ready to take part in the Verdun offensive on February 21st, 1916. Due to the soft ground the gun pits for the heavy pieces had to be well prepared in advance. Fatigue parties used girders and trunks to lay the foundations for the gun and prepared shellproof dugouts for the gun crews.**
**Verdun.**
**February 1916.**

**21-cm-steel mortar being brought into position. In February 1916 the German High Command tried to break enemy resistance by using overwhelming artillery power for the first time at Verdun. Even heavy siege guns were transported from fortresses in Germany to the forests of Verdun.**
**Top right: Transport of the barrel with a special wagon into the prepared gun pit.**
**Bottom left: The gun carriage equipped with wheels is entering the position directly behind the barrel transport.**
**Bottom right: Ready to fire.**
**Verdun.**
**Spring 1916.**

**Above: Deep 21-cm-steel mortar gun pit in the Somme battle. The gun pit is two metres below the surface to prevent the mortar from being damaged by hostile fire. The maximum fire range of this gun was 7700 metres. Protection against bad weather conditions was necessary at long-term positions. This gun pit is constructed like a garage so the gun can be pulled back under shelter.**
**52. Infantry-Division.**
**Pusieux, Somme.**
**November 1916.**

**Above: Improved gun pit of a heavy field howitzer 13. The pit is strengthened against enemy shellfire by using rails, trunks and wickerwork.**
**France.**
**1915.**

**Opposite**
**Top left: Heavy field howitzer 02 ready to fire. The gunner on the right side is pulling the trigger with a rope.**
**52. Infantry-Division.**
**Pusieux, Somme.**
**1916.**

**Top right: Well camouflaged and dug-in gun pit of heavy field howitzer 13 north of Reims. Camouflaged pits were a simple but effective measure to protect guns against hostile observation and shelling.**
**Menneville, Aisne.**
**1917.**

**Bottom left: 10-cm-gun 14 completely destroyed by a barrel burst. None of the gun crew survived the explosion.**
**France.**
**1917.**

**Bottom right: Field gun 96 being repaired at an ordnance depot behind the frontline. Guns were seriously worn out by the intensive firing. Limited industrial capacities forced the German artillery to use guns beyond their normal working life. As a consequence worn-out gun barrels reduced firing accuracy which often resulted in the shelling of their own trenches.**
**Western Front.**
**Undated.**

**Right: Barrel bursts were a permanent deadly risk for gunners. The escalating artillery battle on the Western Front consumed a steadily growing amount of shells. In a very short space of time industry had to convert its limited pre-war production levels to mass production levels, using millions of unskilled workers. This resulted in a high percentage of defective shells which exploded prematurely when fired. The barrel of this heavy field howitzer 13 has been completely blasted.**
**Western Front.**
**Undated.**

**Below: Operating heavy field howitzer 02. Firing the heavy shells was hard work, as was the maintenance and cleaning of the gun. The complex mechanism of a howitzer had to be maintained carefully and the barrel needed regular cleaning.**
**France.**
**1915.**

Above: German long-range gun that shelled the French town of St. Dié at the Vosges sector. The city, ten kilometres behind the frontline, was an important place in the French rear area.
East of St. Dié, Vosges.
Winter 1915/16.

Top right: Firing 21-cm-mortar during Operation Michael. The high fire accuracy of the 21-cm-mortars on pre-registered targets allowed the necessary fire preparation to be reduced to a few hours. This ensured the momentum of surprise for the German attack.
Somme.
March 1918.

Right: Dump of heavy shells captured during Operation Michael. While storming the British positions at the Somme the Germans seized vast amounts of booty.
Somme.
March 1918.

Opposite: Battery commander with the gun crew of a heavy piece at the Western Front. Sand bags have been used to reinforce the gun pit. The gunner on the left has opened the breechblock. His colleague on the right hand side of the breechblock is holding the tool used for setting the shell fuse. Before being fired each shell fuse had to be set by hand.
Western Front.
Undated.

Chapter Eleven

# MORTARS - Guns of the Trench War

Mortars, or "*Minenwerfer*" as the German Army called this weapon, were a typical weapon of the trench war at the Western Front. The modern mortar force originated from the Russo-Japanese War in 1904-1905. The siege of the fortress Port Arthur had resulted in several months of gruelling trench war. Under the conditions of close combat the Japanese artillery had not managed to take part in the battle without endangering their own infantry when shelling the Russian positions. To destroy Russian defences the Japanese engineers developed simple mortars instead. The high-angle fire of these improvised guns proved to be very effective in breaking the Russian resistance. The mortars allowed heavy loads of high explosives to be thrown into the enemy positions that were close to their own entrenched infantry. The heavy loads, falling nearly vertically onto their targets, crashed into enemy trenches, dugouts and obstacles and opened the way for the attacking infantry. All important military powers sent official observers to Manchuria in 1904-1905. Some like Ian Hamilton, John J. Pershing and Max Hoffmann later became famous leaders in the Great War. The Russo-Japanese War was also the object of detailed studies by military scientists and staffs in the pre-1914 era. However, the mortar lesson was only understood in the German Army.

The Engineer Committee of the Prussian Army developed a modern-style mortar in a relatively short time. The heavy mortar (calibre 25cm) was introduced in the German engineer forces in 1910 and the medium mortar (calibre 17cm) in 1913. The medium mortar was typical for a weapon of this system. The modern construction was a muzzle-loader that included a barrel recoil system, a rifled bore, and a panoramic telescopic sight. Six different charges were available. The mortar was not fired from wheels like a normal gun but from a steel gun-platform after the wheels had been removed. High-angle fire with an elevation angle between 60-70 degrees increased the destructive power of the mines and allowed mortar crews to use any topographic advantage, dead angles of hilltops for example, when choosing a fire position. This new weapon was top secret and was to prove an unpleasant surprise for the Entente armies in 1914. On August 12, 1914, for the first time, heavy mortars pounded Fort Fleron near Liege. Some days later Fort Boussois near Maubeuge came under heavy mortar fire. Medium mortars proved their effectiveness for the first time at Antwerp.

As the mortar had originally been constructed for siege warfare the trench war that was beginning at the Western Front offered plenty of new opportunities for the young, and rapidly growing, mortar force. At the beginning of the war forty-four heavy mortars and 116 medium mortars were available. The production of the light mortar started in autumn 1914, but this type was still not yet ready for combat at the outbreak of war. In November 1918 the German forces operated 1200 heavy, 2400 medium, 12,400 light and 700 so-called "*Fluegelminenwerfer*". In accordance with the peace treaty of Versailles Germany had to destroy 28,449 Minenwerfers. At the outbreak of war special mortar squads (*Minenwerferabteilungen*) operated the mortars. Later each division had its own mortar company that eventually grew to battalion size. The infantry regiments organized light mortar units at first. By dissolving divisionary mortar units each regiment got its own mortar company.

The German mortar force proved to be an ideal weapon for the trench war. Mortars were used as heavy infantry weapons for close combat in cooperation with the infantry in the trenches. From 1914-16 the production capacity of the German industry could not compete with the infantry's growing demand for mortars. As a result the troops at the front, using their own initiative, developed several types of primitive mortars. These guns became known under the names of "*Wagner-*", "*Albrecht-*", "*Genter-*", "*Magnus-*" and "*Heidenheimwerfer*" and their quality and the effect of their shells were very varied. For example the "*Magnus* mortar" fired big tins filled with pieces of metal. Its piercing capability was low but the fragmentation had a terrible effect on the enemy infantry. Germany's industry contributed some more simple mortar models. One of them was the "*Lanz-Werfer*". This light smooth bore 9.13cm-gun was introduced in 1915. It was notorious with the troops for its poor ballistics that resulted in many duds. Before the war the Lanz factory produced farm equipment. At the Western Front light and medium mortars were the backbone of the German mortar force. The guns were easily disassembled and transportable even on rugged terrain. The light mortar needed a crew of ten men to carry the gun and equipment, the medium mortar twenty-two. When arriving at a fire position the light mortar was ready to fire within a few minutes whereas the medium mortar took half an hour to be assembled. The fire range of the light mortar varied from 50 to 1300 metres. The medium mortar could fire at ranges from 180 to 1040 metres while the maximum range of the heavy mortar was 600 metres. However, this could be doubled if only a half charge was fired. Firing 100 mines per hour the light mortar achieved an extraordinary high fire sequence while the medium mortar fired only 30 mines in the same time. Nevertheless, due to the different weight of mines (light; 4,75kg, medium; 53kg) medium mortars fired a total of 1590 kg per hour, three times the shell load fired by the light mortars during the same time. German "Minenwerfer" were responsible for a considerable share of the shelling at the Western Front. Per month, 20,000 heavy 120,000 medium and 1,500,000 light mortars were fired.

Mortar fire was very efficient in close combat trench war. The high fire sequence of light mortars meant they could be used against hostile manpower and light fortifications. The medium mortar was more effective than the heavy field howitzer. Medium mines destroyed obstacles within a circle of four metres and even crashed dugouts that were protected by three metres of earth. The tremendous blasts and the terrible destruction caused by the mine shelling had a demoralizing effect on the enemy forces. Mortar fire was used effectively as barrage fire. The impact on the enemy infantry was increased by firing mines that were equipped with time fuses which exploded five metres above the surface of the ground and produced considerable fragmentation and a shock wave. Due to their role as close combat weapons the mortars were normally in fire positions in the forward trenches. Carrying the guns was no problem for the mortar crews. Transporting ammunition was however the arduous task of the infantry. Fatigue parties spent whole nights carrying mines to the mortar pits. To transport 100 medium mines to the gun pits – this is the ammunition fired by one mortar within three hours – the men had to shoulder a burden of five tons of steel and high explosives.

**Top right: "Albrecht-Moerser" at the Somme before the British offensive. The design of this mortar type is very simple and the barrel is the product of crude workmanship. The barrel is fixed at a heavy base in order to absorb the blast when fired.**
**52. Infantry-Division.**
**Somme.**
**May 25, 1916.**

**Right: In the forward fire zone mortars were operated from shelters and dugouts. This medium mortar is positioned inside a concrete shelter. The gunner is greasing the projectile before charging the gun.**
**Belgium.**
**1917.**

**Opposite**
**Left: Covered medium mortar position. Nearly three metres below the ground surface, this mortar pit has been reinforced by girders, wickerwork and sandbags. The mines have been dumped in the wicker baskets behind the gun. The fatigue parties used these baskets to carry the projectiles.**
**France.**
**1916.**

**Right: Medium mortar in open fire position at the Ypres salient. The leather cover protected the muzzle and optical devices against bad weather conditions.**
**Infantry-Regiment 126.**
**Ypres, Flanders.**
**1915.**

**Above: Mortar crew with disassembled medium mortar. The repair of minor defects and the maintenance of the gun were the job of the mortar crew. In order to transport a mortar, the crew had to disassemble it completely.**
**Lingekopf, Vosges.**
**Summer 1915.**

**Top right: Light mortar crew with ammunition and cleaning tools. Training and maintenance were essential for the light mortar units. Note the handy light mines which made high fire rates and quick firing possible.**
**France.**
**1917.**

**Right: Light mortars under repair at a mobile ordnance repair shop in the Champagne sector. The ordnance repair shops behind the front were responsible for the repair of difficult defects and the exchange of special parts.**
**Souhain, Champagne.**
**December 1917.**

Weihnachten

**Above: Impact of a heavy mine. The mine explosion is blasting a cloud of earth and smoke into the sky leaving only devastation at the point of impact.**
**France.**
**1917.**

**Top right: Infantrymen bringing medium mines to the mortar pit in the forward trench. Mortars were close combat guns and had their positions in the forward trenches where horse-drawn or motorized transport was impossible.**
**Western Front.**
**Ca. 1916/17.**

**Right: Special construction for the mortar ammunition transport in the Vosges Mountains. The transport of medium or heavy mines was extremely hard work for the trench garrison, especially in difficult or mountainous terrain. This mortar crew found their own solution by constructing a kind of lift for the mines.**
**Vosges.**
**Summer 1915.**

**Opposite: Mortar section of the Landwehr-Infantry-Regiment 123 with their guns. The soldiers often sent photos showing their companies or sections home to their families.**
**Minenwerferabteilung, I. Battalion, Landwehr-Infantry-Regiment 123.**
**France.**
**December 1917.**

13

**Right: "Lanz-Werfer" in position in the dense forests at Verdun. The construction of the "Lanz mortar" was very simple and cheap. Even factories without experience in the production of guns could produce it. The "Lanz mortar" had a simple carriage without a hydraulic recoil system or optical devices. The transport and positioning of the gun was easy. A few planks were sufficient for the bed.**
**Verdun.**
**1916.**

**Opposite**
**Top left: Training of a mortar crew at a training ground behind the front line. In such an open position a heavy siege mortar would never be used. This photo allows a good view of the construction of the carriage and the big planks necessary to stabilize the gun.**
**Northern France.**
**Undated.**

**Bottom left: Charging a "Ladungswerfer" in position at the Vosges Mountains. This was one of the different models of improvised mortars used by the German Army to satisfy the pressing demand for mortars at the front. This model is constructed according to the classical pattern of mortars without any modern technical devices.**
**Vosges.**
**1917.**

**Right: Heavy "Albrecht Mortar" in a covered fire position. These improvised heavy guns were constructed from 1915-1916 to make up for the lack of standard medium and heavy mortars. As they had no hydraulic recoil system and were mounted on a simple carriage these mortars could even be produced by ordnance depots behind the front.**
**52. Infantry-Division.**
**Somme.**
**1916.**

**Right: "Lanz-Werfer" in position at a forward trench at the Somme. The blast of a heavy shell has buried the mortar under earth and debris.**
**52. Infantry-Division.**
**Somme.**
**1916.**

Chapter Twelve

# TANKS

The crucial problem of the trench war at the Western Front was how to break the deadlock. The high fire intensity, deep wire entanglements, successive lines of trenches and the slowness of the infantrymen who were heavily packed with weapons, ammunition and tools made any attack a slow and costly business. Even in successful attacks the attacking force was usually completely worn out by the time they had occupied the enemy trench. As a result it was often easy to push them back to their start line with organized counterattacks. To re-supply and to relieve the depleted attack forces on the heavily shelled and cratered battlefield was an unsolvable problem and depended completely on manpower. Cross-country vehicles that could have mastered the shell-torn ground did not yet exist. Advance became a matter of mere metres instead of kilometres. The slow progress in the big offensives at Verdun and the Somme in 1916 or at Flanders in 1917 were typical examples of this tactical deadlock. Attack operations were reduced to what the British side called the tactic of "bite and hold." The response to the deadlock could only be to find a technical solution. This was the origin of the tank. An invention of the Great War, the tank was an armoured vehicle. With its caterpillar wheels it was capable of moving across difficult terrain and it was able to crash obstacles and trenches with its weight and the power of its engine. Armed with machine guns and quick-firing guns, and served by a crew of half a dozen men, the tank was able to deal directly with machine gun strongpoints and clear the enemy trenches with its flanking fire. The British derived the idea from their armoured fleet. The tank was designed as a "land ship" to cruise the broken battlefield, protected by its heavy armour against hostile fire, sweeping the enemy positions with its own guns.

In Britain the first prototypes, called "Little Willy" and "Big Willy", were developed in 1915. Big Willy became known in 1916 under the name "Mark I". This rhombus-shaped tank was eight metres in length, with a 10mm thick armour (later models were 12mm and 14mm thick), a weight of twenty-eight tons and a crew of eight men. Four of the crew were occupied with running the tank. The tank commander was responsible for guiding the vehicle. He signalled his orders by hand to the man who served the gearing-unit and to the two others who handled the breaks at the caterpillar-tracks. The deafening noise in the tank's interior prohibited any spoken communication and the heat and rumbling made running a tank a strenuous business. The engine provided the tank with 105 metric horsepower, allowing a maximum speed of four miles per hour. From February 1916 onwards a "male" version was produced, armed with two 5.7-cm-guns and four machine guns and a "female" version, armed with five machine guns. By December 1916 150 tanks had already arrived at the British Expeditionary Forces. Up until 1918 successive types, Mark I-V, were produced; of these Mark IV became the model that was used most often. 420 male and 495 female Mark IV were produced. In 1915, independent from the British tank project, France also started developing tanks. Engineers from the Schneider-Creusot Works studied the problem of how to convert armoured cars into cross-country vehicles. The solution they came up with was to equip the chassis of an American Baby-Holt tractor with an armoured box that was armed with two machine guns and a 3.7-cm-gun. This vehicle had a weight of 13.5 tons and became known as the Char Schneider M 16. The 3.7-cm-gun was later replaced by a 7.5-cm-gun. The engineers of Schneider-Creusot's rival, St. Chaumond, designed their own tank model at the same time. The St. Chaumond tank had a weight of twenty-three tons and was armed with a 7.5-cm-gun and four machine guns. Compared with the British Mark tanks, the French types had less cross-country mobility.

The British Mark tanks and the French Schneider and St. Chaumond M 16 were heavy tanks. In 1917, in response to the need for medium and light tanks British industry started to produce the Whippet tank with a weight of fourteen tons and a length of 6.10 metres. The crew of three men had three machine guns at their disposal and the engine provided the tank with ninety metric horsepower allowing a maximum speed of 8 1/2 miles per hour and a radius of action of eighty-six miles. Starting in November 1917, the French Ministry of War embarked on the production of the light tank Renault M 17/18; 3177 tanks of this type were produced between then and the end of the war. The M 17/18 weighed only 6.7 tons and was only 4.88 metres long. An engine of thirty-nine metric horsepower allowed a maximum speed of five miles per hour. This light tank was heavily armoured with 22 mm of steel and armed with a machine gun and a 3.7-cm-gun. Nevertheless, it was relatively cheap, technically reliable and suitable for mass production. Of all these tanks improved versions were produced in the following years; these appeared on the battlefields of the Western Front in 1917 and 1918 in growing numbers. A large number of M 17/18 tanks in particular took part in the offensive operations of 1918 in France and Belgium.

The tank made its first appearance during the battle of the Somme and was a real shock to the Germans who met the driving castles without any adequate weapons to fight them. Only direct hits by gunfire could crash the armour of the tanks. However, tanks only appeared in small numbers at the beginning and they turned out to be slow und unreliable machines. In attack operations many tanks cracked because of technical failures long before they met the enemy. The best tactical use of the new weapon had also yet to be learned. High Wood, Flers and Ginchy became the scene of the first tank attacks on September 15th, 1916. There only thirty-six tanks were involved. At Flers, the initial rush of four tanks led the British infantry into the village. Some miles to the west, at the German strong point High Wood, an attack with four tanks resulted in complete failure due to unsuitable tactical organization. Shellfire-free corridors were reserved for the tank advance but the terrain, which was too broken even for the tanks, meant that the job of taking High Wood was again left to the infantry who had to pay dearly for it. When tanks made their first appearance at the Western Front they only had tactical success. This gave the German soldiers the urgently needed time to develop methods to fight the tanks. Even today some critics maintain that the British used the tank too early on and in too small numbers, instead of waiting and launching an overwhelming mass attack, surprising the German Army in 1917.

The debut of the French tank force on April 16th, 1917, in the disastrous attack at the Chemin des Dames sector, was a complete failure. In the early morning one hundred and twenty-eight heavy Schneider and St. Chaumont tanks, armed with 7.5-cm-guns and machine guns, started to cross no-man's land to crush the German line. The majority of them were lost due to technical failures. Many others got stuck in deep trenches and mud. In both cases the machines were doomed to become an easy target for the German guns. Only forty-seven tanks survived the German shelling and entered the German positions. This time the tanks were no shock. The Nivelle Offensive had already lost the momentum of surprise as it had been delayed several times by terrible weather conditions. Moreover, the new German defence scheme of a defence in depth, which meant holding the forward trenches by dispersed sentries only and forming the real defence in a deep system of trench lines dotted with pillboxes and machine gun nests, turned out to be a serious challenge even for the new tank force.

The first mass attack of tanks took place at the Western Front at Cambrai in November 1917. The Tank Corps was allowed to use its tanks according to tactics that conformed to this new weapon for the first time. After a short bombardment 300 tanks attacked and forced their way into the German defences. Some of the tanks broke through as far as the outskirts of Cambrai. The surprise attack was an impressive success and nearly broke the "Hindenburg line". However, the British did not take advantage of their success. A few days later a German counterattack pushed the British back to their starting line. The successful German counterattack obscured the message of Cambrai that mass attacks of tanks that used the momentum of surprise could break even the strongest defence.

The German trench fighter got over his tank shock and learned how to kill the monsters. Captured tanks were studied carefully in order to find their weak points and special weapons were developed, like the Mauser M-98 anti-tank rifle, to deal with the new threat. Direct artillery and mortar fire became the main weapons for destroying the tank's armour. However, the dangerous tanks remained something special for the German infantry. Many photos show soldiers looking at destroyed tanks with a mixture of bewilderment and pride. Tank wrecks appeared as a trophy and became a kind of "tourist attraction" for the soldiers on the battlefield. In the battles of the summer of 1918 tanks became a normal feature at the front and increased the Allied pressure on the cracking German Army. The German Supreme Command, misled by the general failure of the Allied tank weapon in 1916/17, did not appreciate the role of the tanks and failed to see their value in offensive operations. A serious tank production programme was never initiated in Germany. After the war it was argued that German industry, lacking in raw materials and industrial capacities, would not have been able to compete with the Allied tank production programmes. However, at the same time, the German navy spent plenty of steel and labour to build new battleships which never met the enemy. These resources would have been sufficient to build a considerable German tank fleet. Instead, the German Army only established a small tank force, using a few captured British tanks and a small number of German constructions. The design of the German tank A7V began relatively late, in December 1917, and by September 1918 only twenty tanks of this type had been produced. Compared with the nearly 6000 tanks produced by the Allied industries in the war this was a negligible number. With its weight of thirty-two tons, 30 mm thick armour and a crew of eighteen men, the AV7 surpassed all Allied models. The engine provided the tank with 200 metric horsepower, allowing a maximum speed of ten miles per hour. However, the majority of German soldiers never got to see this formidable tank in action on the battlefield. On the contrary, the German generals stressed the importance of improvised anti-tank weapons and drew up special batteries for close combat against tanks. Machine gunners received special ammunition and the infantry was trained to blow up tanks by using bundles of stick bombs.

**German soldiers having a look at tank C-23 tank destroyed in the battle of Cambrai. Most of the 300 tanks involved in the attack were destroyed. C-23 was knocked out by an impact on the top of the right gun turret. The gun turret shows some camouflage painting.**
**Cambrai, Somme.**
**November/December 1917.**

**Above: Wreck of a destroyed British tank used as a German dugout. The flag indicates the command post.
Northern France.
1917/18.**

**Back of a destroyed tank at the Australian trenches captured by the Germans near Bullecourt on April 15th, 1917. The Australians marked their trenches with signs that were meant to help their troops find the way inside the position.
XIV. Reserve Corps.
Bullecourt, Somme.
April 15, 1917.**

**Below: Quiet moments. A few soldiers on their Sunday trip to look at a tank wreck. The tank has partly sunk in the soft ground and has been disarmed. The trees bear signs of heavy shelling.
Flanders.
1917.**

Englische Tanks.

**Opposite**
**Top left: The tracks were one of the weak points of the tanks. The weapons of this British wreck have already been removed.**
**Northern France.**
**1917/18.**

**Top right: After the attack. British tank stopped by gunfire inside a destroyed village.**
**Northern France.**
**1917/18.**

**Bottom left: Cannibalized British tank behind the German lines. The beam at the heck was meant to help the tank when crossing trenches.**
**Cambrai, Somme.**
**1917.**

**Bottom right: British tank captured by Grenadier-Regiment 123 near Bullecourt. After the battle. The grenadiers are looking for where the tank was hit. Two impacts have broken holes into the left side of the tank. The German soldier on the left is wearing a signal pistol.**
**Grenadier-Regiment 123.**
**Bullecourt, Somme.**
**April 1917.**

**Right: Sunken British tank wreck at the Somme desert. The soft ground sealed the fate of the tank. On the left side the name of the tank is legible. All around the wreck there are dispersed petrol cans.**
**Somme.**
**March 1918.**

**Below: Tank wrecks dispersed at the Somme desert after this area was reoccupied by the Germans in March 1918. Nearly two years after the Somme battle shell holes and trenches are covered by new vegetation.**
**Somme.**
**March 1918.**

**Bottom right: British tank wreck as it was left after being severely hit into the right side in 1916 or 1917. The Germans captured the wreck in the spring offensive of March 1918. After its destruction the wreck was obviously disarmed and used as a dugout. The dugout entrance is visible under the right gun turret.**
**Somme.**
**March 1918.**

H
46

**Right: Like a stranded battleship. The idea of armoured battleships cruising the battlefield of the trench war was the inspiration for the construction of tanks. The shape of some of the tank models, like this French Schneider-Creusot at the Aisne sector, remind one of this.**
**Aisne.**
**1917.**

**Opposite**
**Top left: British tank crew burnt alive in their tank wreck. This and similar horrible scenes attracted the curisosity of German amateur photographers in the tank battle at Cambrai.**
**Cambrai, Somme.**
**November/December 1917.**

**Top right: Group of disabled British tanks knocked out by German artillery on the road to Cambrai.**
**Cambrai, Somme.**
**November/December 1917.**

**Bottom left: Sightseeing. Wrecks of French Schneider-Creusot tanks that were destroyed when they passed a German trench in the Aisne offensive. The wrecks have already been disarmed.**
**Aisne.**
**1917.**

**Bottom right: French tank sunken into a German trench. This is a thirteen ton Schneider-Creusot tank. The tank was armed with two short-barrelled guns at the front and with two machine guns at the side. The photographer has marked the time and place on the wreck with chalk.**
**Aisne.**
**May 15, 1917.**

**Right: Destroyed French Schneider-Creusot tank marked by his crew with the symbol of a cloverleaf.**
**France.**
**1918.**

Chapter Thirteen

# AVIATION AND TRENCH WARFARE

At the outbreak of the war the German air force was only three years old. The German air force grew up from nineteen aircraft in 1911, to 6100 officers and 55,000 other ranks with 4800 aircraft in November 1918. This considerable fighting force was eventually organized into 145 "*Flieger-Abteilungen*", eight bomber groups, two squadrons of giant aircraft, sixty-five fighter wings and thirty close-support fighter wings. During the first few months of the war the German Army aircraft were limited to reconnaissance missions. Even this was often not understood in the army and corps staffs. A deep suspicion reigned against these "technical toys" and infantry reports were preferred. Often it was only the pilot's initiative which brought valuable reconnaissance data to the headquarters. But even then there was no exchange of this data between corps, army and OHL staffs, and decisive information was disregarded when it was of no direct importance for their own mission. In August 1914 each of the eight German armies and all twenty-five active army corps had one "*Flieger-Abteilung*", made up of six aircraft, for air reconnaissance. The German OHL, the cavalry corps and the reserve corps had no aircraft at their disposal. However, already in the early days of September, the lack of air reconnaissance at the Marne turned out fatal for the German Army. Without a tool for direct reconnaissance, the OHL lost the control over the advancing armies, and – to make things worse – at the decisive outer German right wing, a reserve corps had to fight its way blind without air reconnaissance. The German leadership misunderstood the military situation and the fatal order for retreat was given.

When the trench war began the role of the air force grew rapidly. Reconnaissance was still the main task of aircraft and the captive balloons. The shell-torn battlefields became a complex system of trenches, dugouts, obstacles and battery positions, where one's own forces and the enemy's were nearly invisibly dispersed. The growing fire intensity of the infantry arms and the artillery confined ground observation to the narrow perspective of loopholes. And even those scarce observation results often did not reach the headquarters when shellfire cut the telephone lines and killed the runners. Air reconnaissance became a vital part of the battle command. Contact patrols and gun spotters located their own infantry and the hostile infantry on the battlefield and directed the shelling of their guns. The infantry in the shell-torn country signalled their positions to the low flying aircraft by laying out ground panels and the pilots, still without a wireless in their aircraft, dropped their reports directly over the gun positions or headquarters. With this simple method a pretty effective degree of communication was obtained. The captive balloons were the other branch of the air force. The balloons could hold their positions for a long time as they were anchored to the ground. Connected by telephone with staffs and artillery, the balloon observer reported back the situation on the battlefield in real time and even directed the shelling against moving targets. As a means of close battle support reconnaissance aircraft and captive balloons came under corps and divisional control. At the Western Front each German infantry division disposed of one or two balloon squads consisting of a balloon, a mobile motor winch, vehicles for equipment and gas, an anti-air machine gun and a few 3.7-cm-automatic guns. The infantrymen called their balloon the "divisional sausage" or even "virgin's dream", referring to the shape of the sausage balloons. As well as direct observation, photographic reconnaissance was also the job of the air force. Aerial photographic equipment was considerably improved and the air cameras produced photos with high resolution. Plotting from air photographs provided staffs and infantry with data for detailed trench maps and produced air photographic maps which were indispensable expedients in the labyrinthine world of the trenches. Next to tactical reconnaissance special wings were used for long-distance reconnaissance far behind the front. The observation of traffic density, wagon concentrations at railroad stations or the growing size of hut camps behind the front gave valuable hints about the strategic plans of the enemy and disclosed interesting targets for the bombers.

Bombers were the first aircraft that showed that the air force could take an active role in the war beyond reconnaissance. On August 14th, 1914 the French air force sent Voisins bombers to attack the German hangars at Metz for the first time. In the autumn the French Voisins wing was reorganized and from spring 1915 it waged a systematic bombing campaign against Germany. A weapon to stop the bombers and the reconnaissance aircraft was desperately needed. It was soon realized that there was a great need for fighter aircraft and these would develop into the most famous branch of the young but as yet unarmed air forces.

In the first months of the war the crews of two-seater airplanes carried out their first experiments with rifles and revolvers. The observers fired their rifle against passing hostile aircraft without support. And even this provisional armament achieved some results. On the 5th of October 1914 the observer of a French Voisins bomber shot down a German Aviatik two-seater. But the real fighter aircraft with a pilot steering his machine and firing his gun at the same time in frontal attacks was yet to come. Before the problem of synchronizing the propeller and the machine gun had to be solved. Initially, the observer, in a two-seater airplane, took over the role of the air gunner who fired his machine gun from the nose or tail position to avoid the propeller. The first real fighter aircraft firing through the propeller appeared at the Western Front when the French pilot Roland Garros protected the blade of his propeller with metal shields against bullets from his own gun. In this way Garros avoided shooting his own propeller to pieces when the non-synchronized bullets hit it. Garros used his solution successfully against the German pilots for several weeks before he crash-landed behind the German lines. Garros did not manage to destroy his plane and the Germans picked up Garros' valuable idea and asked the famous engineer Anthony Fokker to copy it. Instead, Fokker and his engineers developed a new synchronizing gear and created an offensive aircraft which became known as the "Fokker Plague" which ruled the skies over the Western Front in the winter of 1915/16. Only the appearance of new aircraft types like the DH2 and the Nieuport 11 enabled the Allies to win back air supremacy. From that time on an arms race was fought between the aircraft engineers of both camps. Air supremacy changed sides each time a new fighter model was taken into service at the Western Front.

A great variety of aircraft types, weapons and ammunition arrived at the Western Front and were used by reconnaissance, fighter, bomber, spotter, patrol and close-support fighter pilots for their respective missions. For example, an attack against sausage balloons required an aircraft with excellent low flying qualities and the capabilities of firing rockets or tracer bullets to set the enemy balloon aflame. The different branches of the air force and the growing air force organization required specialized combat control. Already in March 1915 the "Chief of the Air Force" took over his duties at the Supreme German Headquarters. He had to advise the OHL on all questions regarding the air war and he was responsible for supplies and technical development. However, operational control of the flying units was still the business of the OHL, the armies and the army corps who each received a special staff officer for air war matters. On October 8th, 1916 *General* v. Hoeppner became "General in Command of the Air Force" and an intensive process of reorganization of the German air force began. The new Air Force Commander had far reaching responsibilities and formed special reconnaissance, fighter, bomber, spotter, patrol and close-support fighter wings. He advised the OHL on air force matters and the distribution of the flying units at the different theatres of war.

The pilots at the Western Front were admired as the "knights of the skies". The infantryman, who lived in the dirt and despair of his shell hole, envied the pilots who patrolled in the clear blue sky and, after having accomplished their missions, flew home to a rearward airfield where clean billets and hospitable casinos awaited them. However, the pilots' life was not as comfortable as it seemed from the ground. The loss rates of pilots were much higher than those of the infantry and in the autumn of 1917 their average life span was three months before they were shot down, killed, wounded or burned alive. The pilots' lack of experience, especially the younger ones, often proved to be fatal. Well aware of this situation the pilots were under even more stress than the infantrymen under drumfire. The commanders' attitude towards parachutes made the situation even worse. Only the balloon observers had parachutes. Parachutes were denied to pilots as it was feared that they would bail out prematurely in critical situations. Low flying missions were quite risky because of ground fire and the passing artillery shells in the air. Technical failures, like a burning carburettor or hits at the engine, often set the aircraft aflame and left the pilot the "choice" of burning alive or jumping to his death. The majority of the pilots preferred the latter. Missions were normally flown at altitudes of between 3000-6000 metres. The pilots sat in open cockpits where no oxygen masks or heatable flying suits were available to cope with anoxia and the exposure to the cold. World War I pilots served at the limit of their physical endurance and often beyond the technical limits of their aircraft.

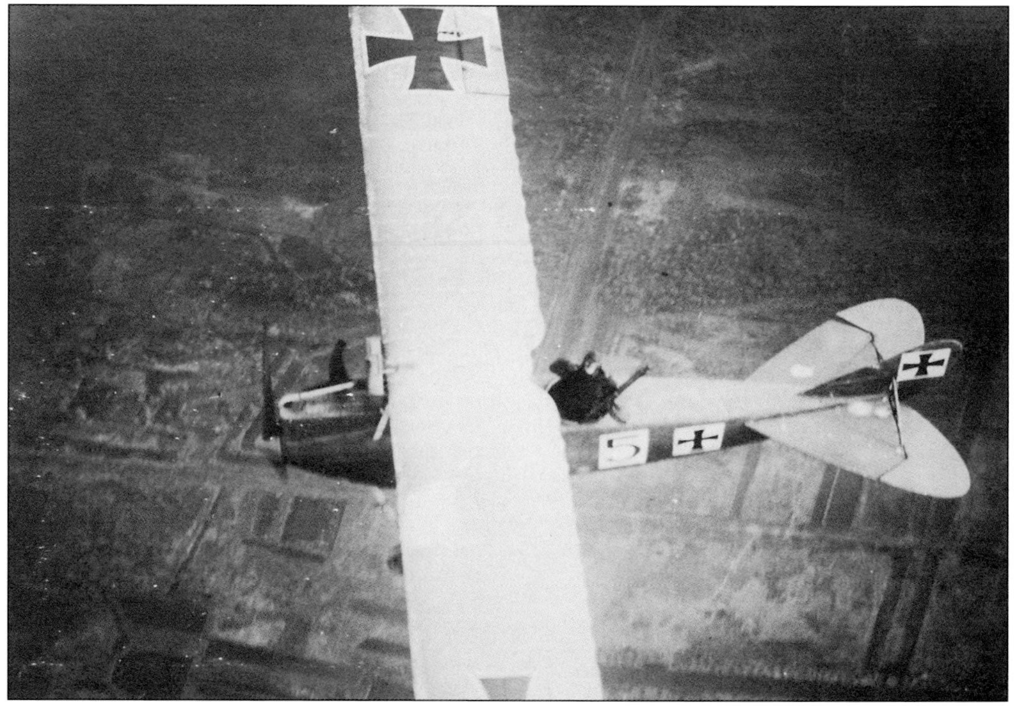

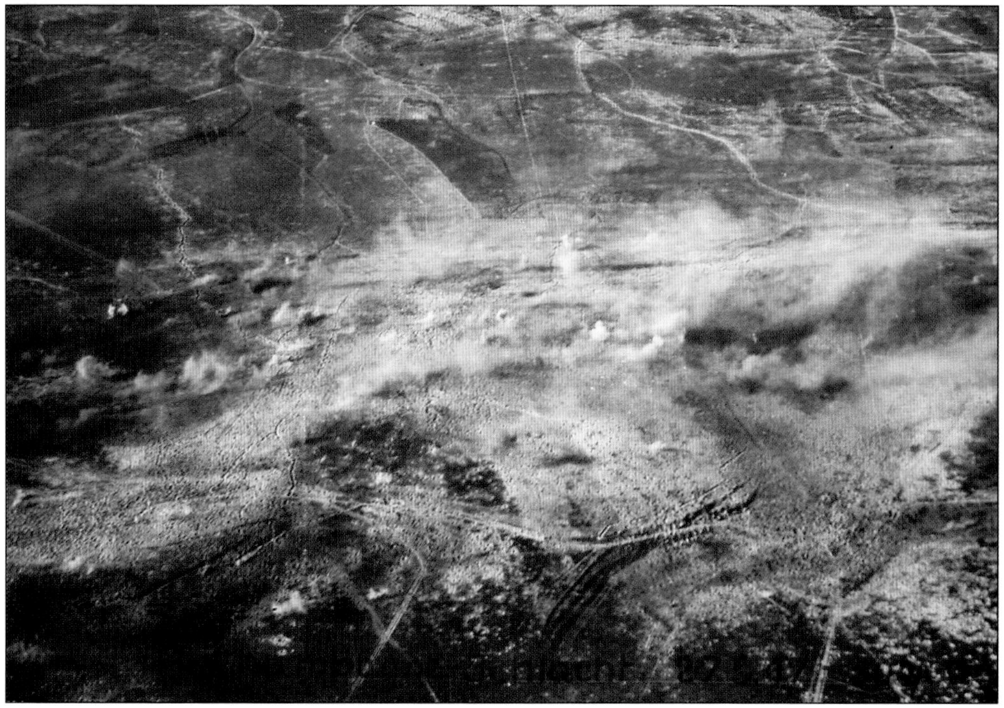

**Top left: The far-reaching eye of the front. German reconnaissance planes crossing the frontline at a high altitude for a long-range reconnaissance operation behind the British line.
Northern France.
1918.**

**Above: German reconnaissance aircraft over the enemy rear area. Pilot and tail gunner had to report all enemy traffic and activities on the ground and take aerial photos. At the same time, the tail gunner had to observe the sky for hostile fighter aircraft which were a permanent threat.
France.
1917.**

**Left: The battle at the Western Front as the airmen saw it. Part of the Champagne sector under heavy artillery fire in May 1917.
Champagne.
May 27, 1917.**

**Above: Early morning. Two German aircraft being prepared for take off. Behind the planes one can see the tents used as shelters for the planes. Western Front. 1917.**

**Right: Pilots of Feldfliegerabteilung 234 at the airfield Goudelancourt les Pierrepont. The airmen of the reconnaissance units were not as renowned as fighter pilots but they did an important and dangerous job. Without air reconnaissance the military leadership was blind. Feldfliegerabteilung 234. Goudelancourt les Pierrepont, Aisne. Winter 1917/18.**

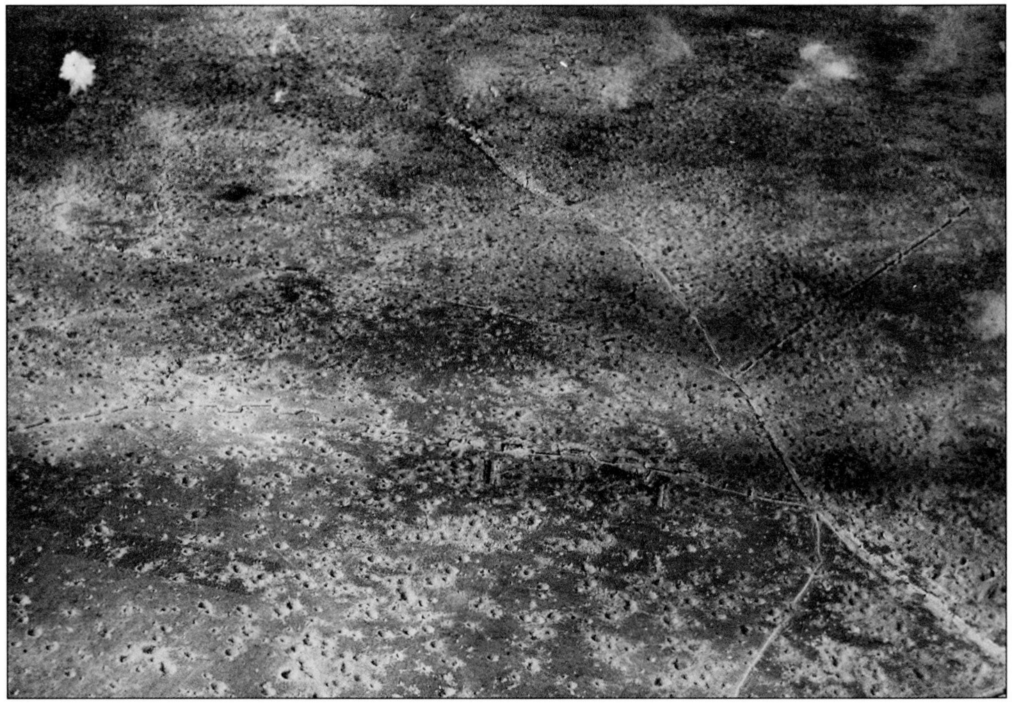

**Left:The weapons of the reconnaissance pilots. Different kinds of special cameras for air reconnaissance. Technology for aerial photography developed in the Great War and reached a high standard.
Feldfliegerabteilung 234.
Aisne.
Winter 1917/18.**

**Above: Sector of the 220. Infantry-Division at Croisilles south of Arras. The infantry fought the war at the Western Front in a labyrinth of shell holes and trenches. Without aerial reconnaissance, leadership in the battle and artillery control would have been impossible.
Sector of the 220. Infantry-Division at Croisilles, Artois.
June 16, 1917, 10.40am.**

**Opposite: Party at the casino of Feldfliegerabteilung 234. The infantry envied the exclusive life of the pilots behind the frontline. However, the pilots' job was much more dangerous than the infantrymen's life in the trenches.
Feldfliegerabteilung 234.
Goudelancourt les Pierrepont, Aisne.
Winter 1917/18.**

**Opposite**
**Top left: The end of a mission. Crashed German aircraft.**
**France.**
**Winter 1917/18.**

**Top right: Wreck of a crashed French aircraft at the German trenches south of Laon. Many planes were downed in the battle zone or they crashed into no-man's land.**
**Aisne.**
**Summer 1917.**

**Two at bottom: French aircraft shot down somewhere behind the German lines at Alsace. The victorious German pilots and curious infantry examine the aircraft's remains. The French pilots' dead bodies were recovered from the debris.**
**8. Landwehr-Division.**
**Alsace.**
**October 1915.**

**Above: Divisionary sausage balloon being prepared for lifting. Each division had its own sausage balloon for the observation of the sector.**
**Rouvres, Woevre plain, Lorraine.**
**1916.**

**Top right: Sausage balloon observer in his basket, ready for lifting. The sausage balloon observer had his observation post in a basket under the balloon from where he could observe the complete sector. In contrast to the pilots, the observers had a parachute and could bail out if a fighter aircraft downed the balloon.**
**Manre, Champagne.**
**Summer 1915.**

**Right: Filling of a sausage balloon. After having been assembled the balloon was filled with gas from the gas wagon on the left side of the balloon. The gas was inflammable, and in the case of a fighter attack the balloon would be destroyed by fire within minutes.**
**Infantry-Regiment 126.**
**Verdun.**
**June 1916.**

**Opposite**
**Top left: Sausage balloon changing position during Operation Michael, observed by advancing German infantry. When sausage balloons had to take over a new position the balloon crew dragged the balloon with ropes over land. This is an Austrian balloon. Some Austrian units took part in the attack in March 1918. III. Battalion, Infantry-Regiment 144, 223. Infantry-Division.**
**La Fére, Oise.**
**March 1918.**

**Top right: German troops passing the old frontline at the Chemin des Dames after the breakthrough in May 1918. A sausage balloon is observing the advance.**
**Chemin des Dames, Aisne.**
**May 1918.**

**Bottom left: German survey unit of the 28. Reserve-Division staff analysing new aerial photographs and compiling data in order to update trench maps. Aerial photographs were the basis for military surveys and for detailed trench maps for the leadership and the troops.**
**28. Reserve-Division.**
**Champagne.**
**October 20, 1917.**

**Bottom right: Aerial photograph of Fort de la Pompelle north of Reims. The fort was held by French troops and it was an important objective in the attack at Reims in June 1918. World War I photographic technology could produce photos showing all details of the enemy position.**
**Fort de la Pompelle, Champagne.**
**Summer 1918.**

**Wagon-based printers for the production of trench maps. The army corps and the divisions had their own survey units and mobile printers to provide the troops quickly with updated trench maps. The topography of the trench war battlefield was in a permanent state of construction and destruction so the majority of the trench maps could only be used for a few weeks.**
**France.**
**1917.**

**Above: Improvised anti-aircraft machine gun. Because of the lack of a special air defence, the infantry at the frontline had to take matters into their own hands and they converted machine guns into anti-aircraft guns. These soldiers fixed their gun at the top of a stake to keep enemy aircraft at bay.**
**Verdun.**
**Autumn 1917.**

**Top right: German field gun 96 converted into an anti-aircraft gun. This gun crew found a daring solution to converting their field gun. By designing a special construction the gun obtained the necessary angle and could revolve. The beam under the barrel served as a counterweight that was used to absorb the recoil when the gun was fired.**
**France.**
**1917.**

**Right: 8.8-cm-air defence gun mounted on a car. In 1916, only sausage balloon units had special anti-aircraft guns at their disposal. Balloons often became the target of fighter aircraft and depended completely on anti-aircraft cover.**
**Verdun.**
**March 1916.**

Chapter Fourteen

# SERVICE OF SUPPLY AND THE RAILROAD

At the Western Front the railroad was the backbone of the service of supply. The trench war consumed the production of whole industries. Trains poured a never-ending flow of arms, ammunition, food, equipment, construction material and men into a combat zone of unprecedented size. The rapid fire of modern guns and rifles in particular resulted in a massive consumption of shells and ammunition that could only be transported to the battlefields by railroad. To fill the battle zone that extended over hundreds of miles millions of combat troops had to be sent into battle. The transport of just one German division by rail took thirty trains. Belgium and Northern France offered the German Army the facilities of a modern railway system to fulfill these supply demands. The railway supply alone made modern war possible. At the same time railway supply was one of the reasons why the war degenerated into trench war and attrition from autumn 1914 onwards. When the offensive battle at the Western theater of war lost its momentum and the Western Front developed both opposing armies depended on their railroad supply to recover. Troops and supply depots were replenished with supply in abundance that thousands of trains delivered to the railheads. Supply in abundance and its easy availability lured the army commanders and quartermasters into immobility and attrition battles. From that time on the fighting armies depended on their railway supply lines and a network of railheads close to the battlefields. By 1918 neither the German nor the Allied Command had succeeded in ridding themselves of this dependency that nailed the armies to their railroad supply lines and restricted their freedom of movement to a radius of some dozen miles around their railheads. As a result the railway system set the limits for the military operations at the Western Front. Major operations could only be launched in sectors that had an efficient railway system that allowed the assembly and supply of troops and artillery by rail. A renowned example of operational planning that ignored the limits of railway supply lines was Ludendorff's attack at the Chemin des Dames on May 27th, 1918. This had originally been planned as a limited attack of the 7th and 1st Armies with the intention of attracting Allied divisions from Northern France to the south. However, Ludendorff was misled by the attack's surprising success and strengthened the storm divisions on their unexpected rush to Paris instead of stopping his troops at the Vesle River as had been intended. The advance ended in the first days of June on the northern banks of the Marne River forming a seventy-mile deep bulge between Noyon and Reims. The Marne bulge turned into a trap for the Germans who were cut off from their supply base. Only two railway lines led into the bulge; one of them passed Soissons, and the other one passed Reims. The destroyed tunnel of Margival blocked the Soissons railway line and Reims was still under French control. The service of supply of the 7th and 1st Armies depended completely on the insufficient transport capacities of trucks and horse-drawn vehicles. The repair works at Margival, the opening of a new secondary line and the attack at Reims on July 15th did not manage to open the supply lines into the Marne bulge.

Railroad supply had played an important role in strategic planning since the Franco-Prussian War of 1870/71. The main purpose of the railroad was to bring the troops to the theater of war. For the assembly of troops by rail intensive preparations were carried out in the pre-war period by the Railroad Department of the German General Staff in cooperation with the civil railroad administration. The Director of Railways (*Chef des Feldeisenbahnwesens*) General Groener was responsible for this task. At the outbreak of war mobilization of the troops meant mobilization for the railway too. During the first few days of war the old peacetime rail timetable was still valid and passenger and freight trains of different velocity were on duty. As a first step freight trains were cancelled and wagons prepared as troop transports. Meanwhile at the assembly areas close to the border railway engineers established military railheads. On the third day of mobilization the military rail timetable came into force resulting in a complete change of system. From that time on all trains were run with the same slow velocity bringing troops and supplies to their respective theater of war according to a prearranged timetable.

Civil railroad traffic came to a near standstill. It was not until strategic concentration was finished that civil traffic was reopened. Special disembarkment commissioners awaited the arriving troops at the disembarkment districts in order to coordinate the transport needs of the troops with the available railroad capacities. This was necessary because from the beginning of the fighting troop commanders urged for additional troop and ammunition transports in their respective sector or expected the disembarkment of troops not at the prearranged railheads but close to the scene of battle. Some even tried to interfere personally in the railway management. The Director of Railways resisted any such interference in order to guarantee the functioning of the system. After the successful assembly of the troops at the border the disembarkment commissioners took over as liaison officers between the army commands and the military railways.

In the first months of the war however the railway system of Belgium and Northern France was partly blocked by destroyed tunnels and bridges that had been blown up by the retreating Belgian and French armies. Officers of the railway engineers accompanied the advancing armies and reconnoitered the condition of the railway lines. Where they discovered damage or destruction German railway construction battalions were ordered forward for the necessary repair works. The railway construction battalions carried out intensive work during the first few months of war in order to open the blocked railway system again. But the job was tremendous and the reconstruction work had to be focused on the main lines. Even on the repaired sections railway traffic was difficult because the signal system was still out of order and the railway officers had to guide the traffic by telephone. As a consequence, during the first few weeks of war several armies had to depend on the same railway line for their supply and the railway construction battalions failed to follow up the advancing troops. At the beginning of the Marne battle the armies of the German right wing nearly lost contact with their railway supply line far behind them and supplies of food and ammunition became scarce. Such was the situation that the German *Major* Henoumont wrote after the war that "in the case of further advance the supply situation would have become critical" (cit. Schwarte: *Die militaerischen Lehren des Grossen Krieges*, p.310). However, the German troops retreated from the Marne thus coming closer to their railheads and supply depots. With the beginning of the trench war the supply situation improved. Railheads and railway lines were established close behind the front. The railway management in the occupied areas was reorganized. In the beginning it was carried out by the neighbouring German railway boards. Later on a network of military railway boards was established by the Director of Railways to deal with problems of construction, maintenance and administration of the railway system in Belgium and Northern France. In 1916 the "Railway Transport Department West" (*Etra West*) was set up at Charleville for the supervision of the railway system at the Western Front. Similar departments were responsible for the Eastern and Southern theaters of war.

The military railway system at the Western Front had two main problems to cope with. Firstly, in order to meet the Allied offensives with adequate strength, troops had to be transported quickly from one part of the Western Front to the other. In order to enable this railway lines running parallel to the front had to be opened. A reserve of rolling stock was assembled that was ready to pick up troops and move them to their respective operational area by order. To speed up the embarkment of troops loading stations and loading ramps were constructed everywhere behind the front. Thus the German Army was successful in pushing back all Allied blows by sending reserve troops into battle by rail.

The second problem was the provision of enormous numbers of ammunition and supply. In spite of the fact that enormous numbers of goods had to be handled the dispatch of goods was still old fashioned. The invention of the container was reserved for the future. From 1914-1918 the service of supply was characterized by repeated loading, unloading and reloading. Fatigue parties had to do most of this manually at the railheads, which were frequently the targets of hostile shelling. Millions of artillery shells were transported by train to the railheads behind the front. Fatigue parties unloaded the trains there and put the shells, packed in wooden boxes or wicker baskets, onto horse-drawn vehicles, trucks or narrow gauge railways. These transported the ammunition to ammunition dumps behind the front or directly to the gun pits, where the gunners had to unload the vehicles. All this had to be done at night. The gunners often had to carry every single shell to their guns, despite adverse weather conditions and hostile shelling. But their work was not over yet; the empty wooden boxes, wicker baskets and cartridges still had to be sent back for recycling. It was the infantry's dangerous job to bring up small arms ammunition, bombs, mortar shells and construction material to the forward line. Each night tens of thousands of men participated in the fatigue parties that transported supplies to the trenches like a never-ending ant's trail. At the frontline the manpower of the infantry was the main factor of the service of supply. There was no shell, bomb or piece of wire or timber that made its way into the trenches without the work of the infantrymen. However, this was no one-way traffic system. The increasing crisis of raw materials forced the German Army to clear the battlefield of lost equipment, arms and ammunition wherever it was possible. Clothes, boots, field packs, blankets, gas masks, helmets, arms, tools, ammunition boxes – everything, no matter what their condition – were collected by fatigue parties in the combat zone and from the dead bodies. The goods were sent by railway to special collecting points in Germany where women were busy with the dangerous job of sorting the contaminated materials. If beyond repair the object would be used as raw material but a lot was cleaned and repaired and reissued to the troops. Many new recruits received just such low quality second-hand clothes, boots and equipment when they joined the army.

Directly behind the frontline a special branch of the railway, the narrow gauge railway played an important role in the service of supply. A small gauge of 600 or 1000mm was characteristic of the narrow gauge railway; the wagons could be drawn by locomotive, horse or even by manpower. Rails and iron sleepers were prefabricated and laid in pieces of several meters length. Special small army locomotives and "brigade wagons" were used for bringing the troops and ammunition close to the frontline. On their way back the narrow gauge trains evacuated wounded soldiers. The brigade wagons were multi-purpose vehicles that could be quickly transformed from an ammunition carrier into a hospital wagon, or disassembled completely for easy transport. The "German Railway Transport Department West" reported that narrow gauge railway transported between 200 and 300 tons for each division at the front per day. From 1914-1918 railway engineers constructed a dense network of lines and railheads of this miniature railway behind the front in order to connect the standard-gauge railway with supply dumps, camps, gun pits and the trenches. Even in the final phase of the war between October 1st, 1917 and March 31st, 1918 the three German railway boards at the Western Front constructed 931 kilometers of 600mm and 273 kilometers of 1000mm gauge railway. In 1918, the German narrow gauge railway ran 550 locomotives and 6500 wagons on this rail network to provide the front with shells and food.

**German military railway transport from the Verdun sector to the battle at the Aisne on a stop at the station of Sedan. Railway transport formed the backbone of the German transport system behind the Western Front and enabled the German High Command to send the rare reserves to battle hotspots quickly.
Sedan station.
May 20, 1918.**

2

Tür

**Opposite**
**Top: Military transport at a railhead behind the Aisne sector. Officers had the privilege to travel in passenger coaches while the rank and file had to be content with goods waggons.**
**Aisne.**
**1917/18.**

**Bottom left: German officers in front of their transport waggon. The vehicles are loaded onto platform cars. Congested railway lines caused many stops along the way.**
**Aisne.**
**1917/18.**

**Bottom right: The troops spent days on traveling to their respective sectors. These officers kill the time by playing cards.**
**Aisne.**
**1917/18.**

**Below: Heavy artillery on the move to Priesterwald in the Lorraine sector stopping for a rest at a station near the Moselle River. Without railway transport the mass use and supply of heavy artillery would have been impossible.**
**Moselle valley.**
**May 1915.**

**Top left: Soldiers unloading their vehicles and equipment at the military ramp at Baroncourt railhead ten miles behind the Verdun front. Railway transport meant plenty of work for the soldiers because they had to do the loading and unloading themselves under the supervision of their officers.**
**Baroncourt, Verdun.**
**September 1916.**

**Above: Fatigue party unloading wagons at a railhead in France. At the railheads, all military freight had to be reloaded by hand onto horse-drawn or motorized transport vehicles for the final passage to the front.**
**France.**
**1916.**

**Left: German railhead in France. Dumps of corrugated iron, wire netting and timber for the construction of trenches and dugouts are ready for truck or horse-drawn transport to the frontline.**
**France.**
**Summer 1917.**

**Opposite: Shed construction by a German fatigue party at a railhead in Northern France. The intensive supply traffic for the Western Front demanded the construction of a system of railheads and warehouses for storing supply goods. POWs waiting to be transported to a POW camp.**
**Northern France.**
**Summer 1916.**

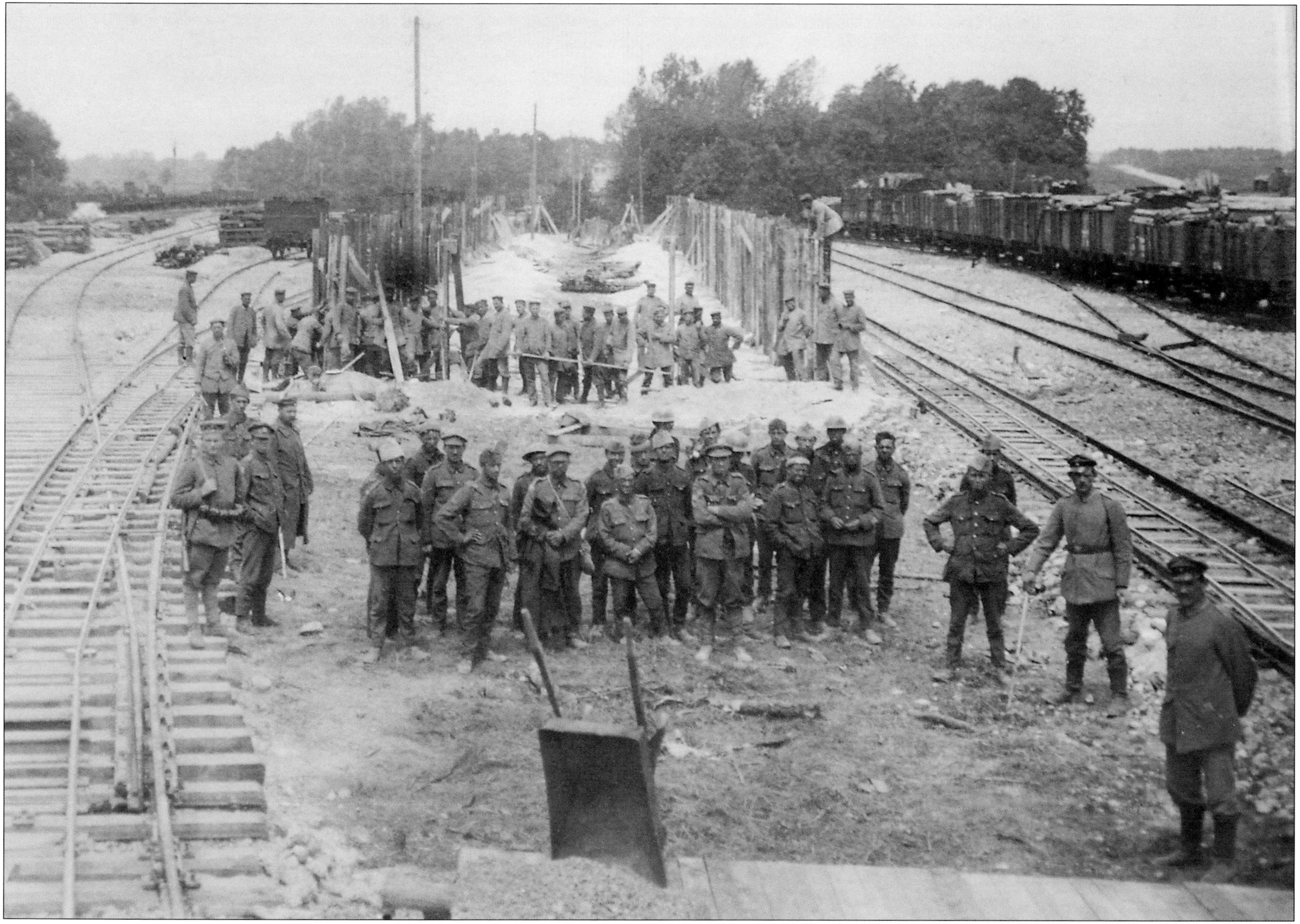

**Above: Light railway engine at Béthincourt during the battle of Verdun. Directly behind the frontline huge amounts of supply and ammunition had to be moved. In most sectors a dense network of narrow gauge railways connected the supply dumps with the gun positions and communication trenches.**
**Eisenbahnbau-Company 20.**
**Béthincourt, Verdun.**
**March 1916.**

**Opposite**
**Top left: Heavily shelled railhead at the Somme. Railheads close behind the front were frequently the targets of artillery fire.**
**Somme.**
**1916.**

**Top right: Railhead at Pozières after the explosion of an ammunition train. Ammunition transport often resulted in accidental blasts that destroyed complete railheads.**
**Pozières, Somme.**
**April 1918.**

**Bottom left: Fatigue party of Russian POWs clearing the site of an exploded ammunition train. Tens of thousands of Russian POWs were used for the maintenance of the railroad system and the supply roads behind the front.**
**Verdun.**
**1916.**

**Bottom right: German railroad engineers reconstructing a railway in the "Somme desert." In March 1918 the Germany Army again seized the Somme battlefield of 1916 where the road and rail networks had been completely destroyed. Their reconstruction was the necessary condition if the German Army were to maintain this area.**
**Somme.**
**April 1918.**

**Top right: Crowded accommodation of a railway construction company. Railway engineers generally lived in wagons, thus allowing them a high degree of mobility.**
**Eisenbahnbau-Company 96.**
**Western Front.**
**April 1915.**

**Above: Construction of a light railway 200 metres behind the frontline at the Ypres sector. The engine is pushing a wagon loaded with rails. Narrow gauge rails were prefabricated and easily laid.**
**Infantry-Regiment 126.**
**Hooge, Flanders.**
**August 1915.**

**Left: Narrow gauge railway behind the Groenenburg position, between Zillebecke and Zandvoorde, at the Ypres salient. These small lorries were used for material or ammunition transport. If no engine was available men or animals had to pull the lorries.**
**Infantry-Regiment 126.**
**Groenenburg, Flanders.**
**April 1915.**

**Below: Railroad engineers constructing a narrow gauge railway behind the Verdun sector. The embankment is already prepared and fatigue parties are laying the prefabricated rails under the supervision of engineer officers.**
**Eisenbahnbau-Company 20.**
**Eastern bank of the Meuse River, Verdun.**
**February 1916.**

**Opposite**
**Top: German supply columns in Northern France. Behind the front, horse-drawn transport had to take on the major part of the transport business.**
**Northern France.**
**Summer 1915.**

**Bottom left: Supply road passing the village of Epehy in the Somme sector.**
**Epehy, Somme.**
**April 1918.**

**Bottom right: German army truck of the 4. Ersatz-Division with its crew. Motorized transport was rare in the German Army. Note the wheels. German trucks had no tyres but different types of substitutes like iron wheels.**
**4. Ersatz-Division.**
**Flanders.**
**July 1916.**

Karcherstraße
nach Gratreuil
und Ripont.

**Opposite**
**Top left: Road construction during the Verdun battle. The service of supply depended on a fully functioning road and rail network. The soft ground of deep forests directly behind the frontline, rural tracks and destroyed railroads demanded plenty of construction work.**
**Verdun.**
**February 1916.**

**Top right: Supply road called "Karcherstrasse" behind the front in the Champagne sector near Ripont village. It was not only the battlefield which seemed empty in daylight. Supply roads that were under enemy observation could also only be used at night. The tracks in the sand show how active nightly traffic was.**
**Karcherstrasse, Ripont, Champagne.**
**Summer 1917.**

**Bottom left: Barbed wire dumped at the main road of the village of Thelus, south of Vimy Ridge. Night fatigue parties would later collect the wire and bring it to the trenches. The construction and maintenance of wire entanglements consumed much barbed wire.**
**Thelus, Artois.**
**October 1915.**

**Bottom right: Machine gun ammunition and mortar dump under the cover of trees behind the frontline. Machine gun ammunition was provided in portable boxes. The mortars are so-called "Lanzwerfer".**
**France.**
**1916.**

**Right: Infantry unit with an infantry gun on the way to the front. Trucks were used for the quick transport of counterattack forces to the battlefield.**
**France.**
**Autumn 1918.**

Chapter Fifteen

# ANIMALS AT THE FRONTLINE

Next to the millions of soldiers, millions of animals also lived and died on the battlefields at the Western Front. Horses, mules, donkeys, dogs, carrier pigeons and canary-birds served with the troops and accomplished important duties like transport and communication or they served as gas alarms in mining operations. Cattle and pigs were held as livestock by the troops behind the front to supplement the official rations. Even pets like dogs and cats picked up from the destroyed towns and villages lived with the troops in the dugouts or at the rear area camps. However, the infantrymen at the Western Front also had to share their trenches and dugouts with masses of unwelcome fellow occupants: Millions of rats and mice. These rodents were the plague of the Western Front which profited from the corpses of men and animals and from rotten food supplies dispersed everywhere on the shell-torn battlefields. Even the "empty battlefield" of the Western Front offered plenty of space for different kinds of animals to live with the men in the trenches.

At the Western Front transport depended mainly on horse-drawn transport. Motor trucks and cars only took over an increasing part of the transports very gradually. This was especially the case on the Allied side of the front. On the German side motorization and mechanization lagged behind the technical capacities of the Allies. Motor tractors were seldom seen and horses had to draw even the heavy artillery up until the end of the war. Trucks were mainly used for the speedy transport of infantry reserves to threatened sectors of the front. Horses, donkeys and mules accomplished the bulk of transportation. Behind the front fleets of horse-drawn supply wagons brought ammunition, shells, construction material and food to the supply dumps every night. Artillery fire and the shell-torn roads meant a high death toll and an incredible strain for the horses. Sudden shelling often killed dozens of horses, particularly at the railheads. When guns had to change position under fire the horses were sent forward to pull the guns into their new gun pits. Donkeys and mules served as pack animals or pulled the wagons of the narrow gauge railways when locomotives were not available. Pack animals were also used when narrow tracks prohibited any transport by wagons or where the construction of narrow gauge railway tracks was impossible, as was often the case in the Vosges Mountains. Behind the front, but still in the range of hostile guns, the infantry, the artillery and the service of supply had large stables for their horses. The animals spent the daytime there and were taken care of by grooms. In spite of their location, in woods or under camouflage nettings to provide cover against enemy observation, hostile shells frequently hit the stables and killed or wounded horses. Hundreds of thousands of horses lost their lives at the front; they were either killed by artillery shells, disease or exhaustion. Medical care and food supply for the horses, mules and donkeys became a crucial task for the armies as the animals were extremely necessary for maintaining their mobility and supply. In the German armies, corps, divisions, brigades and regiments commissioned veterinary officers and veterinary surgeons were responsible for the shoeing of the horses, the control of the horses' fodder and the control of epidemics. To improve the food supply for the animals the German Army farmed deserted farmland behind the front. When on rest and recreation behind the front, the German infantrymen were often busy with agricultural work and making hay for the horses. But even the added military farming could not assuage the damage inflicted by the strenuous living conditions imposed on the German army horses. By the spring of 1918 the animals were generally in bad health and often too weak to bear the additional work demanded by the beginning of the war of movement.

Animals also played an important role in the maintenance of the communication systems at the Western Front. Direct battle command at the Western Front was conducted by telephone. A sophisticated system of telephone cables connected the various headquarters behind the front with the combat forces in the frontline down to the company commander in his dugout at the forward trench. If they were not buried several metres deep the telephone cables were very vulnerable to shelling. However, there was usually no time and labour to be spent burying the cables; consequently the first victim of any major combat at the Western Front was the communication system. When communications collapsed men and animals had to take over. Even under heavy shelling runners had to deliver orders and reports. Many of these men were killed on their lonely missions. Messenger dogs and carrier pigeons were used to reduce these human losses. But dogs were only partly successful. Messenger dogs had to be trained intensively in preparation for service at the front. Because of their height they had an equal risk of being hit by bullets or shell splinters when they were passing the combat zone and the loss rate of these valuable animals was high. The use of dogs required special dog sentries who were responsible for the care and shelter of the animals. The service of carrier pigeons was less complicated. Even on the shell-torn battlefields the soldiers could transport these animals in small cages on their backs and the cages were easily sheltered in the dugouts of the forward command posts. In June 1916 one of the carrier pigeons became famous when it brought back the last message from the besieged Fort Vaux at Verdun. Cut off from all communications the French garrison was half suffocated and dying of thirst when the Germans began to force their way into the fort's interior with high explosives and flame-throwers. The fort's commander Raynal sent his last carrier-pigeon to the French headquarters at Verdun asking urgently for rescue: "Still resisting but under intense attack with gas and smoke. Rescue urgent. This is our last carrier-pigeon." Contact ceased and three days later Fort Vaux surrendered.

The shell-torn deserts of the Western Front had their own plague: Rats and mice. Profiting from the dead bodies of men and animals that were decomposing everywhere in no-man's-land or on the communication tracks behind the trenches, these rodents lived closely and quite undisturbed together with the infantrymen in the trenches and dugouts. When returning from their daily meal of rotting corpses, the rats and mice infested the food in the soldiers' field bags, or ran across the faces of the sleeping infantrymen. Only gas attacks were dangerous for them, chasing the rats and mice with deadly clouds out of their holes and forcing them to run for their lives. Post-war German regimental histories report that when the British Army shelled the German positions and rear area at the Somme for seven days before their attack on July 1st, 1916, several villages were also heavily shelled with gas. Rats and mice came out of their holes and corners and lay dead everywhere about the place. Sometimes the soldiers were so fed up with their unloved fellow occupants that veritable rat hunts were organized. Then dozens of soldiers would kill all rats and mice within reach with sticks and spades and in this way the rat population would be reduced to a bearable level for a few days. The killed rodents were sometimes collected and tied by their tails to a rope to be photographed like hunting trophies.

When the civilian population fled from their shelled villages behind the front, the cattle, chickens, dogs and cats were often left behind. Cows, pigs and chickens did not survive for a long time. Hungry soldiers searched all over the ruined houses and farms and caught the animals, a welcome additional food supply. Reports and letters from the first months of trench war are full of anecdotes referring to such extraordinary dinners. Stray dogs and cats were picked up by soldiers fond of animals and they lived together with the men at rear area camps or in the dugouts at the frontline. For the officers, hounds were a question of prestige and an expression of their traditional life style. Many of these officers spent their leisure time behind the front hunting together with colleagues and their hounds. Some soldiers had a little cat in their field pack, which shared life and dangers with their master. If their master was killed the dogs and cats usually found another home quickly enough.

**German train columns behind the front. Due to the lack of motorized transport horse-drawn transport was the main means of transportation for ammunition and supply between the railheads and the front.**
**France.**
**1915.**

**Left: German soldier and his foundling kitten. In the deserted towns and villages plenty of pets were left behind by the evacuated civilian population and lived together with the soldiers.**
**Reserve position at the sunken road near Angres, north of Arras, Artois.**
**1915.**

**Opposite**
**Top left: Resting German transport column at Longpont crossroads in the Marne salient in 1918. Columns were shelled at this crossroad a few days before and left a killed horse behind. At the front horses were in permanent danger of being injured or killed.**
**Longpont, Aisne**
**June 1918.**

**Top right: Main street of Forges, three miles behind the frontline at Verdun. An ammunition column came under fire here and lost its load and horses.**
**Forges, Verdun.**
**April 1916.**

**Bottom left: Damaged houses and killed horses in the town of Albert a few days after capture by the German troops in the course of Operation Michael.**
**Albert, Somme.**
**March 1918.**

**Bottom right: This German railhead was heavily shelled in the preceding night. Vehicles and horses of the waiting transport columns were all annihilated.**
**France.**
**1916.**

**Left: Pack mule carrying mortar mines behind the frontline position. Where bad road conditions prohibited wagon transport, horses and mules were used for the transport of heavy loads.**
**Champagne.**
**1917.**

RUE DES TERRASSES

**Opposite**
**Top left: Horse with its foal at a rear area camp in France. Administration and service of supply behind the front had all kinds of animals for transport and food supply.**
**France.**
**1917.**

**Top right: Stables of train columns behind the frontline at the forest near Manancourt at the Somme. Each frontline division had large camps for its transport units in the rear area.**
**Waldlager Manancourt, Somme.**
**January 1917.**

**Bottom left: Artillery vehicles and horses at Camp Manancourt. The camps behind the front offered protection against enemy reconnaissance and bad weather conditions.**
**Waldlager Manancourt, Somme.**
**January 1917.**

**Bottom right: Train horses killed by a direct hit to their stable north of Verdun. Long-range artillery often shelled camps and rear area facilities.**
**Munitions-Kolonne 22.**
**Consenvoye, Verdun.**
**March 1916.**

**Above: Mule transport at the Vosges Mountains. Mountain tracks and snow forced the German supply service to depend on pack mules for bringing ammunition and food to the frontline positions.**
**Schnierlach, Vosges.**
**January 1915.**

**Right: Donkey drawn narrow gauge railway behind the Champagne front. Due to the lack of engines animals were used to pull the wagons.**
**Champagne.**
**July 1916.**

**Food carrying party with transport donkeys at noon. Hot food was served for the frontline troops once a day if the situation allowed. Carrying parties had a difficult and dangerous job bringing the food directly into the trenches. The only help for crossing broken terrain, craters and trenches were the donkeys.**
**Champagne.**
**May 1918.**

**Quiet moments behind the front. German officers sitting together with beer and their dog. Many officers had their own dogs with them.**
**Western Front.**
**1915.**

Chapter Sixteen

# BEHIND THE FRONT - Rear Area Life

The troops at the Western Front lived in a regular system of exchange between front line service, reserve position and rest and recreation behind the front. Next to the dense structures of the service of supply, the quartermasters of the "groups" also had to build and maintain the billets and the hygiene facilities for the rest and recreation of the troops in their respective sectors. The rear area offered the soldiers baths, delousing stations, shops, service clubs, cinemas, theatres and even bookshops. However, the troops' feelings were sometimes mixed when they learned that relief was coming, especially when they were serving in "quiet sectors" with well-constructed dugouts. The reason for this was that behind the front the housing conditions were often exceedingly substandard because the rear area administration occupied the best billets and left only dirty and cold quarters for the front line forces on relief. Behind the front the troops found their billets in villages and little towns. When the villages had been evacuated by their civilian inhabitants houses and barns were mostly in a rotten condition. The troops that quartered temporarily did not care for the unpleasant billets and heated their quarters with any available wooden furniture and doors in the cold season. In this way many houses were cannibalized. The houses and barns were often only equipped with uncomfortable bunk beds constructed on wooden frames with wire netting. The civilian population of the still inhabited villages had to accept the quartering of soldiers who lived together with them in their homes. The rural regions of Belgium and France however, did not offer enough billets for quartering thousands of troops. As a result the rear area administration constructed barrack camps everywhere behind the front in the cover of wooded terrain. The typical hut-camp consisted of wooden barracks. Duckboards bridged the mud between the huts. The accommodation consisted of bunk beds, a few crude tables and benches, a few washbowls, a round iron stove and a broom for cleaning the billet. Between sixteen and twenty-four men inhabited such an uncomfortable billet, which nevertheless looked like a sweet home to the trench soldiers when they were relieved after several weeks of service in an active sector. For millions of men at the Western Front the years that they spent in the atmosphere of crowded shelters and barracks became part of their collective war experience.

Often front line troops on relief faced not rest and recreation but drill and practice marches which were meant to improve discipline and order which, many officers argued, had deteriorated in the trenches. A Bavarian company-sergeant-major described ironically in a letter from June 1916 how he experienced relief behind the front in the Vosges Mountains near the city of Colmar: "My dears! We are expecting to be relieved. The so-called relief will be twenty-five roll calls and fifty reports and inspections per day. Twice a vaccination against typhoid fever. Fatigue duty to produce 500 fascines between 5am and 2pm. Then inspection of the rifles. Three hours march to Colmar in the valley for bathing and four hours back up the mountain. We will come home from the bath, sweating, and covered with dust, perfectly refreshed for the next thirty days. The beautiful life of a warrior! The day often starts at 3am. To make things easier we sleep in our uniforms and take off only our boots. If in the middle of the night one of the young officers decides to issue an order to the company that he forgot to deliver and which could wait till the next morning, I have to run in the darkness from barrack to barrack, wake up the men and issue the order. Often orders are changed three times and issued to the men again and again, until the men threaten that the next visitor will be kicked out of the barrack" (cit. Remus collection).

A typical German rear area organization was that of "*Gruppe* Prosnes" which held the line between Cornillet Hill and Aubérive village in the Champagne sector during the summer of 1917. The group received its name from the severely disputed village of Prosnes. The sector was characterized by a range of dominating hills between Nauroy and Moronvilliers which controlled the Suippe valley in the north and the highway Reims-Verdun in the south. "Cornillet Hill", "Luginsland", "Hochberg" and "Fichtelberg" became renowned during the Champagne battles and were frequently cited in the German Army reports. The Prosnes group constructed a dense system of defensive positions behind the forward trenches. Two reserve lines ran south of the Suippe River at a distance of 2500 metres from each other. The 3rd reserve line was 7500 metres behind the forward trenches on the north bank of the river. The rear area facilities were covered further north in the wooded terrain of the hilly country between Retourne and the Suippe River and extended over an area of forty-four square miles. Thousands of barracks and hutments filled the thin pine-groves and formed little cities with all the necessary accommodation. "Gruppe Prosnes" depended completely on barrack camps to billet the troops because there were only two villages – Aussonce and la Neuville – in the rear area zone. Neither village offered sufficient quarters for the troops in the group's sector which consisted of forty to fifty thousand men. Like the combat zone, the rear area was divided into four sectors numbered XI-XIV. Each sector was organized in a different number of camp districts. Sector XIII consisted of twelve camp districts, while sector XIV had only five. This depended on the different size of the camp districts and on the extension of the wooded terrain. Approximately eight miles behind the forward line, the rear area facilities had to be camouflaged in order to avoid hostile shelling. Barrack camps near the front could only be erected under the cover of vegetation. Within the camp districts a number of different barrack camps existed. These camps were designated within the camp districts by numbers or letters but they were mainly known in the troops by names like "Badisches Lager" or "Mecklenburger Lager" which referred to the home states of the troops that had first been billeted there. Others were called "*Kaiser Lager*" or "*Kronprinzen Lager*", honouring the imperial house, or "*Mudra Lager*", referring to a famous German general. Each camp had its camp commander, administrative facilities, kitchens, wells and hospitals. For example, sector XIV counted fourteen wells and sector XII seven hospitals. The numbers in the other sectors varied depending on the geological conditions and the size of the camps. Labour forces from the group constructed the barracks and engineers were responsible for the drilling of the wells. Newly arrived infantry divisions in the sector of the Prosnes group had to first occupy their designated rear area sector. For the newcomers the camp districts were confusing labyrinths and special camp maps were issued to them. Based on the camp assigned to them by the group command, the regiments ordered some companies into the battle line that had to relieve the front line forces in the following night. The companies' administration, service of supply and rolling kitchen remained behind in the camps, under the command of the company-sergeant-major who was responsible for organizing and sending food and supplies to his company in the forward line and for receiving and billeting the company when on relief in the rear area. Often serving in the same sector for months many regiments developed a close adherence to their camps.

During the second half of the war the intensive use of the provisory hutments and barracks, storm and rain and the increasing lack of labour and construction materials led to a progresive degeneration of the camps. In the first few days of July 1918, when the 239. Infantry Division assembled its troops north of the Suippe valley for the offensive scheduled to start on July 15th, the men were billeted in the old camps of the Prosnes group. Gerhard Scholtz, then a nineteen-year-old artillery lieutenant, found the barracks half ruined and stripped of their doors, windows and furniture. The roofs were full of holes and consequently Scholtz thought it "quite ridiculous" that they bothered to go inside for the night. It made no difference whether they slept indoors or out. Even in the barrack they could see the bright night sky above them. These hutments no longer offered any protection against rain or winter (cit. Scholtz: *Die Schlacht im Westen*, p.114-117).

**Opposite**
**Left: Rear area traffic in the village of Ornes a few days after the capture of the village during the attack on the fortress of Verdun. Several weeks later the village was completely destroyed by artillery fire.**
**Ornes, Verdun.**
**March 1916.**

**Right: Typical German hut camp in the rear area. The villages and towns of the rural areas in France and Belgium often did not offer enough quarters to billet the troops. Huge barrack camps were constructed and became home for the troops behind the front.**
**France.**
**1917.**

**Below: Hut camp of an engineer training unit in France in July 1918. As well as resting the frontline troops on relief, the rear area camps had to house the services of supply and training units**
**Pionier-Feld-Rekruten-Depot 1.**
**July 1918.**

245

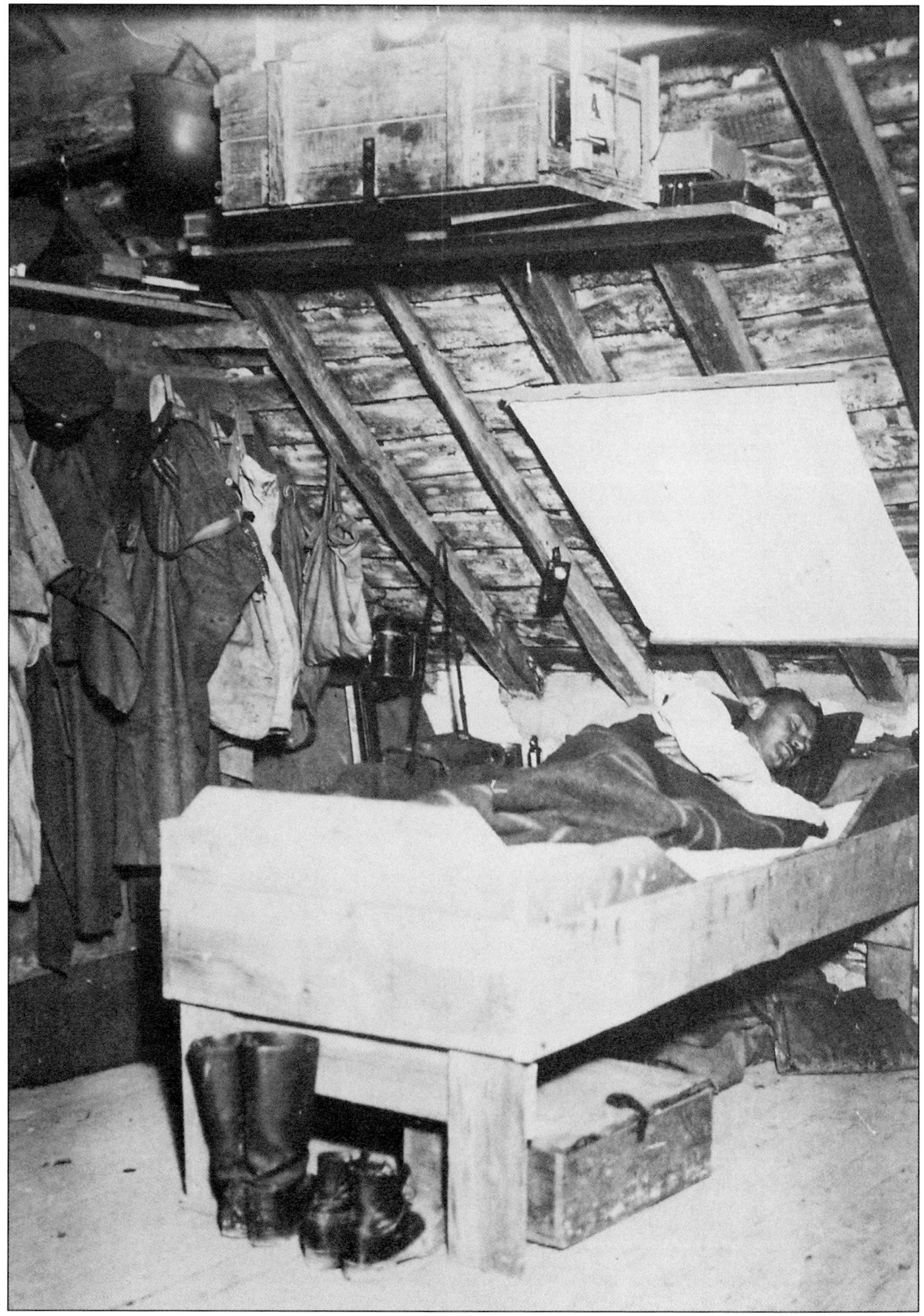

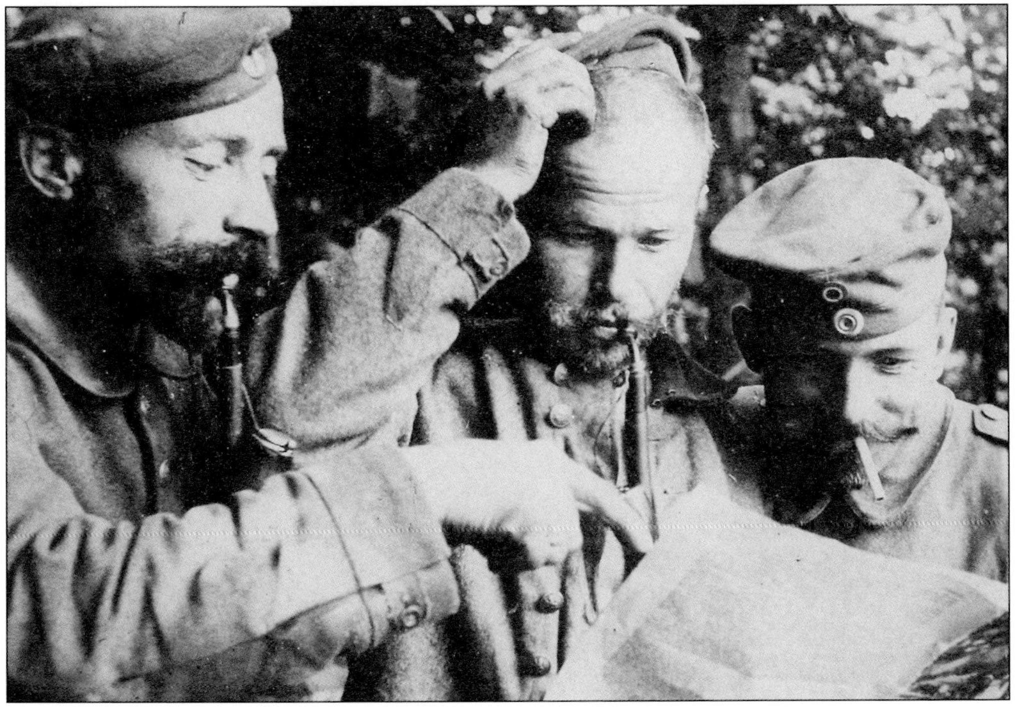

**Opposite**
**Top left: Camouflaged German camp in the Argonne forest. The dense woods and deep ravines of the Argonne forest concealed an elaborate network of camps.**
**Charlepaux Mill, Argonne.**
**Summer 1915.**

**Bottom left: Campsite for resting German infantry in 1915. At the beginning of the war infantry were frequently housed in tents. Part of each soldier's personal equipment was a tent square. By combining a few tent squares tents could be constructed easily.**
**France.**
**Summer 1915.**

**Right: Officer's quarter in the loft of a village house. Compared with the crowded billets of the rank and file this quarter is quite luxurious.**
**France.**
**October 1917.**

**Left: In wooded areas the German forces constructed log cabins made of local trees. These log cabins were furnished with elaborate verandas and other decorations.**
**Lorraine.**
**Spring 1917.**

**Bottom left: Quiet moments behind the front. Newspapers became more and more important for morale and propaganda purposes. Armies and divisions published their own periodicals.**
**France.**
**1916.**

**Below: A view into the interior of an officer's log cabin at a rear area camp behind the Lorraine sector.**
**Lorraine.**
**Spring 1917.**

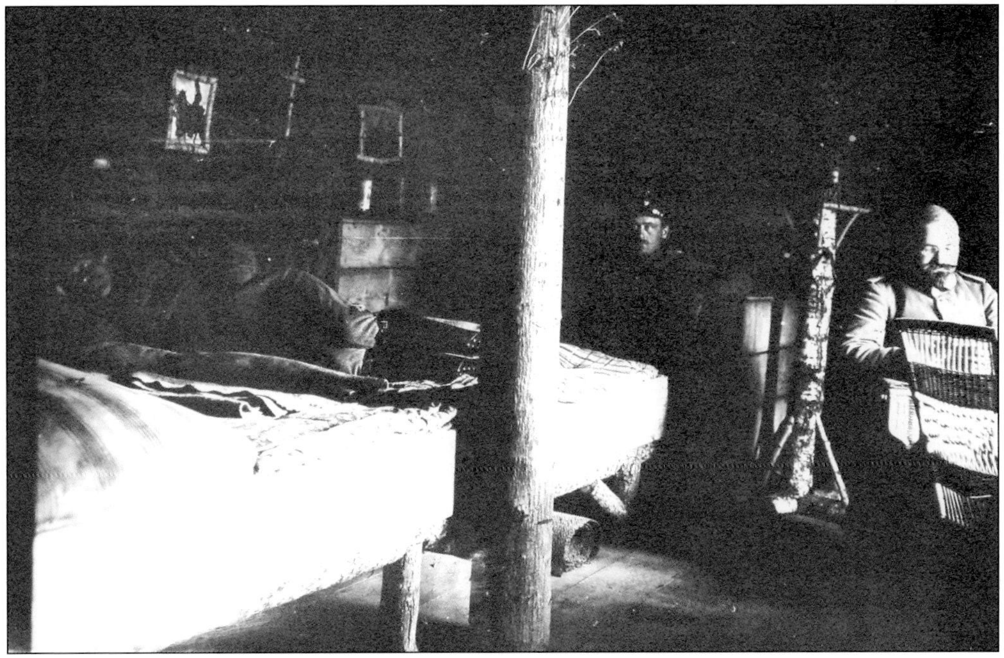

**Top left: Christmas Eve at a barrack camp in the rear area near Avaux village 5 miles behind the Aisne front. Christmas was an important day for the German soldiers at the frontline and in the rear area.**
**Avaux, Aisne.**
**Christmas 1917.**

**Above: Headquarters of the Brigade-Ersatz-Bataillon 84 in the Vosges sector. The timber forest of the Vosges Mountains provided plenty of building material for elaborate buildings. Note the wire netting on the roof for camouflage purposes.**
**Brigade-Ersatz-Bataillon 84 Offenburg.**
**Markirch sector, Vosges.**
**Summer 1916.**

**Left: Military band playing at Condé for the resting troops. Rest and recreation behind the front included musical performances by military bands.**
**Condé, Argonne.**
**April 25, 1916.**

**Above: Performance of a military amateur theatre as part of a holiday behind the front somewhere in France.**
**France.**
**1916/17.**

**Top right:Typical German festival with beer, fried sausages and a brass band in the rear area somewhere in France. Such festivals are a typical part of the German national custom and were indispensable for the troops at the front.**
**France.**
**1916/17.**

**Right: Army cinema at Thonne les Près. Cinemas played an important role in the entertainment programmes for the troops' comfort and welfare at the Western Front.**
**Thonne les Près, France.**
**1917.**

Ortskommandant:
Leutnant Becker
Wache
Schusssicherer
Keller.
Ortskommandantur

**Opposite: Guards of the town major in front of the town headquarters in an unknown village near Reims. In the combat zone a town major maintained order and discipline of the billeting and passing troops.**
**III. Battalion, Infantry-Regiment 471.**
**Near Reims, Champagne.**
**September 1917.**

**Right: German Army street signs at a village near Laon. The dense military traffic behind the front demanded a system of army street signs and signposts.**
**5th Company, Infantry-Regiment 151.**
**Samoussy, Aisne.**
**July 1917.**

**Below: Ammunition columns and trains passing a road fork somewhere in Northern France. In fulfilling their duty behind the front the services of supply frequently became the target of hostile shelling.**
**Northern France.**
**1917.**

DROMARD LUDET
Verkaufsstelle
des
I. Batl. Fuß. Art. Rgts. 10
Limonade 10 Pfg
Selters 5 Pfg

Feldbuchhandlung
Soldatenheim

**Opposite**
**Top left: Military stores of a heavy German artillery unit. Military stores were always an attraction and a meeting point for the troops.**
**I. Battalion, Fuss-Artillery-Regiment 10.**
**France.**
**1916/17.**

**Top right: Members of a German field post office. Field post was the only way for the soldiers at the front to keep in touch with their families at home. The field post service was part of the service of supply and very important for keeping up morale.**
**Deutsche Feldpost 324, 1. Armee.**
**Champagne.**
**May 1917.**

**Bottom left: German field post office at Anizy le Château north of the Aisne front. The military field post system did not only have to transport letters and postcards but plenty of parcels as well. Families at home sent food, clothes and other presents to their soldiers at the front.**
**Anizy le Château, Aisne.**
**May 1917.**

**Bottom right: German Army bookstore and soldier's home in the rear area. At the Western Front, the German Army built up a system of facilities to serve the social, physical and intellectual demands of the troops.**
**France.**
**1916/17.**

**Below: Troops' comfort and welfare centre in the Verdun sector. The facilities consist of a photographic studio, a delousing station and a bath.**
**Gibercy, Verdun.**
**1916.**

**Above: Interior of a German Army bookstore at the Western Front. Army bookstores offered a wide selection of books and newspapers for the troops but these were subjected to army censorship.**
**France.**
**1916/17.**

**Opposite**
**Top left: Toilets for the rank and file at a rear area camp. The crowded living conditions of the front and rear area deprived the soldiers of all privacy.**
**Western Front.**
**1915.**

**Top right: Shoemakers of Ersatz-Infantry-Regiment 51 at work. Army boots were permanently wearing out at the front and had to be repaired repeatedly.**
**Ersatz-Infantry-Regiment 51.**
**Remenauville, St. Mihiel.**
**October 1915.**

**Bottom: German infantrymen and army horses farming land behind the front. Wide areas were evacuated by the civilian population. The scarcity of food motivated the forces to farm the abandoned land.**
**France.**
**1916.**

**Above: Hay harvest near Essey at the St. Mihiel salient. Due to the German Army's dependence on horse-drawn transport haymaking was an essential duty for the forces.**
**Fuss-Artillery-Regiment 8**
**Essey, St. Mihiel.**
**Summer 1915.**

**Opposite**
**Top left: Military review somewhere behind the Western Front. In the autocratic military system reviews were the only occasions for the soldiers at the front to meet their superior commanders and the rulers of their home states.**
**Western Front.**
**1915/16.**

**Top right: General Deimling awarding the Iron Cross to troops of Infantry-Regiment 126 behind the Flanders sector. The Iron Cross was the most prestigious decoration in the German Army.**
**Infantry-Regiment 126.**
**Hooge, Flanders.**
**August 1915.**

**Bottom: The Grand Duke of Baden Friedrich II. inspecting Infantry-Regiment 113 at the front. This regiment had its origin in the Grand Duchy of Baden and the sovereign maintained close ties to his troops.**
**Auménancourt le Grand, Champagne.**
**Autumn 1915.**

**Below: Training ground of Infantry-Regiment 126 north of Verdun. Behind the front the German Army was in a permanent process of training to improve tactical performance and to train new recruits. Experienced forces like Infantry-Regiment 126 had mixed feelings about this training and called the training ground a "children's playground."**
**Infantry-Regiment 126.**
**Mouaville, Verdun.**
**June 1916.**

**Right: Soldiers of Infantry-Regiment 126 exercising attack techniques at the regimental training ground. Ladders played an important role in attacks against forts to bridge the ditches.**
**Infantry-Regiment 126.**
**Mouaville, Verdun.**
**June 1916.**

CHAPTER SEVENTEEN

# MEDICAL AID AND HOSPITALS

It was the fate of many soldiers at the Western Front to be wounded in action or to fall ill. According to the "German Army medical report" (*Sanitätsbericht*) and the statements of the German *Reichsarchiv* 4,215,662 cases of wounded German soldiers were registered in the Great War at all fronts. The majority were wounded at the Western Front: 3,088,743. The Allies paid an even higher price at the Western Front. In the same period the French Army alone reported 3,419,000 wounded soldiers. 300,000 of the French wounded died in hospital. On the German side the situation in the hospitals was better. There, ninety-four out of 100 wounded men survived. According to these statistics 6-9% of the wounded soldiers at the Western Front died. Another important figure was the ratio between the killed and the wounded. In the German Army this ratio was approximately 1:3. This means that of four reported losses one man was killed and three were wounded. A remarkable exception was the period between August 1917 and November 1918 where the ratio increased to 1:4/4.5. Only in 1916, between February and October, when the battles at Verdun and the Somme raged, was this ratio surpassed 1:4.2. These numbers confirm the intensity of the fighting.

A complex system of medical services was necessary to handle such numbers. The medical service of the German Army was under the command of the "Director of Medical Services". He was responsible for 33,359 physicians and 92,000 medical orderlies. 15,000 of them were killed in action, including 1325 physicians. For the evacuation of the wounded soldiers, 174 regular and improvised ambulance-trains were at the disposal of the German High Command. This transport capacity was assisted by eighty-six ambulance trains of the volunteer medical service. The trains had a capacity for 300 wounded men each. For the control of the medical service each army command had a medical staff. The army corps had a corps medical officer who controlled twelve field hospitals of the respective corps. In the reserve corps the number of field hospitals was limited to four. The divisional medical officer of the infantry division was responsible for two ambulance companies. Ambulance companies counted in their ranks thirteen medical officers and 297 NCOs and rank and file, fifty-three horses and fourteen ambulance and supply vehicles. The ambulance companies maintained dressing stations near the front. Regimental and battalion medical officers and their orderlies managed the regimental aid station and the advanced dressing stations in the trenches. Field hospitals and dressing stations were billeted in tents or in dugouts close to the fire zone. In 1916 the infantry divisions were reduced to one ambulance company and two field hospitals. In the rear area permanent military hospitals were established to replace the field hospitals. Most of the transportable wounded were evacuated by train to Germany where they were treated in "reserve hospitals". Many of the reserve hospitals were established in former school buildings, châteaus, factory buildings or monasteries. At the front and in rural areas, where large buildings that would have been appropriate for the use as hospitals were not available, churches were often occupied by the field hospitals. However, the churches turned out to be bad hospitals as most of them were dark, damp and difficult to heat.

In the combat zone the wounded soldiers received first aid from their comrades or medical orderlies. Each soldier carried a first-aid kit on his body containing the necessary surgical dressing. Lightly wounded men had to find the way to the next advanced dressing station on their own; there they received preliminary treatment and a register card containing information about the wound and authorization to go to a collecting point in the rear area. Seriously wounded men were evacuated by stretcher-bearers from the medical service. However, these were often not available and comrades would have to use their shelter half and a rod as provisional hammocks to bring the wounded back to a casualty clearing station. At the advanced dressing stations the wounded received their first treatment and the wounds were bandaged properly. From the advanced dressing stations the stretcher-bearers quickly transported the seriously wounded to the main dressing stations for further treatment. If the dressing station was near the rails of a narrow gauge railway, or if it was accessible for ambulance trucks, the wounded soldiers were evacuated to the main dressing stations by these transport vehicles. But heavy shelling often prevented evacuation and the wounded were left waiting in crowded dugouts till dusk to be evacuated under the cover of darkness. At the main dressing stations a staff of surgeons awaited the wounded and operated the urgent cases. The surgeons had to work under relatively improvised conditions in dugouts, tents or half destroyed villages. Here they extracted the bullets and the shell and bomb splinters from the mutilated bodies of their patients. Between 1914-1918 there was still no cure available against gangrene and tattered limbs usually had to be amputated to avoid the decay of the wounded tissue. Behind the front in France and Belgium a system of field hospitals and military hospitals received the wounded that were sent from the main dressing stations on ambulance trucks and ambulance trains. Serious cases, who needed a longer period for recovery, were sent by ambulance trains to Germany where reserve hospitals received the patients for further treatment.

As well as being responsible for the treatment and evacuation of the wounded the medical service was also responsible for the health, hygienic conditions and treatment of ill soldiers. Vaccinations, regular medical examinations, the construction and disinfection of the toilets in the trenches and the establishment of bathing and delousing stations behind the front helped to maintain the health of the men at the front.

In the first months of the war thousands of wounded soldiers died of tetanus. The wounds were tattered and contaminated with dirt. After they started vaccinating the wounded tetanus disappeared. The troops suffered from colds and influenza, intestinal trouble and dysentery. Typhoid fever also occurred occasionally. What was new was the fact that a growing number of soldiers suffered from various symptoms of nervous stress. The overwhelming effect of drumfire or the experience of being buried alive in collapsing dugouts produced the phenomenon of shell shock and long-term nervous diseases. Nervous breakdowns resulted in chronic bladder, stomach or heart diseases, or in the dumbness, deafness, paralysis or tremors of the patient. When the German Army realised this problem they established special hospitals for cases of nervous disease at Malonne near Namur and St. Solf at Valenciennes. Physicians disagreed on the medical grounds for the nervous diseases. Some argued that the shelling caused physical damage in the nervous system. Others thought shell shock was a psychological problem.

However, the plague of preceding wars, when the number of soldiers dying of diseases exceeded by far the losses of killed and wounded men, seemed to have been overcome by the modern system of health care in the Great War. The only exception was Spanish influenza which appeared at the European battlefields in 1918 and was very contagious. The mobility of the troops was responsible for the spreading of the epidemic. Thus 1918 was the year of influenza at the Western Front and it killed as many people as the war did. Captured Allied POWs passing through the frontline brought the deadly infection with them, which, after years of war and malnutrition, claimed many victims in the German Army and civilian population. The sick rate was high and paralysed complete units at the front. Ulrich Sander reports that when in position at Billy-Montigny, some kilometres east of Lens, 90% of his engineers were sick with influenza and could not leave their underground shelters (Sander: *Pioniere*, p.283). The death toll inflicted by Spanish influenza was high in both camps.

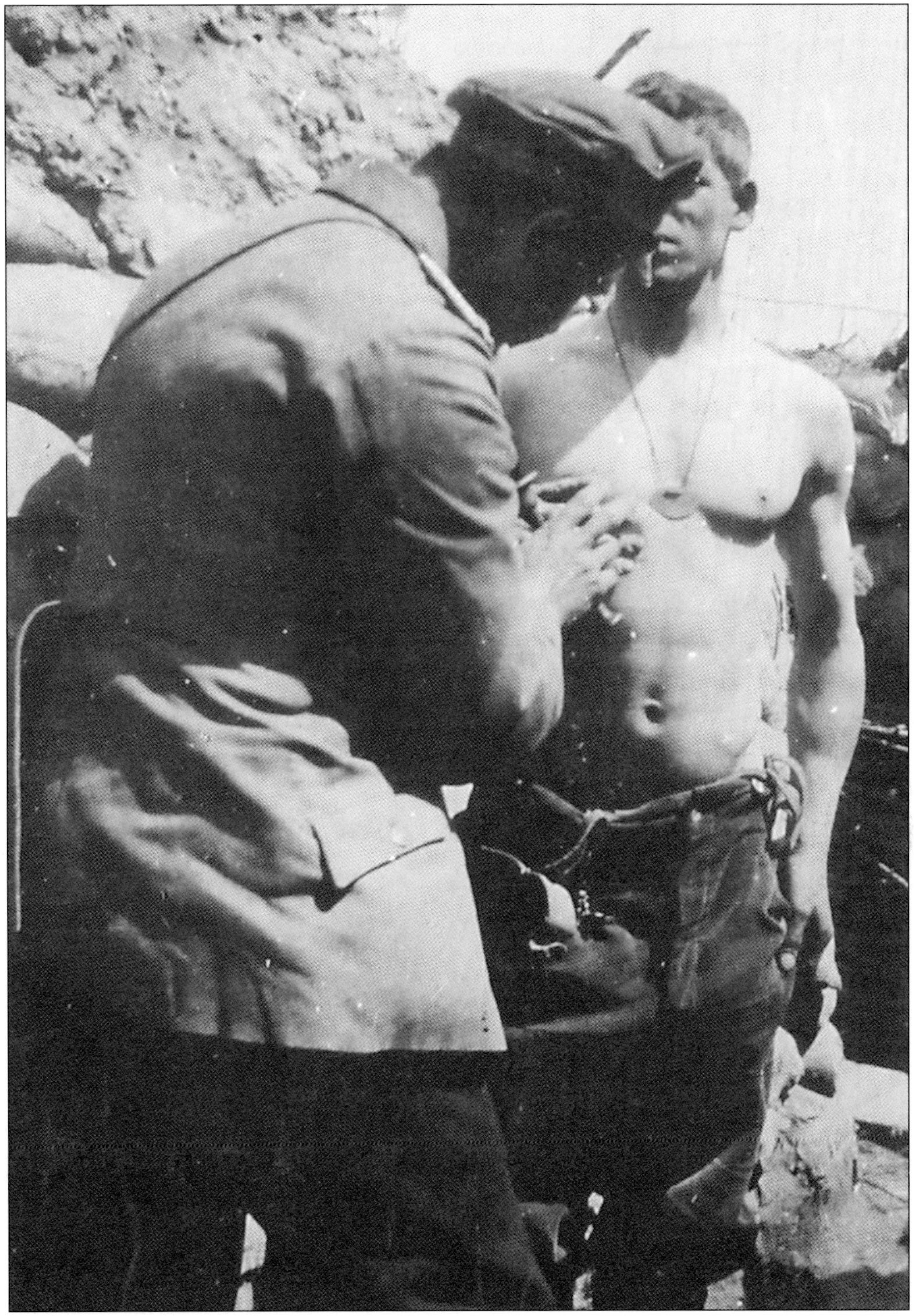

**Health check in the trenches. Military doctors had strict control over the hygienic and health conditions of the soldiers in the trenches.**
**52. Infantry-Division.**
**Somme.**
**1915/16.**

**Right: Rest on the march. German ambulance column at a Belgian village stopping for a rest. Some confiscated civil vehicles are visible between the ambulance vehicles. All vehicles are marked with the Red Cross flag.**
**Belgium.**
**Summer 1915.**

**Opposite**
**Top left: Field dressing station at Juvincourt at the beginning of the Aisne offensive. Wounded soldiers waiting on stretchers for evacuation by ambulance cars. In the background one can see advancing German columns.**
**52. Infantry-Division.**
**Juvincourt, Aisne.**
**May 1918.**

**Top right: Waiting for patients. German field dressing station at Flanders. Stretchers have been dumped under the shelter for emergency cases.**
**Flanders.**
**Winter 1916/17.**

**Bottom left: Medical orderlies loading wounded soldiers into horse-drawn ambulance vehicles behind the frontline. The field dressing station is well camouflaged in the forest.**
**Sanitaets-Kompanie 560.**
**France.**
**Summer 1917.**

**Bottom right: Destroyed German ambulance column after an air raid. Several medical orderlies have been killed between the destroyed ambulance vehicles.**
**Northern France.**
**September 23, 1918.**

**Right: German motorized ambulance vehicles at the destroyed town of Nesles during Operation Michael. Mobility was a prerequisite for the ambulance service.**
**Nesles, Somme.**
**March 1918.**

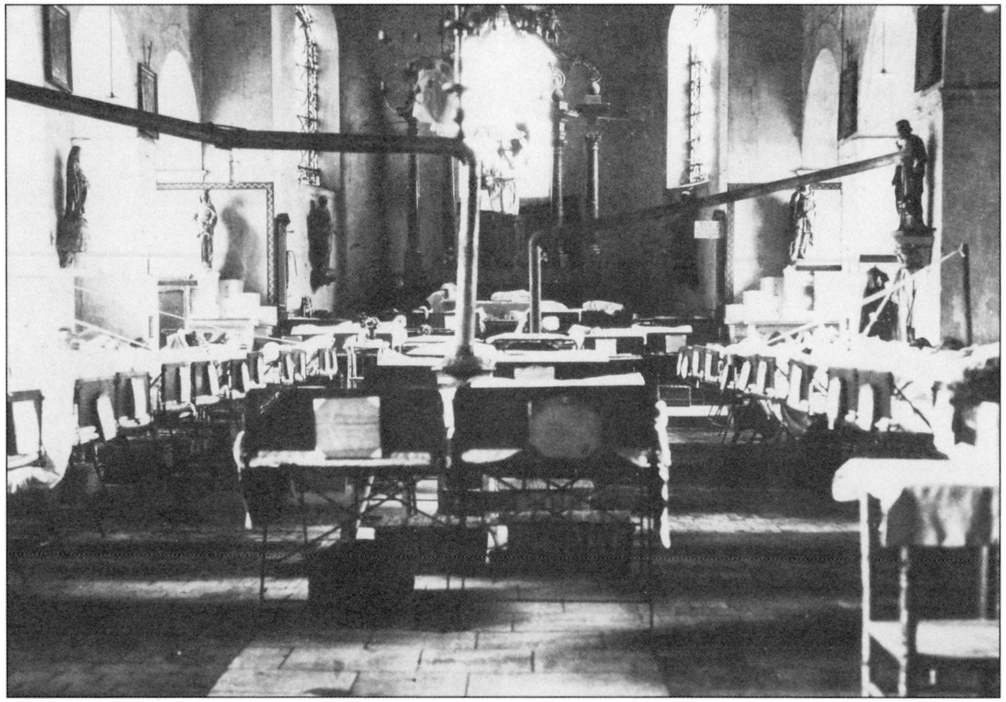

**Left: French church converted into a field hospital. Before major battles special ambulance facilities were set up to cope with the expected stream of wounded soldiers. This church hospital is ready to receive new patients.
France.
1916.**

**Bottom left: Overcrowded field hospital north of Verdun. The battle of Verdun in 1916 sent thousands of wounded men into the hospitals. This hospital was seven miles behind the frontline.
Vilosnes sur Meuse, Verdun.
Summer 1916.**

**Below: After being evacuated to military hospitals in Germany, seriously wounded soldiers often spent many months there for recovery. Many were disabled for the rest of their lives.
Germany.
September 1915.**

**Opposite: Wounded soldiers and medical orderlies in front of hospital barracks. Where larger buildings like schools or churches were not available, barracks were built to house the field hospitals. Above the entrance door a sign is visible with the inscription: "Fearless and Faithful".
France.
1917.**

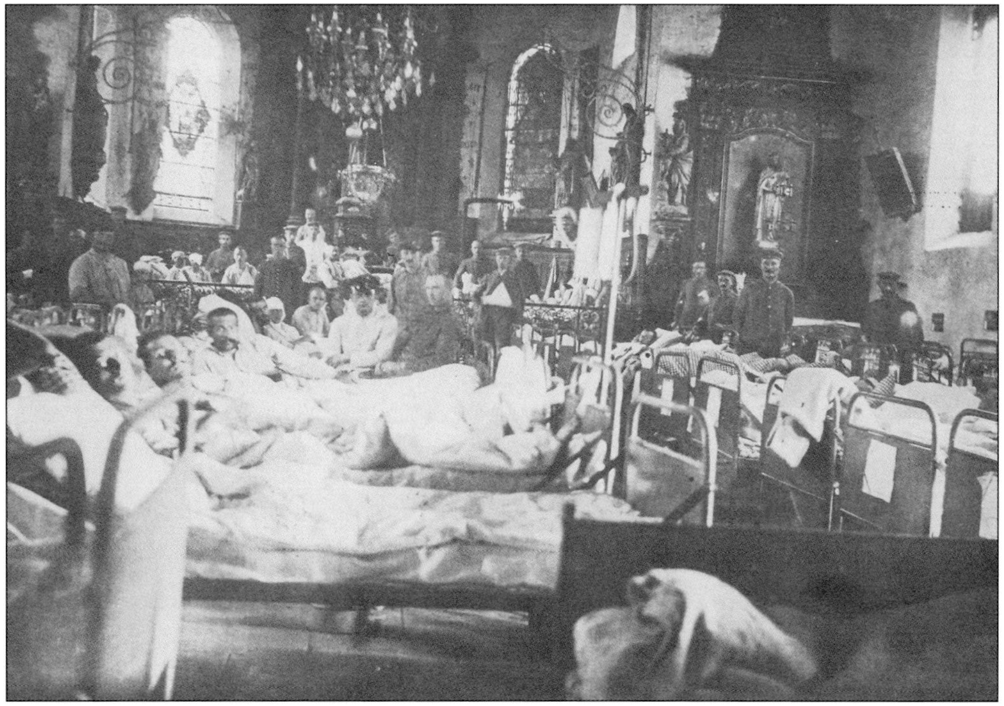

Chapter Eighteen

# THE END -
## What the Western Front Left Behind

According to the ceasefire agreement signed by the Allies and Germany in the headquarters' train of Field Marshal Foch at the forest of Compiègne the fighting at the Western Front ended on November 11th, 1918 at 12am. Some battalions received the order to ceasefire no earlier than 11:50 am, some even later; more lives were thus lost. The ceasefire was greeted by the men at the front with disbelief, astonishment and a huge feeling of relief: They had survived. But even on the Allies' side there was no open expression of joy at the front. The change from violent combat to peaceful idleness was too sudden. On the German side very few realized that the aftermath of the war lay still ahead and that hard times of political disorganization and economic crisis awaited the men coming home from the war. In the night of this last day of battle thousands of Very lights and flares went up at the Western Front and illuminated the darkness. On both sides of the line the soldiers fired their supplies of light rockets into the sky at the end of this memorable day.

When the fighting ceased the shell-torn battlefields of the trench war in Belgium and Northern France were already far behind the German armies which had retired in front of the advancing Allied forces. The fighting armies left the cratered deserts of Flanders, Artois, the Somme and the Aisne and the Allied rear area organization and service of supply took over. During this time, on the banks of the Meuse River, the American Army fought its way through the German defensive zone where four years of trench war in the Argonne forest and north of Verdun had dotted the country with shell holes and trenches. It was only at Lorraine, the Vosges Mountains and the Alsace that the Germans still held the trenches that they had occupied since 1914.

The ceasefire contract stipulated a quick evacuation by the German Army of the occupied parts of Belgium and France including Lorraine and the Alsace. Immediately after November 11th the German divisions left their positions and started their march back to the German border. At this time the American pilot Jimmy Meissner and the war correspondent Webb Miller passed the ceasefire line of the American sector with an aircraft and observed the German retreat from the air. No shot was fired against this single aircraft. On the ground they observed endless grey columns of German infantry and army vehicles that covered the roads. Exploding German ammunition dumps sent their smoke into the sky (cit: Miller: *Ich fand keinen Frieden*, p.72-75). The German infantrymen had only one thing on their minds: To get home. In Germany a revolution broke out. The Emperor had already resigned. In the face of the growing disorganization and the low morale of the tired forces evacuation of the troops, in adherence to the ceasefire timetable, was a priority for the German General Staff. Lacking transport the German Army had to leave behind plenty of valuable war material and supply dumps. Retreating soldiers pillaged the depots.

Not only material and supplies were left behind however. The Allies inherited several millions of square miles of devastated country, hundreds of destroyed villages and towns and a traffic system worn out by four years of war. When the first inhabitants came back to their villages and farms in the former battle zone they were confronted with a vision of unimaginable destruction. Many villages and farms had completely vanished from the surface of the earth. Grey or red dust of stones and bricks pulverized by millions of shells coloured the ground where their houses had once stood. Where ruins had survived, houses and farms had been turned into strongpoints belted with wire. Each cellar had been turned into a shellproof dugout or machine gun post. The farmland was cratered with millions of shell holes, cut by half-collapsed trenches, and was covered by impenetrable networks of barbed wire. Thousands of concrete pillboxes, intact or blown to pieces, dotted the fields. Half-collapsed dugouts and the shafts of destroyed wells hidden between the ruins waited as death traps for careless people. Broken weapons, dispersed small arms ammunition and bombs, and everywhere the duds of high explosives and gas shells made the former battlefields dangerous places for the inhabitants returning home. The vegetation had also reoccupied the shell-torn desert covering the treacherous ground and its dangers with a thick layer of weeds. Many years and a tremendous amount of work were necessary for clearing and reconstructing the fields of the trench war. The first men to work there were German POWs. After the armistice POW camps were erected on the old battlefields to billet the prisoners' working parties. Old wire was used to enclose the camps. The prisoners' job was to cut the rusty wire obstacles into small pieces with wire-cutters, and to fill the trenches and craters with earth. They also had the odious task of clearing away dead bodies and high explosives which were dispersed everywhere along the former frontline. Depending on the soil, some bodies were only half-decomposed, others reduced completely to skeletons and single bones. Still dressed in their half-rotten uniforms and boots, the dead soldiers confronted their living comrades with ghostly scenes of death and horror. The remnants of the bodies were collected and brought to nearby war cemeteries. The unexploded high explosives were very dangerous and still imposed a death toll on the men clearing the battlefield. Ammunition and duds were simply piled up and exploded.

Eight years after the armistice the American correspondent Webb Miller revisited the battlefield at Verdun. In his articles he described the deserted hills on the banks of the River Meuse as being covered with brushwood and weeds which had turned the former farmland into a depressing wilderness. In the former forests young trees grew up between the rotten trunks and stumps of the dead old trees that had been shot to pieces by the artillery. Only a few steps from the path, skulls, bones, rotten boots, the rusty parts of rifles and machine guns, steel helmets riddled with bullets and the rotting remnants of battledresses lay dispersed. Between the forts Douaumont and Vaux an old French priest spent his time collecting the shattered bones of the killed. At Douaumont Hill French workers erected a huge charnel house where the remnants would later be placed. In the 1920s monuments were already under construction at many places at the Western Front. The famous "Lion of Souville", marking the high water mark of the German advance at Verdun, and the concrete block of the "Tranchee des Baionettes" were both finished. At the Somme the "Monument to the Missing" was to record the names of all Commonwealth soldiers missed in action for posterity. Hundreds of other monuments would follow (cit. Miller: *Ich fand keinen Frieden*, p.176-184).

In the 1920s and 1930s the old battlefields became the destination of an increasing flow of battlefield tourists. Veterans who wanted to see the battlefields of their youth again, relatives seeking the graves of their loved ones and mere tourists travelled to the former Western Front. Michelin published battlefield guides with detailed descriptions for tourists and local travel agencies offered special trips to the battlefields. Restaurants and little hotels, which were often decorated with war souvenirs, received the travellers in the ruined towns and villages. Many villages in the former battle zone were not reconstructed. Even eight years after the war others were only partly inhabited, like Vienne le Château at the Argonne forest. Only 600 of the 2000 pre-war inhabitants had come home. But life had to go on. In the following decades an intensive programme of reconstruction and re-cultivation took place. The towns and villages were rebuilt and farmland was cleared of the debris of war. Apparently, there are only monuments and war cemeteries left to commemorate the war in the trenches in Belgium and France. However, even today, trenches, shell holes and the collapsed entries of old dugouts are still visible in the woods of the Argonne forest or north of Verdun. Sometimes, in the evening light, the early shadows reveal flattened shell holes on a meadow on the slopes of Côtes Lorraines'. The thick mountain forests of the Vosges hide forgotten pillboxes in their shade. The earth of the former battlefields is still full of shell splinters, shrapnel, bullets and wire. But where once tens of thousands of men were killed in the trenches of the shell-torn Western Front battlefields, farmers now grow potatoes and corn.

**Abandoned German position at the Aisne in autumn 1918. A zone of hundreds of miles of an incredible devastation passed through Belgium and France when the fighting ceased.**
**Aisne.**
**Autumn 1918.**

**Opposite: Only some months after the cease fire nature is already recapturing the battle zone and covering the traces of war with fresh vegetation.**
**France.**
**1918/19.**

**Left: The "Somme desert", renowned for its wartime destruction. All the infrastructure having been razed during 1916-18 the inhabitants found a veritable desert when they came home.**
**Somme.**
**1918.**

**Bottom left: Unknown village somewhere at the Aisne. Four years of shelling and trench war made such places an unpleasant site even for their military inhabitants. Just what the civilian inhabitants felt when they came home after the war has never been written about.**
**Aisne.**
**1918.**

**Below: The town of Etain was behind the German lines. The level of destruction is typical of what happened to so many towns in Belgium and France.**
**Etain, Verdun.**
**1918**

**Opposite: Ruined church Sainte-Pierre at Roye one year after the war ended. The inhabitants came back. Children gazing at a roundabout amongst ruins.**
**Roye, Somme.**
**1919.**

**The same place under German occupation in 1917/18.
Roye, Somme.
1917/18.**

**"Le tourelle" outpost near Fort Douaumont in 1933. Even fifteen years after the war only some weed and bushes covered the shell torn ground. Veterans of the third battalion of the French Infantry Regiment 74 erected a monument at this site. The battalion lost 72% of its effective holding this position for some hours.**
**Fort Douaumont, Verdun.**
**1933.**

**Postcard from Verdun. "Le Lion de Souville" monument marks the site of the high watermark of the German attack at Verdun in 1916. Millions of bursting shells pulverized the earth and burned the vegetation. Note the danger sign. Contaminated with non-exploded shells and chemical ammunition the former battle zone is still dangerous.**
**St. Fine Chapelle, Verdun.**
**1933.**

**Only one of hundreds dispersed along the former Western Front: War cemetery near Arras: 34,500 individual graves and 18,000 buried in mass graves. But many never got a grave. Maison Blanche, Artois. 1933.**

# BIBLIOGRAPHY


Bloem, Walter: *Vormarsch/Sturmsignal!/Das Ganze halt!* Kriegserlebnis-Triologie 1914-1918, Leipzig 1939.

Buchner, Adolf: *Der Minenkrieg auf Vauquois*, Deutenhausen 1982.

Buckreis, Adam: *Der Weltkrieg und die Zeit nach dem Kriege*, Nuernberg.

Bull, Stephen: *Aspects of war. Trench warfare*, New York 2003.

*Champagne-Kriegszeitung/VIII. Reserve-Korps: Bilder aus der Champagne und von der Aisne*, Zweite Folge 1916.

Chef des Generalstabes des Feldheeres: *Einzelheiten ueber Stellungsbau 15.12.1916*, Berlin 1916.

Chef des Generalstabes des Feldheeres: *Grundsaetze fuer die Abwehrschlacht im Stellungskriege 1.9.1917*, Berlin 1917.

Churchill, Winston: *Die WeltKrisis 1916/18*, vol. 1-2, Zuerich/Leipzig/Wien 1928.

Cooper, Bryan: *The ironclads of Cambrai. The first great tank battle*, 2002.

Cooper, Duff: Haig. *Ein Mann und eine Epoche*, Berlin.

Eisenhower, John S.D.: *Yanks. The epic story of the American Army in World War I*, New York 2001.

Ettighofer, Paul: *Verdun*, Wiesbaden 1985.

Ettighofer, Paul: *Eine Armee meutert. Frankreichs Schicksalsstunde 1917*, Guetersloh.

Hoffman, Rudolf: *Der deutsche Soldat. Briefe aus dem Weltkrieg*, Muenchen 1937.

Falkenhayn, Erich v.: *Die Oberste Heeresleitung 1914-1916 in ihren wichtigsten Entschliessungen*, Berlin 1920.

Foch, Marschall: *Meine Kriegserinnerungen*, Leipzig 1931:

Foerster, Gerhard/Paulus, Nikolaus: *Abriss der Geschichte der Panzerwaffe*, Ost-Berlin 1982.

Frauenholz, Eugen v. (Ed.): *Kronprinz Rupprecht von Bayern – Mein Kriegstagebuch*, Muenchen 1929.

Fuehren, Franz: *Die Hohenzollernfusiliere im Weltkrieg 1914-1918*, Berlin 1930.

*German Army Handbook, April 1918*. Ed. by David Nash. London 1977.

Goerlitz, Walter: *Kleine Geschichte des deutschen Generalstabes*, Berlin 1977.

Goodspeed, D.J.: *Ludendorff. Soldat, Diktator, Revolutionaer*, Guetersloh 1968.

Groom, Winston: *A storm in Flanders. The Ypres salient, 1914-1918*, New York 2002.

Grosser Generallstab: *Die Schlachten und Gefechte des Grossen Krieges 1914-1918*, Berlin 1919.

Hart, Liddell: *Foch. Feldherr der Entente*, Berlin.

Heigl's *Taschenbuch der Tanks*, vol. 1-4, Muenchen 1935.

Hindenburg, Paul v.: *Aus meinem Leben*, Leipzig 1934.

Hirschfeld, Gerhard/Krumeich, Gerd/Renz, Irina: *Keiner fuehlt sich mehr als Mensch... Erlebnis und Wirkung des Ersten Weltkriegs*, Essen 1993.

His, Wilhelm: *Die Front der Aerzte*, Bielefeld 1931.

Hodges, Arthur: *Lord Kitchener*, London 1936.

Hoepner, General v.: *Deutschlands Krieg in der Luft*, Leipzig.

Horne, Alistair: *Des Ruhmes Lohn. Verdun 1916*, Minden.

Immanuel, Oberst: *Siege und Niederlagen im Weltkriege. Kritische Betrachtungen*, Berlin 1919.

Johnson, J.H.: *Stalemate. The real story of trench warfare*, London 2004.

Juenger, Ernst: *Das Antlitz des Weltkrieges*, Berlin 1930.

Kaltenegger, Roland: *Das Deutsche Alpenkorps im Ersten Weltkrieg*, Graz 1995.

*Kamerad im Westen. Ein Bericht in 221 Bildern*, Frankfurt a.M. 1930.

Keegan, John: *The First World War*, New York 1999.

Kriegs-Bild- und Filmamt: *Der Weltkrieg im Bild*, Berlin-Oldenburg 1931.

Kronprinz Wilhelm: *Meine Erinnerungen aus Deutschlands Heldenkampf*, Berlin 1923.

Kuhl, Herman v.: *Der Weltkrieg 1914-1918*, vol. 1-2, Berlin 1929.